Leisure and Recreation Concepts

Leisure and Recreation Concepts
A Critical Analysis

*Sine potentia verborum se
nonscere non potest.*
— Ancient Saying

Jay S. Shivers
University of Connecticut

Allyn and Bacon, Inc.
Boston   London   Sydney   Toronto

Library of Congress Cataloging in Publication Data
Shivers, Jay Sanford.
Leisure and recreation concepts.

1. Leisure—Philosophy. 2. Recreation—
Philosophy. 3. Leisure—History. I. Title.
GV14.S48   790'.01'35   80-15483
ISBN 0-205-06992-4

Printed in the United States of America

Contents

Preface   vii
Acknowledgments   xi

I — Leisure Origins and Subsequent Development   1

Chapter 1   Leisure—An Introduction   3
Leisure and Human Development, 3   Homo Sapiens and Leisure Development, 7

Chapter 2   Ancient Civilizations and Leisure   21
The Rise of Civilization, 22   Near Eastern Contributions to Western Culture and Leisure, 25   Sumer and Akkad, 26   The Kingdoms of Egypt, 27   Babylon, 32   The Hebrews, 35   Ancient Western Civilization and Leisure, 37   The Hellenic Age, 38   The Greeks and Leisure, 39   The Romans, 42   Life and Culture in Early Rome, 43   Life and Culture after the Roman Conquest, 44   Early Imperial Society, 46   Late Imperial Society, 47

Chapter 3   Leisure after the Fall   51
Work and Leisure in Medieval Europe, 52   Days of Toil and Holidays, 57   Town Air Is Free and Provides Leisure, 57   The Burger's Leisure, 62   Aristocratic Life and Leisure, 64   The Influence of the Renaissance on Culture and Leisure, 68   The Spirit of Leisure, 70   The People's Leisure Activity, 70   Aristocratic Leisure and Recreational Experience, 72   The Reformation, Calvinism, and Leisure, 75   The Monk, Church, and Schism, 76   The Rise of Calvin, 77   Leisure Activities of the Masses in the Sixteenth Century, 80   Leisure Activities of the Aristocrats in the Sixteenth Century, 81   Leisure in Colonial America, 83

Chapter 4   The American Experiment   87

Invention and Humanism, 87   Leisure and Recreational Activity after the
Revolution, 89   Industrialization and Social Issues, 91   The New Leisure
and Recreational Service, 92   Creativity and Leisure, 93   The Economics
of Leisure, 95   Urban and Suburban Development Fosters Recreational
Service, 96   The Acceptance of Leisure and Recreational Activity, 98

Chapter 5   Reflections on Leisure   103

Leisure as Recreation, 103   Leisure as Pleasure, 106   Leisure as Rejuvenation, 109   Leisure as a State of Being, 111   Leisure as Function, 115
Leisure as Social Stratification, 119   Leisure as Time, 123

Part II — Intellectual Forces that Shaped Recreation and Leisure   129

Chapter 6   Formation of an American Philosophy
of Play and Recreation   131

Henry Barnard's View of Play, 132   Luther Halsey Gulick on Play and
Recreation, 133   Philosophical and Psychological Advances in Theory of
Learning, 140   William James on Play, 140   John Dewey's Consumma-
tory Concept, 143   John Dewey's Concept of Play, 144   Reaction to
Dewey's Ideas, 150

Chapter 7   An Analysis of Play and Recreation Theories   157

Instinct as Motivation, 158   Instinct Theories of Play or Recreation, 160
Hedonism as Motivation, 166   Homeostasis as Motivation, 172

Chapter 8   Recreation—Definitions and Concepts   179

Problem of Inadequate Conceptualization, 179   Play and Recreation, 199
Summary, 207

Index   211

Preface

Is leisure an outcome of civilization or has it a history that predates writing? How long has leisure been associated with human
activity? How has leisure assisted human evolution? Any study of
leisure must attempt to answer these and other pertinent questions.
Knowledge of leisure as a modern phenomenon has been well documented, but prehistoric leisure has been either ignored or misunder-
stood. An understanding of leisure in terms of human behavior
obliges a look at the origins of leisure and the influence that this
time segment has had on human life. If we are to learn about cause
and effect relationships that have impact upon human behavior, it
is necessary to uncover both evolutionary and developmental designs
concerning leisure use throughout the human epoch.

Human beings are curious animals, both in terms of intellectual
questioning and in uniqueness. They are unlike all other animal
forms, particularly in their ability to abstract ideas and to develop
language. These two features, which characterize modern people,
combined with symbolic communication, permit a transmission of
knowledge that includes both past and future as well as the meaning of life and death. When we know of human descent, as Darwin
informs us, or of human ascent, as Bronowski teaches, then we are
in a better position to understand ourselves and the reasons we act
in certain ways.

Some of our leisure behavior is of ancient origin. It is possible
to postulate that cultural affectation occurred because of leisure.
Only an investigation of human evolution and development can

provide us with some of the answers to questions that have been perplexing human beings for thousands of years. Leisure as a basis for culture may be much more than a philosophical orientation if, as a result of animal experimentation during leisure, adaptation occurred which ultimately produced the Homo genus. Of course, the interpretation placed upon leisure, the use of free time, and the facets of culture that were produced by not having to expend constant effort to survive, all have meaning in this context. Whether culture grew out of leisure or leisure was a consequence of cultural manifestations must be explored. Reciprocity between leisure and culture may have been mutually beneficial, but historical exploration is necessary to determine which produced or supported the other.

The leisure element in all human epochs tends to document the uses to which free time has been put. Additionally, a study of classical leisure is important for assisting the student in understanding more about the phenomenon of recreation. In performing such an analysis, the nature of recreation and its definition might be determined. Through normative critical analysis the foundations for a philosophy of recreation may be established.

This presentation is not merely a summarization or accounting of the abounding play, leisure, and recreation definitions and theories. Rather, it has been designed to promote a clearer concept of the word "recreation" and to integrate a positive selection of ideas in this particular area of thought that may be systematized into a philosophy of recreation. It is concerned with what recreation is, rather than how it is accomplished.

Historically, recreation has come to mean those activities performed in leisure, time not spent on vocation, education, or life-sustaining pursuits. Just as history has attached the idea of specific activities to recreation, so too has custom identified certain activities with the field of recreational service. During the course of its existence as a field of applied social service, this field has assumed responsibility for certain forms of activity carried on in leisure and thereby termed recreation. Through history and habit, recreation has come to be defined in such a restricted sense that its justification for being is largely negated.

The establishment of a discipline for the field depends on its relationship to concepts that are traceable to early Greek philosophy, Renaissance exploration, Enlightenment humanism, and contemporary philosophies of the American culture. With these ideas to build on, a discipline of learning, set in the framework of rational value judgments that refer to ethics in human development and behavior, has been stated.

Recreation is defined in terms of human behavior. It is any consummatory experience, nondebilitating in character. As a human experience it has thus been broadened from restrictive definitions to include potentially all human activities. In this light, the implications for education, both professional and lay, are tremendously enlarged. At a time when recreational service curricula in institutions of higher education are preparing future leaders in this field, a single meaningful statement of the conceptualization of recreation and its place in the firmament of American thought needs to be voiced.

This text offers the reader a world view of recreation that may be assimilated personally. It analyzes leisure, play, and recreation theories and forms an entirely new concept of play/recreation as both process and product of the homeostatic condition in human beings. It has employed the philosophical method of asking essential questions about why and how people achieve recreation.

Acknowledgments

This book is dedicated to my wife, whose loyal support and sustaining love have enabled me to continue my efforts through discouraging times. I also wish to acknowledge my son, Jed Mark, for his impatient reading of my manuscript. And last but not least, I wish to acknowledge the assistance of my secretary, Miss Mary Lou Nye, without whose aid a clean manuscript would never have been produced.

I
Leisure Origins and Subsequent Development

Chapter I
Leisure – An Introduction

In ages when people have had and used leisure positively, cultural advancements have been largely made. The arts and sciences, but particularly the humanities, have developed extensively out of the creative use of leisure. Free time, constructively used, advances society, enriches individual life, and produces massive cultural development accreted over time.

One of the most illuminating methods for understanding present concepts is to view them from an historical perspective in order to appreciate their progression from distant origin to contemporary meaning. Leisure was a part of culture before civilization developed and has been a part of human society from a time prior to when people learned how to communicate with one another.

LEISURE AND HUMAN DEVELOPMENT

Leisure was integral to human culture since the human brain was capable of conceiving the difference between survival activities and activities which developed without compulsion. In the beginning there was only survival. Until human beings learned how to make fire at their own discretion, preserve whatever food they could find or kill, have an adequate water supply, built or locate an easily defensible habitation against marauding foreign groups and savage animals of the infra-human species, their every thought focused on just staying alive.

It is now conceded that human beings have been on earth at least two million years longer than was previously thought. With the popularization of recent anthropological findings of Richard Leakey, we now have startling evidence that our immediate precursors probably existed at least two million years ago and that the *Homo* line was separate and distinct from those of other primitive primates for approximately six million years.[1] This simply means that human beings evolved along parallel, but not the same tracks, as other hominid forms. It may also be inferred that humans' larger brain capacity offered greater opportunity to think abstractly and to comprehend cause and effect relationships more quickly than other species.

While there is no solid scientific evidence to determine when prehistoric humans first possessed leisure, certain speculations can be made about the effects of free time on subsequent human development. It is probable that much, if not all, of primitive humans' first activities centered on survival. We may imagine the kinds of daily activity that had to be undertaken. Food, shelter, potable water supplies, and defensible positions against the attack of hostile others were necessary. How long total survival activities remained the sole preoccupation is unknown, but it is obvious that by the time of *Homo habilis,* free time was available. The pebble culture people must have had leisure to conceive of the tools they shaped from pebbles and rock shards[2] some 2.5 million years ago. Although necessity may force an individual to acquire new skills or invent new tools, leisure is an essential factor in any such invention. Without the time to think about a given problem and its possible solution, i.e., to play with ideas, it seems improbable that tools could have been shaped for specific use.

The significant transition from *Homo habilis* to *Homo erectus,* considered to be the direct lineal ancestor of modern human beings, occurred during the Lower Pleistocene period. *Homo erectus* spans a period of more than 1.5 million years, or to approximately 100,000 years ago. These prehistoric humans wandered over what is today the central plains of Europe. They had learned to use fire at their

---

[1] *Time,* "Puzzling Out Man's Ascent," (November 17, 1977), pp. 64-78.

[2] Raymond A. Dart, "On the Osteodontokeratic Culture of the Australopithecine," *Current Anthropology,* Vol. 12, 1971, p. 233.

own discretion. This knowledge enabled them to do what no other animal had previously done—adapt the environment to accommodate their needs instead of adjusting themselves to the natural setting. The dwelling places of *Homo erectus* could now be warmed and somewhat illuminated. In this newly constructed zone of safety, they enjoyed relative security. As well as providing new opportunities for living, fire may have been even more important as a contributor to human intellectual evolution. There are theories that indicate that by changing humans' habits, the use of fire also modified their brain structure and improved their ability to learn and communicate.[3] Having learned to domesticate fire, *Homo erectus* could seek protection from inclement weather in caves and crevasses, and could thus withstand the rigors of their harsh environment and survive.

When humans took to the caves, they had to dispossess bears, lions, and other carnivores. Penetrating caves to the deepest recesses was possible with the light and warmth that fire provided. Unusual evidence suggests that fire was used in hunting.[4] The cooking of food, certainly meat, is assumed to have originated during the time of *erectus.* The ability to consume softer, cooked foods may have reduced the musculature of the jaw and its skeletal composition, thereby enabling morphological changes that resulted in a skull that permitted more space for cranial expansion and a larger brain.[5]

The psychological changes, which probably developed along with physical modifications, could have come from the use of fire. Cooking may have prompted behavioral restraints. Less impulsive behavior would occur when food was cooked. Instead of eating raw food on the spot, more food was taken to the dwelling places, there to be allocated, cooked, and eaten. This was more enjoyable and required formalized constraint or regulation. Consequently, there was bound to be an advance in the ability to communicate.

It may also be assumed that fire played an important part in changing one of life's basic rhythms. Instead of being directed by an internal biological clock, which produced a twelve-hour cycle of waking and sleeping, *Homo erectus* was required to break that cycle

---

[3] Phillip Tobias, *The Brain in Hominid Evolution* (New York: Columbia University Press, 1971). Cf. also, Frank E. Poirier, *Fossil Man An Evolutionary Journey* (St. Louis: The C. V. Mosby Company, 1973), p. 153.

[4] Sherwood Washburn, ed., *Social Life of Early Man* (Chicago: Aldine Publishing Co., 1961), pp. 176-193.

[5] C. Loring Brace, "Environment, Tooth Form and Size in the Pleistocene," *Journal of Dental Research,* Vol. 46, September-October, 1967, p. 809.

to tend the fire. This biological adjustment produced an artificial environment that other animals did not have. Humans no longer depended upon the sun's movement for light and heat. The evening hours could now be illuminated, at least to some extent, and other activities that ordinarily would be postponed until daylight could be expanded.

Domesticated fire brought a new leisure into the lives of *Homo erectus*. Now there was time to think about activities that were increasingly complicated—coordinated hunting activities, animal and tribal migration patterns, and cultic or ritualistic ceremonies that were forerunners of religious experiences. With fire, human beings gained time that was free of danger, insecurity, and environmental pressure. With this new time they could use their developing minds to plan imaginative activities, to attempt enlarged communication with peers, to content themselves with such enjoyable activities as eating cooked foods and performing activities that offered the physical pleasure of mental stimulation. Incremental leisure was one outgrowth of the ability to handle fire.[6]

The shift away from full-time engagement in survival techniques brought about a measurable increase in absolute free time. Surely this occurred over a long period since brain development took place simultaneously. The biological clock, directed by a cluster of nerve cells buried deep within the hypothalamus, could no longer hold sway as evolving humans overcome this instinctive natural cycle.

Current writers who theorize that prehistoric humans continued to dote upon circadien time as the natural order of events fail to understand that the biological cycle was broken long before the appearance of *Homo sapiens*. If anything, the nomadic existence forced upon the paleolithic hunters was freely chosen in comparison to alternative life styles, e.g., farming; but their leisure could only be obtained when survival needs had been met. It was not until fire became a tool that something of a settled leisure condition could be counted upon. It is invalid to state that "the governance of cyclical, natural time was inherently leisurely."[7] It was not only *not* leisurely, it was hurried, troubled, and early dying in that those unfortunate enough to belong to this cultural epoch rarely lived beyond 18 years of age. It must have been unique to have group members live to 30

---

[6] John Pfeiffer, "When Homo Erectus Tamed Fire He Tamed Himself," *Human Variations*, ed. M. Bleibtreu and J. Downs (Beverly Hills, Cal.: Glencoe Press, 1971), pp. 193-203.

[7] James F. Murphy, *Concepts of Leisure: Philosophical Implications* (Englewood Cliffs, N.J.: Prentice-Hall, Inc., 1974), p. 6.

or 40 years. Such individuals were looked upon as ancient sages of the community.

The nomadic way of life still prevails in modern times, and the nomads gear their days to the herds and the seasons they follow. However, these nomads have habitual settlements, artificial illumination, and other creature comforts that take them a long way from mere survival techniques. That they have leisure is unmistakable, but it is no more guided by cyclical or circadien time than any other people who do not live without fire or other artificial illumination. In short, any attempt to conceptualize leisure as an attitude or as indistinguishable from either work or survival activities must be considered suspect.

Homo erectus roamed the earth for approximately 900,000 years. During those millennia certain physiological changes must have been evidenced. Toward the end of the Middle Pleistocene, new evolutionary hominids began to appear. Some scientists have suggested that because of varying environmental conditions met, the origin of modern racial groups can be dated to this Middle Pleistocene hominid expansion. The later *erectus* and early *sapiens* populations evolved contemporaneously. Whatever future discoveries disclose, there is substantial evidence that evolutionary humans were craft making individuals and the tools they fashioned as well as the sites of their dwellings became the names by which these people were known.

During the late third glacial period the first modern humans appeared and swept all before them. Traces of modern humans may go back several million years, but their evolvement in present form took place about 100,000 years ago. The upper Pleistocene hunters of Europe displayed cultural acceleration and technological progress to an extent that dwarfed all preceding *Homo* forms. Additionally, the unfolding to full fruition of aesthetic senses, which had only been displayed in incipient states among the *erectus* population, played an extremely important part in enabling subsequent generations to mark their passage. Significantly, it is in the aesthetic field that knowledge of *sapiens'* leisure has been made known.

HOMO SAPIENS AND LEISURE DEVELOPMENT

The remains found in the grotto of Cro-Magnon in Dordogne, France, indicate that these late Peleolithic people brought the human race a matchless step forward. They were artists who drew and painted on any smooth surface that could take their materials, as their drawings on cave walls and cliff faces attest. They not only drew and painted, but carved as well. Quite a bit of information is known about some of the populations residing in European regions, particularly in France where many artifacts, habitations, tools, and cave art have been uncovered. However, late Paleolithic humans traveled into North and South America and Australia. Furthermore, human development continued in Asia and Africa as well. During the 30,000 years of the Late Paleolithic period, *Homo sapiens* lived in small groups as hunters and gleaners. To all outward appearances, they looked very much like contemporary hominid populations.

In diversity, taste, and style, Cro-Magnon culture far surpassed its predecessors. In all likelihood, these people did not fear attack by other hominids or animals, at least not as much as their ancestors did. Upper Paleolithic people hunted the hairy mammoth as well as bison, reindeer, horses, and aurochs. With their greater intelligence and the moderate environment in which they lived, a more secure life was possible. Thus, when the urgency of the hunt was over, there was leisure. What they did with their leisure has been recorded for posterity. The cave dwellings and assembly places of the Cro-Magnards were alive with pictorial representations of the animals they hunted, tamed, or ate. Ivory, bone, and clay carvings and statuary also attest to their artistry. Although their drawings show neither depth perception nor frontal views of any image, they nevertheless display a high degree of skill and vividness still preserved in the caves of Spain, France, and Yugoslavia.[8] That they used a variety of pigments to make various hues is seen from the cave paintings as well as from opened graves. Color was a primary medium that they used in life and death. Body decorations were painted on, and evidence suggests that the females of this species were well coiffured.

Upper Paleolithic people inherited many of the Neanderthal tool techniques, and although continuing along some of the same lines, they were responsible for the production of fine stone tools and for delicately worked bone articles. The most striking change was the manufacture of blade-tools used in working bone and wood. Among the variety of tool types were burins or chisel-shaped blades

---

[8] Alexander Marshack, "Exploring the Mind of Ice Age Man," *National Geographic* Vol. 147, January, 1975, pp. 74-81.

employed as engraving utensils for working bone, wood, or antler. Another functional tool was the borer, which was worked to a sharp, narrow point and used as a drill. Notched blades were probably used for preparing arrow or spear shafts by shaving the wood. Different scrapers were employed to hollow out wood or bone, scrape hides, remove bark from wood, or to plane workable objects. Among the implements recovered are projectile points that could be fitted to a wooden shaft and used as a hunting tool or a combat weapon. Even daggers were known and shaped by these people.

Upper Paleolithic tool kits are sharply differentiated by the inclusion of such items as polished pins or awls made of bone or antler. Between 17,000 and 12,000 years ago, during the period known as the Magdalenian, such objects as hooked rods employed as spear throwers, barbed points, harpoons, fishhooks, needles with eyes, bodkins, belt fasteners, and other assorted tools were of common manufacture. Frequently, such implements were highly decorated with hunting scenes, animals, and lines. All of this suggests that elaborate wearing apparel, probably of tanned hides and furs, was a part of life.

The numerous traces of artistic work that Cro-Magnon people left behind tell us much about the daily life, ceremonial practices, and stresses that confronted these people. The Upper Paleolithic hunters continued to worship animals, particularly the cave bear. Their interest in attempting to gain control of a world which, despite their intelligence, they could not quite understand permitted them to seek explanations that relied upon supernatural and magical conformations. The cave art that they created has its aesthetic merits, but it is likely that these art forms were designed to obtain control over natural forces by sympathetic magic.[9]

> Upper Paleolithic man made dramas out of his rituals. To ensure a plentiful supply of bears, reindeer, horses, and bison, he made images of them in clay or paint within his deeply recessed caves. He then danced in front of or around these images while praying to their spirits not to be hostile or angry with men, but to provide them with food as good parents should. At the end he symbolically killed the animals, either by sticking spears into the soft clay or perhaps by throwing weapons at those that were painted. The reality of the dance and the rituals thus became a cause-effect relationship that would create a future supply of food. Bison and herds of deer and

---

[9] Grahame Clark, *The Stone Age Hunters* (New York: McGraw-Hill Book Co., 1967).

horses were painted as if early man were driving them off the tops of cliffs or trapping them in marshes or within narrow, highbanked streams. By depicting what had taken place in the past, man hoped to ensure the duplication of it in the future.[10]

Another indication that the paintings were functional rather than aesthetic is the fact that many pictures are superimposed on top of each other. At the Lascaux cave in France, some paintings are four layers deep. In addition to painting, Cro-Magnon people also sculpted. They wrought relief outlines on cave walls and engraved animal outlines. Some statuettes depict the female figure in ivory, bone, fire hardened clay, and stone.[11] These figures, of which the prime discovery is the "Venus of Willendorf," a four-inch high limestone statuette with a wavy coiffure and exaggerated female curves, represent fertility symbols. If there were time to paint, draw, and establish some system of burial, and for women to be provided with elaborate hair styles, there must have been much leisure. The tiny statuettes of female figures with wavy hairdos imply that the artists used contemporary females as models. For a woman, who had so many time-consuming domestic chores to perform for survival, to have had the time to sit patiently and do up her hair in elegant ways, shows that these people lived comparatively secure lives and had well established social customs that allowed for free time expenditure. Well defined specializations probably required certain activities to be accomplished by male or female group and family members. Certainly some activities might have been combined, i.e., hunter and craftsman or shaman and artist. But it is more likely that those with artistic skills and talent might have been clearly differentiated from other clan or tribal members so that they could give full time to their efforts in recording group activities, rites, and seasonal changes.

As in more modern times, specialization permits specific periods of work coupled with periods of rest and relaxation. The degree of the late Paleolithic people's specialization endowed them with sufficient time to make tremendous cultural advances. This may be inferred from their technical progress in tools, dress, habitation, and social customs. Of salient concern is the secure position they attained in the various dwelling places they controlled throughout their

---

[10] David Rodnick, *An Introduction to Man and His Development*, (New York: Appleton-Century-Crofts, 1966), p. 29. Reprinted by permission of Prentice-Hall, Inc., Englewood Cliffs, New Jersey.

[11] Alexander Marshack, "Ice Age Man," pp. 65-89.

30,000-year history. The places were strong points, had good water supplies, and were the migrating passages for herd animals. Permanent habitations were common, although some groups lived in parasitic relationship to migrating herds of reindeer and wandered with the animals as the herd went through its seasonal pasturing cycles.

Security, specialization, and social custom were all forces that saved time and freed these populations from incessant searches for survival. Out of this primitive arrangement, although exceedingly advanced over those of earlier Paleolithic forebears, leisure developed. A culture that could spare highly skilled group members from foraging for food so that they could paint, draw, or sculpt was richly equipped to function in its environment. It may be construed that the artists did not perform in their leisure, but were actually working for the welfare of the group through the functional use of art—i.e., art as magic. If this were the only possibility, the leisure position would be less tenable. However, other nonfunctional art forms, designed purely for the enjoyment they gave to the user, were also manifest. These may be called chattel art forms. Chattel art refers to aesthetic devices found on artifacts not associated with cave or ritual art, but used as decorations on utensils and clothing, fasteners, or other bodily adornments. In this way one may view such aesthetic representation as a form of self-expression rather than as a means for coping with daily life.

Whether art is functional or self-fulfilling, the aesthetic force does not spring full blown into the world from a vacuum. Even genius requires some nurturing. Upper Paleolithic artists must have had some apprenticeship before they could have performed at the level of skill preserved in some of the caves and on artifacts that have been discovered. This practice for skill requires leisure. Without the necessary free time, which had to be made available for the develop-ment of the original artists and their subsequent disciples, the skills of painting with various colors, carving, engraving, and sculpturing could not have occurred. The attainment of sufficient skill to become the group's artistic retainer must have taken much time and special-ization.

If the chattel art view is correct in any respect, it illustrates the use to which leisure can be made in the advancement of culture. Accretions of culture are probably a direct outgrowth of the leisure possessed by the inhabitants of a particular period. One might even say that the degree to which any culture has attained a measure of leisure, with all of the ramifications that leisure implies, will assuredly be displayed in the progress of its social institutions, advancement of technological devices, and demonstrations of its varied capacities in the production of aesthetic creations.

The Upper Paleolith people were great travelers and moved across the various land bridges then connecting the continents, thereby spreading very early to all parts of the old and new worlds. There is as yet insufficient evidence to date precisely the movement and settlements that were made by the Paleolithic hunters. Possibly, hominids trailed animals into the new world through an unbroken land bridge joining Asia and Alaska between 40,000 and 50,000 years ago. Other scientists argue that the latest dates that may be comfortably assigned to the remains that have been found range from 15,000 to 30,000 years ago. Whatever the truth, it may be said that early humans covered the earth through successive waves of migration. Through carbon dating, some new world artifacts are given the old date of 37,000 years, and there is every reason to believe that more recent findings will support the supposition that human entrance into the new world probably occurred over 40,000 years ago.

The way of life of such hunters lasted for many years in some parts of the world. In other parts, the human race entered a period of significant modification. This occurred about 10,000 years ago when the final glacial period came to an end and the climate associated with the modern era developed. The period of change is known as the Mesolithic or middle stone age. The people of the Upper Paleolithic age, the precursors of modern human life, carried the human race far beyond what had been attained up to then. More importantly, they bequeathed to their descendants an anatomy that permitted articulate speech. The brain was that of modern people. In their time they had become artists, craftsmen, and hunters *par excellence*. From them stretches an unbroken genetic line through all the succeeding human epochs. With the end of the last Ice Age, the Mesolithic era began.

The brief Mesolithic period, which lasted from between 1,000 to several thousand years, depending on the people and the region they inhabited, was a time of more efficient food organization, the invention of many tools, and the development of fishing as a supplement and substitute for meat. Some populations had long eaten shellfish, but shore dwellers now began to eat them as a staple. People learned how to spear fish, and then developed hooks, nets, and weirs to catch them. Smoked fish evidently took hold both to preserve the food and to enhance the taste.

As people began to learn about obtaining food from the sea, new regions were exploited for settlement. Woodlands, with all of their natural resources for constructing shelter and hunting, became inhabited. The invention of the dugout canoe provided the means of transportation over formerly impassable rivers or large inland lakes and further assisted in catching fish.

Among the inventions created by Mesolithic humans were the bow and arrow. This device had never been found in nature and constitutes what might be called an invention. Additionally, stone axes, adzes, and mattocks were fabricated so that trees could be cut down to furnish housing materials as well as implements and fuel for heat, light, and cooking. All of these items provided the Mesolithic people with greater control over their environment. The bow assisted greatly in hunting the kinds of animals that provided their protein staple, but domesticating the dog made it easier to track, corner, and retrieve game than had theretofore been possible. Additionally, the dog served as a guardian and pet.

Despite innovations in tool manufacture and habitation, these people continued to rely on hunting as their major means of obtaining food. Wood, stone, and bone remained the basic materials for implements. Slowly and inexorably the world's population increased. The hunter's way of life, which relied on sparse population and an almost inexhaustible supply of open space and animals, waned. A need for another food source began to be felt as a growing population placed increasing strain on both the diminishing herds of animals and the territorial range in which the hunters circulated to obtain food.

As the hunters depleted the animal supply, they generally moved to other regions that could support them. With more and more people appearing, the potential for hunting was considerably reduced. Famine was a real threat to the Mesolithic hunters. For the first time a new method of obtaining food would have to be attempted. People had long known where and when certain grains grew best. The cause and effect relationship between planting and harvesting had been observed and used to supplement diets during the late Paleolithic period and were transmitted to Mesolithic peoples through graphic records on cave walls, bone carvings, as well as the spoken word. However, the hunting way of life was preferred and it was not until diminished animal resources and land encroachment by increased population forced some hunters to cease and desist in their mode of living that agricultural efforts were realized. The

so-called agricultural revolution radically changed human existence.
As John Pfeiffer states:

> Man's first major food crisis occurred before written records, before
> the coming of crowds and mass production and cities. It began 10,000
> to 15,000 years ago, when there were fewer people in the whole world
> than there are today in New York City. It produced man's first and in
> many ways most drastic revolution, the shift from hunting and gather-
> ing to agriculture from a nomadic life to a settled farming existence.[12]

The people of the Mesolithic grew wild barley and wheat; in time
they also cultivated many wild vegetables and fruits. Here was the
initial attempt at large-scale farming and with it came the invention
of tools particularly adapted for plowing, cultivating, and reaping a
variety of grains and other plants. With settlement came the need
to farm intensively, because population increased much faster than
it had when the nomadic life style prevailed. The need for irrigation
developed as larger settlements used all of the available space for
producing more and more food.

Farming ties the population to a specific place. No longer did the
nomadic life influence the majority, although it was and still is
followed by a number of different people roaming through various
parts of the globe. The cultivation of crops permitted the establishment of villages, which itself required the adoption of new customs,
codes, and innovative techniques if the human population was to
survive the stress of living in close proximity.

The Mesolithic was a short-lived period linking the Upper Paleolithic with the Neolithic. There was an upsurge in ritual and sexual
taboos as the establishment of a steady source of food provided
more time for nurturing social behavior and speculating about a
spirit world or life in the hereafter. With settlement, a great deal of
thought had to be given over to housing. A variety of residences, from
mud-daubed huts to tipis and long houses, was in use. The first
permanent community was settled 9,000 years ago in Jericho, in
what is today Israel. With the establishment of Jericho the world
was forever changed.

The Mesolithic lasted until about 3000 B.C. in western Europe.
To the north it continued for at least another 600 years. The Meso-

---

[12]John Pfeiffer, "The First Food Crisis," *Horizon*, Vol. XVII, Autumn, 1975, p. 33. ©
1975 by American Heritage Publishing Co., Inc. Reprinted by permission.

lithic ended earlier in southwestern Asia and the Middle East. Sometime between 5000 and 7000 B.C. a new life force came into being with the development of farming and the village settlement. The Mesolithic receded and gave way to the Neolithic in which most of the world's inhabitants remained until the advent of the twentieth century.

The Mesolithic was a transitional period, and many of the mores founded in the Upper Paleolithic were retained. People's leisure was predicated by the kind of life they led, and the inception of a farming ethic together with village existence did much to change the time schedule by which people lived. Now the pressures of proximity and limited space called another problem into being. The passage of time and increasing population spawned a desire for annexation; this can be seen from the ossified remains of Mesolithic people who died violently with arrows through head or body as marauders attempted to cope with the pressures of survival in a rapidly receding nomadic existence. The cyclical relationship that was to be repeated throughout subsequent history was initiated.

In the beginning there was a need to survive. Survival could only be accomplished by obtaining cooperation from at least one other person. Such cooperation led to trust and a better chance of performing those activities that ensured basic survival. Group living, starting with the incipient family and spreading to clan, tribe, and eventually to community, was effected. Living in collectives produced greater cooperation and coordination, which necessitated communication. Communication and enlarged groups required some codes of governance or sharing among the membership, and this in turn became a force for developing a social contract. As soon as survival was ensured, a minute amount of leisure became available. With cooperation, coordination, and communication the lot of early humanity was facilitated and more leisure enhanced its life and led to innovations in materials and ideas. The heritage of human life continued to be passed along over the millennia and was radically changed during the latter Mesolithic. In all subsequent history there will be the added ingredient of the ultimate human atrocity—subjugation by war. Approximately 8,000 years ago a new race of people and a new life began to develop with farming as its distinguishing trait—Neolithic.

The Neolithic age is characterized by five distinct features: 1) the polished stone implement; 2) agriculture; 3) the use of pottery and weaving; 4) domesticated animals; and 5) cookery. As with preceding periods, Neolithic refers to the tools made by the people of this time. The Neolithic culture, however, included other developments. Jericho, previously alluded to, became the first walled town. In this community some people built their own houses, with roofs, pavements in front, hearths, and food storage sections. Religion also played a role in this ancient culture, for special rooms were cordoned off for gods and rituals. Not only farming, but animal husbandry was practiced.

In their respective settlements along the rivers and beside lakes, people were learning how to shape new materials. The accidental discovery of fire-hardened clay led to the making of pottery. The pottery industry proliferated, and before long many people were making pots of different shapes and sizes and decorating them with carvings and paints. Neolithic people also invented the loom, which enabled the fashioning of woven garments and has remained relatively unchanged these thousands of years. In time, spinning flax, cotton, and later, wool provided the materials for clothing. Agriculture, village life, domesticated animals, pottery, weaving, spinning, and polished tools—these comprised the Neolithic culture that the peoples of the Near East had taken up. This culture was soon promulgated among other people, who learned about it from migrant groups or from individual travelers or traders.

Neolithic culture was not universally adopted by all the people then living. In some instances it was violently resisted as opposing traditions. In others it was never taken up. Nevertheless, the Neolithic culture was absorbed by much of humankind, especially the residents around the Mediterranean basin and in central Asia, India, western Europe, and the Far East.

The chief tool of the Neolithic was the handaxe, which also made an excellent weapon. Neolithic people used bow and arrow in hunting and fighting. Perhaps protection against bands of bow and arrow wielders compelled the inhabitants of Jericho to build their surrounding walls. Because they had the bow, they probably also had some form of stringed instrument. There is little doubt that if they carved whistles from bone, then they also used hollow reeds as pipes upon which to play. They knew how to stretch skins over hollow tree trunks and over drum bases made of pottery. There is no evidence concerning when people began to sing, but inasmuch as they had musical accompaniment and verbal communication, songs must have been sung.

That people always had some leisure cannot be challenged. How they used that leisure is quite another question. It is also appropriate to ask whether culture was accumulated as a result of leisure or whether culture preceded leisure.

During the Neolithic age, stone and then metal became a part of life. First copper, probably discovered by accident through the inadvertent use of copper-bearing rocks as part of a camp or cooking fire circle, then in like manner the alloys of bronze and brass were smelted. Presumably people began to smelt copper as early as 5,000 years ago. Trade in preservatives such as salt, bronze weapons, and tanned skins, and a variety of ornamental minerals, e.g., jade, silver, and gold, was carried on over great distances.

The passing of several millennia led to other discoveries of energy sources. People in primary culture knew only the energy of their own muscle power. In the Neolithic age, they hitched animals to plows and sledges. Among the animals domesticated for this drudgery were the ass, camel, reindeer, and horse. Even with these animal helpers, people continued to supply the muscle necessary to accomplish everyday tasks. In the Upper Neolithic era the invention of the wheel and sails for small craft revolutionized the way in which goods and people could be moved over the surface of the land and the waterways that bound the world together.

Before the advent of the wheel and the use of metals, a more distinctive change took place in the Neolithic. Agriculture brought the first of the surplus food supplies that supported specialized laborers who performed in trades or fields other than farming. In settlements where goods and labor were exchanged or bartered, there was a need to maintain records and to account for transactions. Out of such experiences in these settlements grew the stimulus that would later find outlet in the habitations where civilization began.

That Neolithic people had time to think and invent is self-evident, for only when individuals can stop their intensive preoccupation with survival can a culture flourish. Neolithic people possessed a great deal more leisure than had any of their predecessors. With it they developed speech, primitive writing, some art, metal tools, agriculture, primitive religious rituals, symbolism, and tribal taboos. Much the same settled way of life was being led by Neolithic people 10,000 years ago as was being led by peasants in some of the rural areas of Europe in the early eighteenth century. The age of the Caucasian in Europe, of which the Neolithic period was the first phase, was still going on until the modern era of power-driven machinery. In fact, remnants of the Mesolithic period could still be observed in several parts of the world where culture resisted modern infringement or was isolated.

When people first tamed fire and could tell somebody else how to build a blaze from pyrites and tinder materials, when the older generation was able to pass on instructions concerning the handling of sharpened stones, wooden implements, pottery, and eventually metals, when food could be cultivated instead of chased, then people had leisure and culture progressed rapidly. But the cycle, once begun, was repeated over and over again. Initially, survival was uppermost. Survival required cooperation. Cooperation permitted planning and coordinated activities, which in turn provided some respite and, therefore, leisure. With leisure there was time to think, invent, and innovate. Eventually, such activities produced land exploitation, population increments, and the need to expand the food supply. Through the cultivation of crops, instead of hunting and gathering plants, people could establish permanent settlements from which sprung the stirrings of civilization. At each step, because of specialization and tools that made work easier and therefore more speedily completed, leisure increased. Unfortunately, with all of the positive benefits of settlement and social contracts, the land space diminished, thus paving the way for raiders who sought to conquer and take over the rewards that hard work had made possible. Such activity impelled the need for a warrior class which then sought to expand the territorial boundaries of its own settlement at the expense of other communities. This type of activity, with raid and retaliation, returned the community to survival activities, and so the full circle was closed.

We have seen that throughout the development of human culture, some leisure has been present. Anthropologists, among other scientists devoted to the study of the development of humankind, have indicated that recreational experiences, in some form, were a direct outgrowth of the possession of leisure.[13] There are indications that preliterate societies used leisure and recreational activity as both an instructional vehicle as well as a monument to human beings' aesthetic and creative tendencies.[14] When people began to gain some

---

[13] Julius Lippert, *The Evolution of Culture*, trans. and ed. George P. Murdock (New York: The Macmillan Company, 1931), p. 415.

[14] George R. Stewart, *Man: An Autobiography* (New York: Random House, 1946), p. 118.

control over their environment and, by chance, learned to use providentially provided materials as utensils, they fashioned vessels made of clay for containing their food and water. To enhance these purely utilitarian products they decorated them with ocher or other coloring substances; thus they played with their articles, which we now see as artifacts in many museums of natural history. As human personality became more sophisticated over succeeding thousands of years, people expressed their feelings upon the walls of caves as well as on pottery, thus symbolizing and transmitting their ideas concerning the creatures they met and the lives they lived.

The method by which primitive people exerted control over their environment could not be mechanically contrived. Nevertheless, they had human strength at their disposal. Gatherings of families or clans into tribal groups, and tribes into communal living, produced the first step in social organization which ultimately led to the development of law. Tribal customs, based upon certain taboos, superstitions, and the like, served to guide and formulate what was later to be known as the political, martial, economic, religious, educational, and family institutions of the social order. While it is true that there was no differentiation between these varying activities during the emergence of humankind from its preliterate stage to the civilized complexity of more highly developed systems, these practices made way for the social structures that have evolved. The ethos of civilization and culture finds its earliest seeds in the leisure which was first attained as evolution changed an animal into a human being.

The origins of leisure are shrouded by the same factors that obscure the origins of humankind. In whatever era of human evolution leisure first came to light, it offered the unbounded time for individuals to sieze upon their opportunities for self-realization and personal enhancement. It has always been this way. Leisure is free time, and that is all. Whether it is used for personal indulgence, expression, creation, or indolence is immaterial. Leisure remains incontrovertably an element of discretionary time, not limited in any objective way except in terms of how it will be used or allowed to pass.

Thus, leisure is both a personal manifestation and a bridge between prehistoric and modern human behaviors. It has affected culture and social development. How contemporary leisure is perceived has antecedents to all previous times. What we tend to do today, except for the added variables of technology, draws from past cultures and experiences that can be ascertained by the careful analysis of human origins, evolution, and development.

SELECTED REFERENCES

Ben-David, Joseph, and Clark, Terry N. *Culture and Its Creators.* Chicago: University of Chicago Press, 1977.

Coles, J. M., and Higgs, E. S. *Archaeology of Early Man.* New York: Penguin Books, Inc., 1978.

Friedle, J., and Pfeiffer, J. E. *Anthropology: The Study of People.* New York: Harper & Row Publishers, Inc., 1977.

Haviland, W. A. *Anthropology,* 2d ed. New York: Holt, Rinehart and Winston, 1978.

Knudson, S. J. *Culture in Retrospect: An Introduction to Archaeology.* Chicago: Rand McNally & Co., 1978.

Kottack, Conrad P. *Anthropology: The Exploration of Human Diversity,* 2d ed. Westminster, Md.: Random House, Inc., 1978.

Leakey, Richard, and Lewin, Roger. *Origins: What New Discoveries Reveal About the Emergence of Our Species and Its Possible Future.* New York: E. P. Dutton, 1977.

———. *People of the Lake.* Garden City, N. Y.: Doubleday & Co., 1978.

Chapter 2

Ancient Civilizations and Leisure

All of the ancient civilizations with which we are familiar have certain common characteristics. Most, if not all, were established along the banks of rivers whose waters nourished the surrounding lands, thereby enabling settled populations to sustain themselves by virtue of a relatively stable food supply. Agriculture and potable water were the major elements that fostered the growth of the earliest towns, which in turn became the mighty cities of antiquity. Civilization is, of course, the story of the city.

Civilization occurs when a cultural accumulation is attained in which human welfare obtains the greatest focus of attention. It is brought about by invention and sustained by the need for organization, cooperation, and communication. Characteristically, all civilization has developed institutional forms of government, economics, religion, and symbolic devices for language. Where there is a flowering of intellectuality and incremental cultural achievement coupled with the stabilizing influence of science and technology, civilization develops. Through technological invention comes the necessity to regulate or guide conduct, and this permits the rise of standardized action and organization. Out of organization grows governance, specialization of labor, and social thought. For the most part civilization is nurtured and encouraged in an environment in which individuals may interrelate, feel protected from hostile forces, exchange ideas, engage in reciprocal practices, and promote the common good. It is an atmosphere in which aesthetic creations are indulged, trade is promoted, and the cultural heritage is transmitted through formal methods, e.g., literature. Throughout its history civilization has been closely associated with city life. From farming village, initially, to trading center, and then to the realization of all social intercourse, cultural achievement, and technological facilitation, the city has been most congenial to the advance of civilization.

Some of the earliest and greatest human achievements occurred in the Mediterranean basin and the Near East, which are very ancient homelands for the human race. The Upper Paleolithic era is well represented in this region. Most importantly, one of the earliest agricultural sites lies at the eastern end of the Mediterranean. The climate that appeared about 11,000 years ago, which is the climate of the modern world, saw the continuation of cultural advancement, and with it the recession of nomadic ways for the settled life that food cultivation made possible. For purposes of this text, we will focus on the beginning of town dwelling and farming ways of life around 9000 B.C. in the Middle East. Out of this developed city-state civilization and relatively quickly, kingdoms and dynasties. By 4500 B.C. Mesopotamia was well on the path to civilization; Egypt was in the same situation by 4000 B.C. From these centers of notable achievement, ideas rippled outward to adjacent lands.

THE RISE OF CIVILIZATION

By 4000 B.C. many different groups of people were leading their lives in diverse ways. In a great arc from the eastern end of the Mediterranean, across the Turkish plains, and through the highlands of Iraq and Iran, Neolithic peoples had migrated, settled, and were now farming, trading, building communities, and learning to weave, paint, make pottery, and smelt metal. While some nomadic tribes still lived by hunting, the greater part of mankind had settled into the domestication of animals and the stabilized base of an agricultural existence. Populations grew rapidly, and competition for fertile areas became serious. Not for the first time was there strife between groups who controlled food resources and those who were perpetually hungry.

One of the regions that would be continuously fought over was situated at the very heart of the various groups who peopled the land. It was only about 150 miles wide and 600 miles long, and extended from the foothills of northwestern Iraq to the Persian Gulf. This was the "fertile crescent," the land between the Tigris and Euphrates Rivers, called Mesopotamia. For the next 3,500 years, Mesopotamia would witness the ascent and destruction of many kingdoms, cultures, and empires. Sumerian, Akkadian, Babylonian, Assyrian, and Chaldaean would originate, flourish, and then be obliterated. By 4000 B.C., settled communities had existed in the upper reaches of the Tigris. They were the earliest farming communities, and from these rude settlements the civilizations of the Middle East were born.

These civilizations contained continuously inhabited structures and some codes of law by which the dwellers abided. Mesopotamia's southern section flowed through broad plains which, when irrigated, became ideal for farming. The most ancient communities of these civilizations were formed when Eridu, in the delta near the Euphrates River, was founded. The southernmost part of Mesopotamia was called Sumer, and within a few hundred years of the founding of Eridu, many new towns and cities were established. The city-states of Sumer-Eridu, Ur, Uruk, Kish, Susa, Larsa, Lagash, and Nippur have been described as the beginning of civilization.

The growing complexity of life along these riverbanks required some form of governmental organization and far-sighted leadership to forestall chaotic uprisings and disorders when natural calamities, e.g., floods, famine, and plague despoiled the land, or to direct and command the population to its appointed tasks in maintaining the food supply, diking the rivers, and operating an army to subjugate its neighbors or to prevent conquest by others. There emerged a king-priest class that commanded the respect of its followers, first by its prowess in warfare and later as the administrator of the city by virtue of armed forces. The military-leader-turned-governor also had ritualistic functions. He led the community in prayers to the local god or gods and soon concentrated within his person the offices of ruler and priest. From this combined function the king-priest and then the aristocracy emerged. Such individuals grew to dominate and reign over the great masses that populated the cities.

The king-priest's duties included officiating at all ritual occasions, and there is good evidence to suggest that within these communities recreational activity was part of religious festival and rite.[1,2] The king-

---

[1] Sabatino Moscati, *Ancient Semite Civilizations* (New York: G. P. Putnam's Sons, 1957), pp. 55-66.

[2] Edward B. Tylor, *Religion in Primitive Culture* (New York: Harper and Brothers, 1958), passim.

priests came to be endowed with divine stature and were considered descendants of the gods. Since they ordinarily could not participate in the typical activities of their subjects, they had more and more leisure which they used for planning social development. Kings were enjoined from performing menial tasks and were limited to governing, warfare, and hunting for sport. Even the arduous requirements of governance were turned over to priest-ministers and scribes who saw to the daily administration of the city-state.

From this communal development, with its social structure and division of labor, there developed a separate social classification, which in turn initiated definite institutions characterized by an orientation toward the maintenance of life. The formulation of social stratification and the rise of these institutions became a powerful force in organizing all of the people so that the job of daily living was facilitated. Agricultural, political, religious, martial, and other tasks were performed cooperatively with the full knowledge that division meant dissolution and probably destruction by invaders. The well-defined social institutions provided for the creation of king-priest and the establishment of the first aristocracy and leisure class. As the community grew, the two functions were separated. Class and caste division was also nourished by tradition, which looked upon this status as completely normal.

With the stratification of class, the kings used priests as their councilors, and much that the priestly class ordained had the sanction of the king's authority. The priests were probably more intelligent than the average person and passed much of their time in contemplation. Spending time in this manner gave them a chance to develop rituals dealing with metaphysical concepts, originate many taboos based upon seasonal cycles or other natural occurrences, and instigate mystical signs and symbols to give them apparent command of the occult and supernatural world. In this way they were not very different from their Paleolithic forebears.

It is interesting that the priestly order of ancient Sumeria (ca. 4000 B.C.) used games, dance, and other recreational activities to dignify ritual and sacrifice to the gods.[3] In this instance the games held a deadly significance. Human sacrifices were made to propitiate the gods, and it was all done in play-acting form.[4]

---

[3] Johna Huizinga, *Homo Ludens* (Boston: The Beacon Press, 1955), p. 15. ©1950 by Roy Publishers. Reprinted by permission of Beacon Press.

[4] Robert R. Marett, *The Threshold of Religion* (London: Methuen & Co., Ltd., 1914), pp. 42-68.

Artifacts from this culture indicate that children played with dolls. Art was used to express creativeness as well as historically significant happenings on scrolls, tablets, walls, and utensils. Dancing, in the ritual of temple ceremonies, was also used to express emotion, depict events, and explain traditional activities carried on as part of the daily lives of the inhabitants of these civilizations.[5]

Dancing, as a matter of course, has become one of the recreational activities in which all people participate and through which many cultures have contributed certain symbolic steps, movements, or physical attitudes.[6] Nowhere is this seen more clearly than in the "dance of life" creations of specific African tribes. The hunter could no more engage in the pursuit of hunting and killing the lion than he could fly without first performing the dancing rite of this entire experience. The dance graphically tells the story of the hunt, the chase, the cornering of the quarry, the manifestations of courage under threat of claw and fang, the final assault of the hunter, the kill, and then the trophy gathering. Unless the adult, who participates in the hunt, actually goes through this symbolic dance, he feels mortally endangered and cannot perform adequately. The whole idea of dramatizing what is to happen and play-acting real life is part and parcel of reality. One cannot take place without the other. In this situation the play on life becomes as meaningful as the reality of the hunting episode; more so if possible, because the former is the "open sesame" to the latter act. Rhythmical movement, and later dance, probably developed out of the boredom that individuals experienced during whatever free time they had. Although the dance presumably became established as a result of individual leisure, such dancing as accompanied religious ritual was obligatory rather than recreational. The ceremony required the dance and could not proceed without its performance. Nevertheless, dance has almost universally become associated with leisure activity.

NEAR EASTERN CONTRIBUTIONS TO WESTERN CULTURE AND LEISURE

With the growth and complexity of social institutions, there also emerged a trend toward governmental organization with one power-

---

[5] Wilfred D. Hambly, *Tribal Dancing and Social Development* (London: Witherby, 1926), pp. 133-135.

[6] Robert H. Lowie, *An Introduction to Cultural Anthropology* (New York: Rinehart and Co., Inc., 1947), pp. 171-174.

ful ruler to whom all others of the community must pay respect and devotion. From 3600 B.C. in the Mesopotamian and Egyptian societies, this social complexity evolved into a distinct separation of classes. Political and military power was given into the hands of a central figure, the king, the mystical rites were handed to priests, and these rites included most, if not all, of the arts and sciences of the day, including religion. The rest of the populace was left with the burden of cultivating the crops, engaging in commercial and trade enterprises, and generally increasing the material wealth of the state.

Briefly, there arose a series of societies ruled by an individual given divine-right powers. Among these were the Babylonian, Hittite, Assyrian, and Persian empires. Several books could be written on every aspect of these kingdoms' cultural importance, but it is only to the leisure and recreational element that we turn.

SUMER AND AKKAD

During the age of the Sumerian unification, in which the city-state of Sumer rose to power over the southern fertile crescent communities, the area between the Tigris and Euphrates Rivers constituted a most prized possession. For the thousand years between 3600 B.C. and 2600 B.C., countless struggles and periodic wars were waged between the mountain- and plains-dwelling peoples. This strife lasted through several kingdoms, and its intensity did not abate until after 1900 B.C. In the northern section of the Plain of Shiner, the state of Akkad held sway over this region, which then became known as Akkadia.

These two hostile states were decidedly different. The Sumerians had a well-disciplined agrarian civilization, whereas the Akkadians were desert nomads without the military training or organization to confront the heavy infantry of the southerners. During the centuries when these two states engaged in border wars against one another, there was comparative peace within the internal areas. However, sometime around 2370 B.C. the Semitic chieftain, Sargon, known to history as "the Great," led his lean archers against the Sumerian host and defeated them in a conclusive battle. He swiftly consolidated his conquest by invading the entire land, and pushed his claims from Elam in the east to the Mediterranean Sea in the west and the two rivers in the north.

Although the Akkadians had conquered in battle, they were gradually engulfed in a wave of fraternization as they adopted Sumerian ways, including the technique of measurement, arts and crafts, commercial organization, metal smithing, a calendar, and a numbering system. Sargon's forced union of Akkadia with Sumeria changed the Akkadian standards of living and it was the Sumerian civilization that prevailed over the simpler Semitic culture. The Semites left their desert life for town living. With town life there was intermarriage and adoption of the vernacular tongue of the Sumerians as well as their writing style, which was cuneiform.

With the civilizing influence of the towns imposed upon the Akkadians, they settled in the land, and it became the Sumerian-Akkadian empire. When these formerly vigorous and warlike Semitics began to acquire the cultural attributes that had developed over a period of two thousand years in the then independent Sumeria, they ceased to be have-nots and became the leisured aristocracy. They hunted and participated in many outdoor sports and game activities, including chariot racing, but they regarded manual labor, especially agriculture, as the province of inferiors. After several generations, the former conquerors became an integral part of the civilization they had overthrown. There was an exchange of religious, political, and social ideas, and in the process of refinement, the conquerors lost some of the hardy pioneering spirit that had impelled them to fight. Thus, the Semites turned aristocrat, relied more and more on others to enforce their rule, and depended upon mercenaries and lesser hirelings, thus laying themselves open to invasion by other up-coming lean and hungry societies.

The Sargonid dynasty lasted less than two centuries, but it is an era filled with artistic works, among which are the Sargonid seals, cut from stone and depicting men and animals in violent action.[7] The art of sculpturing was raised to its highest form in terms of human development at that stage. As the militaristic thrust and hardihood of the Akkadians were lost as a result of civilizing influences, together with the new found leisure which as aristocrats they enjoyed, fresh incursions of warlike people took place and the Sumerian-Akkadian empire was overthrown in 2300 B.C. under the direction of the city-state of Ur.

---

[7] C. Leonard Woolley, *The Development of Sumerian Art* (New York: Charles Scribner's Sons, 1935), pp. 126-130.

THE KINGDOMS OF EGYPT

It was once thought that Egypt was the earliest civilization because the geography of the land was eminently suited to the encouragement of cultural growth and civilized life. The desert climate provided a year-round growing season, and because the annual flooding of the Nile renewed the soils, soil exhaustion never became a problem. The floods were a natural means of irrigation. With an agricultural base assured and the desert expanses on either side protecting the population from foreign enemies, it appears logical that the inhabitants should multiply, that the ready food resource should free some people to pursue learning, and that additional knowledge would assure more food, more people, and leisure. However, this is not the way it was. It is now known that the earliest civilization began in the Fertile Crescent and spread east and west through subtropical humid lands. Though civilization extended early to Egypt, the Mesopotamian region was cultivated first.

During the Upper Paleolithic, about 10,000 years ago, people began to settle in the Nile Valley. By assimilating the cultural development of relatively nearby Mesopotamia, the Nile Valley dwellers began to farm and the land prospered. Four thousand years ago, Egypt was only a series of towns bordering the Nile River. As the towns grew, headmen or chiefs made their presence known and consolidated the communities so that two countries were born— Upper and Lower Egypt. It was not until 3200 B.C. that Egypt was united by Menes and literally burst into the full splendor that was sustained for the next 27 centuries. Egypt was one of the earliest ancient lands to develop the strains of culture into an impressive civilization. More significantly, it maintained its achievements without letup for more than 2,500 years. Few cultures can make that claim.

From the beginning, the Egyptians had two cardinal points that oriented their lives and regulated their conduct—the worship of the Nile River, from which all life flows, and the central authority embodied in the pharaoh. When Menes moved against Lower Egypt and united the country, the first of 30 dynasties of pharaohs came into being. With the first two dynasties, covering some 400 years, Egypt emerged from prehistoric obscurity and entered the stage of world history. Egypt had three major epochs—the Old Kingdom, the Middle Kingdom, separated by two intervening periods when Egypt found itself ruled by foreign invaders, and the New Kingdom.

Each of the three kingdoms was characterized by cultural advances of its own. The Old Kingdom, from about 2700 B.C. to 2200 B.C., was the era in which the great pyramids were constructed. The Middle Kingdom, about 2000 B.C. to 1800 B.C., brought an expanding political and economic capability. The New Kingdom, between 1600 B.C. and 1100 B.C., was concerned with empire building and the acquisition of power. With the close of the New Kingdom, however, Egypt's days of greatness were over, and the country declined politically and militarily as more and more foreign powers, interspersed with pharaohs, occupied the throne until the fourth century B.C.

The exceptional quality of Egyptian civilization began to develop during the reign of the first pharaohs. Political and social structure jelled into the mold it was to sustain, with rare interruptions, from that time on. The pharaohs were omnipotent. Seen as both king and deity, they ruled at the peak of society. Supporting them were the high officials to whom they delegated authority. Responsible to them, the rank and file bureaucracy was in turn maintained by the entire population, which performed the necessary labor of the kingdom.

The cultural explosion of Egypt's awakening was directly related to the introduction of writing, the *sine qua non* to successful centralized rule. Records could now be kept, edicts issued, regulations published, and history written down. The literature of Egypt was created when poets, authors, essayists, and historians could entrust their manuscripts to papyrus. Mathematics, in terms of calculation, developed simultaneously, and this permitted the computation of weights and measures, land surveys, taxes, distances, and time keeping. There is some truth to the idea that medical science originated in Egypt. A great deal of medicine was tinged with magic and supernaturalism, but some of the practice was, indeed, scientifically based.

Egypt's social order can be compared to the pyramid. At the apex was the pharaoh. In descending order came the high officers of the state, the governmental bureaucracy, and the masses that labored to maintain the kingdom in every known form of trade, agriculture, or service. With all power centralized, labor could be directed to harness the Nile. Irrigation projects were continually initiated so that the life-giving water could be brought to the parched fields beyond the land immediately adjacent to the river. Dike systems were constructed to reclaim thousands of arable acres. As agriculture became more productive, the material wealth of Egypt also increased. By 2600 B.C. Egyptian trading vessels had established a regular trade route in the eastern Mediterranean and Red Seas. Trade with Nubia to the south enriched the treasury with the goods produced by ancient Africa and the East. Copper, gold, bronze, silver, ivory, lapis lazuli, turquoise, and exotic spices were among the commonly traded materials.

The intellectual creativity that had produced writing and calculation now developed architecture. One hundred years after the first pharaoh was enthroned, Egyptian builders had discarded the time-worn use of sun-baked bricks for the sophisticated emplacement of stone. Again the seat of authority was able to demand the manpower necessary to quarry and dress the huge stone blocks and transport them at will. Within two centuries, Egypt's construction capability was such that the great pyramids at Gizeh were completed. In succeeding reigns, the stone builders erected some of the most impressive monuments, tombs, temples, and statuary that the world has ever known. The 800 miles of the Nile from its delta to Abu Simbel are still the sites of these remarkable architectural structures.

Art and architecture went hand in hand. From the Upper Paleolithic, the Nile artisans had created beauty and symmetry that enhanced even the most prosaic items. Flint knives, stone or pottery household vessels, pins and combs of bone and shell were decorated and colored in ways that delight the eye. During the period of the three kingdoms, Egypt's aesthetic quality multiplied and a highly sophisticated art flourished. For the next 3,000 years, Egyptian art knew greatness. Sculpture assumed massive proportions as artists tried to convey immense power through size. Painters added vivid pigments to the works of the sculptors and also covered temple walls, columns, and obelisks with representations of official life, religious, battle, and pastoral scenes, and almost every aspect of both daily routine and imagery that fanciful imagination can convey.

Under the pharaohs' ministrations Egypt prospered, and the people had a relatively good life. Any description of ancient Egyptian society would indicate that the people were happy, industrious, sociable, and, in many instances, rewarded. Occasionally, the social order was broken by war, political unrest, famine, or plague, but in the normal course of events life flowed on serenely. As with all ancient civilizations, the life of the laboring peasant was hard with little free time for the amenities. However, in return for their labor, the peasants knew a security and had fewer anxieties than their Mesopotamian contemporaries, whose lands were periodically despoiled by conquerors. During most of the years the peasantry labored without ceasing from before dawn until dusk and then after a frugal meal tried to sleep. When the Nile River flooded, however, it was festival time, a religious occasion when all work paused long enough for the laborer to celebrate with feasts, games, and ritual.

The aristocracy controlled the land, resided in considerable luxury, and knew immense leisure with all of the recreational activities that wealth, imagination, and retainers could buy. The supreme goal of the Egyptian aristocrat was to enjoy the largesse of the pharaoh. The upper class was part of a small, closed elite—a hereditary caste of priests, soldiers, bureaucrats, and, rarely, a gifted commoner who could rise by dint of outstanding talent. The leisured class of Egypt lived in opulence and comfort that would only be duplicated by the aristocracy of other imperial realms. Servants were a necessity to the aristocracy. Each lordly house kept a full retinue of personal maids, butlers, musicians, cooks, bakers, launderers, dancers, etc. Whenever called upon to do so, they served the meals and attended the banqueteers. All of this wealth depended upon agriculture, and the upper class was rewarded by the pharaoh with huge grants of land.

Feasts were a frequent and often raucous diversion of the wealthy. Guests consumed quantities of rich foods, wines, and beer. Since the women were elaborately coiffed, even to the extent of wearing cones of perfumed burning incense, a great deal of time had to be expended in preparing for and going to dinner parties and the like. The consumption of time for such recreational activities sharply contrasted the unleisured lives of the masses. The formal banquets were not unlike modern nightclub entertainments with each course accompanied by acrobats, wrestlers, exotic dancing, storytelling, and music. Hunting wild animals, fishing, boating, and fowling were among the sports regularly enjoyed by nobles.

For two millennia, the Egyptians met and overcame the problems of war, drought, famine, and pestilence. The civilization they built appeared to withstand the rigors of time and place. But, as with all previous kingdoms, a combination of forces began to erode the power of the central government, and Egypt's decline from greatness was assured. Starting with the 20th Dynasty, a steady reduction of the pharaoh's prestige, a shrinking empire, and the influence of the Iron age toppled Egypt from its preeminence. The nation became prey to internicine warfare as palace intrigue gave way to internal discord and the land was divided. After 1100 B.C., Egypt's role as a world power was forever eclipsed. There would be several remissions as certain Egyptian aristocrats regained the throne and provided a strong power base, but these were relatively rare. More often than not, Egypt was invaded by covetous neighbors and other foreign conquerors who had looked upon the rich agricultural valley as a prize to be seized. From the days of the Hyksos in the later Middle Kingdom, to the overthrow of the ruling family by the Libyans, then the Nubians, the Assyrians, the Persians, the Greeks under Alexander the Great, and finally the Romans, Egypt passed from the scene as an independent state and became a subject province.

The Nile Valley gave birth to the people who created the first great united kingdom, devised the political institutions to rule a dispersed geographical region, initiated the bureaucracy to administer hundreds of miles and thousands of people, and planned, organized, and executed engineering and architectural projects on a large scale. The Nile River kingdom provided the climate, food supply, stability, and wealth so that some people, at least the elect, attained a way of life that included not only work and duty, but leisure and the graphic and performing arts that lent luster, sophistication, and enjoyment to those who lived within the charmed circle of the aristocracy. The dynasties of Egypt are part and parcel of Western civilization because Egypt was a cultural crossroads between East and West as well as the home of people who created the enduring art, literature, and leisure of the good life.

BABYLON

From the west came the Semitic people who settled in a rural village, called Babylon, located on the Euphrates upstream from Ur. After three generations of intermittent warfare these Amorites succeeded in bringing much of what was then western Asia under their political and military control, surpassing Ur as the central seat of government, and having Babylon as its capital city. Under their great king Hammurabi (ca. 2100 B.C.), the first Babylonian empire was founded.

During the period of Hammurabi's dynasty, Babylonia flourished as the greatest commercial and political expression of that time. The arts, particularly literature and graphics, were generally developed to an extremely high form not to be repeated in that ancient time.[8] Members of the upper classes indulged in many recreational activities, specifically hunting, fishing, riding, wrestling, swimming, and the exercise of a variety of weapons for both war and leisure. Typical of the philosophy of Babylon is this illustration told about the hero Gilgamesh.

O Gilgamesh, why dost thou run in all directions?
The life that thou seekest thou wilt not find.
When the gods created mankind,
They determined death for mankind;
Life they kept in their hands.
Thou, O Gilgamesh, fill thy belly,
Day and night be thou merry,
Daily arrange a merry-making,
Day and night be joyous and content![9]

The orientation of "live for today" and enjoyment of life is self-evident. This rationale predates the earliest of the hedonistic philosophers of ancient Greece. It connotes the pleasurable existence that the upper classes could afford as a result of the pyramidal society on which Babylonian culture rested. Documentation of the history of the Babylonian empire's rise, the enterprises of peace and war carried on throughout the 400-year dynastic period, the myths, fine arts, dress, habitation, religion, and literature can be found in many texts as well as archaeological sources.[10] Gradually, Babylon grew decadent. Its militaristic capacity was greatly reduced as it became more highly civilized. Its art was prolific, as were trade and commerce. But the fruits of a leisured society came under the covetous eyes of warriors from the East, and by 1750 B.C., the empire that had been Babylon gave way to the Kassites who ruled, and in

---

[8] C. H. W. Johns, *Hastings' Dictionary of the Bible*, Extra Vol. (New York: Charles Scribner's Sons, 1906), p. 584.

[9] Excerpts from "Akkadian Myths and Epics," trans. E. A. Speiser in *The Ancient Near East: An Anthology of Texts and Pictures*, ed. James B. Pritchard (Princeton, N. J.: Princeton University Press, 1958), p. 64. Reprinted by permission of Princeton University Press.

[10] Archibald H. Sayce, *Babylonians and Assyrians, Life and Customs* (New York: Charles Scribner's Sons, 1900), p. 64.

turn were absorbed into, the Babylonian culture as a whole until the twelfth century B.C.

ASSYRIA

To the north of Babylon, Assyrian power had consolidated. The Assyrians raised warfare to a fine art and under Tiglath Pileser I, they conquered all of Mesopotamia and forced Babylon to submit to them in 1150 B.C. However, their conquest was not absolute and for 400 years a power struggle ensued between Assyrian military might and Babylonian force. It was not until the middle of the sixth century B.C. that a third Tiglath Pileser arose to found the New Assyrian empire with the final conquest of Babylon. The Assyrian empire lasted only until a new crop of lean and hungry men came from the Southeast to overthrow the 150-year-old Assyrian kingdom. The Semitic nomads came from Chaldea and in alliance with the Medes and Persians from the north, they captured Nineveh in 606 B.C. The Chaldean kingdom, with Babylon as its capital, lasted until Cyrus the Persian successfully attacked and defeated it in 539 B.C.

Thus, the story of civilization is repeated in successive centuries as conquest follows conquest in an almost rhythmic pattern, with intermittent warfare occurring as fresh invasions from border races inevitably bring about the collapse of the more settled former invaders. The Sumerians give way to the Akkadians, who in turn interbreed with the Sumerians and lose their identity as a distinct people. The Sumerian-Akkadian empire languishes and is set upon by other peoples. The Babylonians defer to the Assyrians, who in turn give way to the Chaldeans and Syrians; the northern Hittites swallow the Syrians and become Aryanized; the Medes and the Persians then dominate until they are finally subjugated by the Greeks.

The Tigris and Euphrates civilizations existed for some 4,000 years. As Winckler states in his 1907 text, *The History of Babylonia and Assyria:* "Eridu, Lagash, Ur, Uruk, Larsa, have already an immemorial past when first they appear in history." Those civilizations created out of the need for social organization and the cultural appreciation for and use of leisure have left an indelible stamp upon human history. Leisure, not necessity, is the mother of invention. Only when individuals have the time to survey their needs beyond mere survival, and appreciate the significance of creating something aesthetic out of a utilitarian item or something utilitarian out of natural materials, does the veneer of culture thicken to become civilization.

THE HEBREWS

Although the Israelites were never politically as significant as the kingdoms of Chaldea, Babylon, Assyria, or Egypt, their place is recorded in history because Judea, or Canaan, was the most direct route for both trade and warfare between Egypt to the south and the Hittites, Assyrians, Syrians, and Babylonians to the north. The land occupying this position was, therefore, almost constantly undergoing attack and conquest, or, as a tributary state, paying indemnification to some foreign power. As small and militarily insignificant as this country was, it nevertheless had a long and troubled history. However, inclusion is made of this nation and its culture because the writings of this people have made significant ethical and religious contributions to western civilization as well as documentation of leisure concepts and recreational pursuits.

The Patriarchs of the Old Testament came upon the historical scene sometime in 1800 B.C. The Pentateuch, or first five books of the Bible, provide the reader with a basic idea of human history and the record of daily life. It recounts the Flood, which appears widely in ancient Near Eastern histories. This may have been an account of some great submersion that occurred in the Mediterranean valley during the Neolithic era.

Genesis gives a history of the founding fathers, along with Abraham's migration from Ur of the Chaldeas, in which a covenant is made with the deity identified as Yahweh, later anglicized to Jehovah. The next six books of the Bible recount the migration of Jacob's tribe to Egypt, the story of Moses, the exodus and wandering of the Jews in the desert before reaching Canaan, the giving of the laws, and the consolidation of Israelite fortunes in Canaan.

The Hebrews never really held Canaan, for in reading the Bible one learns that the Philistines consistently held the fertile seacoast region of the south and the Canaanites and Phoenicians remained steadfastly in possession of the northern border areas. The initial victories of Joshua were never repeated and the Book of Judges becomes a recital of the trouble, defeat, and failure that the Israelites experience. The people soon lost their faith, deserted to pagan gods, and became a people of many races. Under the leadership of several prophets and heroes they continued to wage intermittent warfare, never completely successfully and usually with a disunited front, against a series of enemies. They were conquered by the Moabites, the Canaanites, the Midianites, and the Philistines.

Then the first king arose.[11] Saul was no more successful against countering invasions than were the judges and priests before him. The Philistines overwhelmed him and his army at the battle of Mount Gilboa. His successors were David (ca. 990 B.C.) and Solomon (ca. 960 B.C.). The end of the reign of King Solomon was also the end of Hebrew plans for expansion and glory. A schism developed between the northern and southern sections of the country as two separate kingdoms, Israel and Judah, were established. The rest of the history consists of regicide, fratricide, religious conflicts, political maneuverings, mistaken alliances, and intrigues that go on for three centuries.

Israel was finally swept into captivity in 721 B.C. by Shalmaneser of Assyria. Judah remained partially sovereign until 604 B.C. when Nebuchadnezzar II annexed it and several decades later transported the majority of the people to Babylon. There the Jews remained for more than two generations. Upon their return in 539 B.C. under the protection of Cyrus the Persian, a great change is noted in the character of this people.

> They went a confused and divided multitude, with no national self-consciousness; they came back with an intense and exclusive national spirit. They went with no common literature generally known to them . . . and they returned with most of their material for the Old Testament. It is manifest that . . . the Jewish mind made a great step forward during the Captivity.[12]

Out of this travail an intellectual awakening began and flourished to the extent that a moral force of intense power was created. Ethical concepts to guide the entire community were established. The capability of human grace and perfectability runs throughout this prophetic religion, and is seen in the subsequent establishment of Christianity and Islam as a direct outgrowth of Judaism.

---

[11] I Sam. 8.

[12] H. G. Wells, *The Outline of History* (New York: Garden City Publishing Co., Inc., 1921), pp. 230-231.

But beyond the creativity and monotheistic aspect of the Jewish religion, there is a dominant meaning for leisure and recreational experiences. The entire concept of the Sabbath or day of rest is applicable here. The statement "Have peace [leisure] and know that I am God,"[13] exemplifies the idea that some time had to be set aside from the ongoing functions of daily life when people were free to worship their creator. People were supposed to work from sunup to sundown in whatever vocational capacity they showed talent, but at some point in their lives, and periodically thereafter, they must give thanks to the God in which they had faith. Every seventh day was devoted to this offering of thanks and sanctification. Thus, the Sabbath was a day of leisure, free from the obligations of toil, and concerned with the revitalization of the individual through prayer, feasting, and appreciation of a god-given world.

Other recreational experiences noted in Hebrew life were the usual hunting and fishing activities as well as the utilization of more warlike and defensive instruments such as the sling, the bow, javelin, and short sword. Many biblical passages refer to a variety of physical activities, and one of the outstanding examples of this is Jacob's wrestling with "the Angel of the Lord."[14] Dancing, singing, and playing musical instruments are also recorded in Hebrew literature. Repeatedly, religious rites are celebrated with song, instrumentation, and dance;[15] but through it all the underlying cultural expression of Jewish life revolves around the Sabbath and the leisure that it brings.

ANCIENT WESTERN CIVILIZATIONS AND LEISURE

Parallel with the ancient Near Eastern civilizations another culture arose on the island of Crete, the remains of which at the capital of Knossos indicate an advanced civilization, much of which is now submerged beneath the Mediterranean. This island civilization is at least as old as that of Sumer, but it was only about 2500 B.C. when political unification occurred. For the next thousand years, the Cretans lived in peace, prosperity, and safety. They developed commerce with every civilized nation in the known world. Secure

---

[13] Psalms 65:11.

[14] Gen. 11: 24-25.

[15] Sam. 6:5, 12-14, 16, 20.

in their island citadel and immune from invasion for more than 3,000 years, the Cretans were free to perfect their leisure habits. Their artisans utilized skills to produce a high form of textile manufacture, sculpture, painting, lapidary work, and amenity conveniences that closely approximate those of our modern life.

Excavations show that the people of Crete were able to devote much time to the leisure arts and that they participated in a variety of recreational activities such as shows, festivals, bullfights, gymnastic exhibitions, dance, swimming, wrestling, and other sports. Crete presents a picture of a vibrant, unrestrained, exuberant life, expressive of good living as illustrated by the luxurious conditions surrounding the aristocrats at the expense of the enslaved masses.[16] It is apparent that security, when survival needs are satisfied, allows for leisure. Wherever humans have been safe for any length of time, they have been able to develop their arts, standards of living, and other cultural benefits to an amazing degree. It is not surprising, therefore, that the Cretans were able to accomplish just such a record in light of their immunity to invasion and comparative freedom from want.[17]

THE HELLENIC AGE

As a sea power Crete probably established colonies on the nearest shores, one of which was the Peloponnesus. From 1600 B.C., specific communities actually rivaled Knossos as centers of Cretan culture, and after the sacking of Knossos in 1400 B.C., Mycenae became the chief city of this branch of old Minoan, or Aegean, culture, known as the Mycenaean civilization.[18] This culture, from which many art forms have been gathered, lasted until the twelfth century B.C., when a final and engulfing invasion from the north by the Dorians completely overwhelmed it and dissolved its manifestations into a dark age of three centuries.

It is abundantly clear that a continuous series of minor invasions from the north harried an indigenous people who inhabited Arcadia and Attica from 1800 B.C. to about 1400 B.C. The incoming Hellenic

---

[16] Helen Gardner, *Art Through the Ages*, 6th ed., (New York: Harcourt, Brace and Company, 1975), pp. 101-120.

[17] M. I. Finley, "The Rediscovery of Crete," *Horizon*, Vol. VII, Summer, 1965, pp. 65-75.

[18] Harry R. Hall, *The Ancient History of the Near East* (New York: The Macmillan Company, 1935), pp. 56-67.

people gradually imposed their language on, and in turn were culturally absorbed by, the non-Hellenes. It is not until the Dorian invasion of 1200 B.C. that a cultural break is noted. The chaotic period of death and destruction, upheaval and internecine warfare terminates, perhaps from sheer exhaustion, in the eighth century B.C., after which classical Greece begins to emerge in a renaissance of culture.

THE GREEKS AND LEISURE

To discuss the influence that Greek thought has had on western leisure theory and philosophy, we must first survey the structure of the Greek mind which conceived and directed such intellectual pursuits of knowledge as ethics, morality, and education. To do this, one must be aware of *ârétè* and the consequences this ideal had on all Greek achievements, including play, and subsequently on what we call recreation.

Ârétè combined the idea of what is best in all things and is worthy of emulation and adoration—complete mastery. The Greeks saw *ârétè* in terms of animate and inanimate objects. A thing had *ârétè* if it was able to perform more than merely efficiently; it had to perform excellently in the manner for which it was created. This view applied to people as well.

The formation of the Greek national character takes its mold from a history of its culture, beginning in the aristocratic arena of early Greece, where human perfection was a coveted ideal towards which the superior class of the society was steadily trained and educated.

> We can find a more natural clue to the history of Greek culture in the history of the ideal of *ârétè*, which goes back to the earliest times. There is no complete equivalent for the word *ârétè* in modern English: its oldest meaning is a combination of proud and courtly morality with warlike valour. But the idea of *ârétè* is the quintessence of early Greek aristocratic education.[19]

The ancient tradition of heroic power was not enough to satisfy the chroniclers of a younger era. Their concept of *ârétè* hinged upon a combination of noble actions and noble thoughts. Human perfection was the ideal that joined exalted deeds with nobility of mind. It is this concept of unity forcing its way into the very foundation of the Greek code of life that has been handed down to us in the modern meaning of recreation.

---

[19] Werner Jaeger, *Paideia: The Ideals of Greek Culture* (New York: Oxford University Press, 1943), Vol. 1, p. 5.

Unity and wholeness seem to be the salient features of the Greek psyche. They are best described by Kitto, who states:

> The sharp distinction which the Christian and the oriental world has normally drawn between the body and the soul, the physical and the spiritual, was foreign to the Greek—at least until the time of Socrates and Plato. To him there was simply the whole man. The Greek made physical training an important part of education ... because it could never occur to him to train anything but the whole man.[20]

The above discussion has been presented because it is ultimately bound up with the subject of recreation. It shows the direct lineal descent, as it were, of modern recreation philosophy with its concepts of the rebirth of harmony within the individual from the idealistically contrived values of excellence and oneness of the ancient Greeks. Such a tracing is necessary to support the thesis that recreation is really the alleviation of the awareness of tension and the reunification or rebirth of the individual in mind and body.

In the Greek cultural pattern there emerged a two-fold reason for the existence of leisure which gave rise to great intellectual, artistic, creative, and other achievements. One was the owning of domestic, factory, and mine-working slaves upon whose shoulders the leisure of the well-to-do rested. The other aspect is the simplicity in which the Greek lived. The standard of living and the basic necessities of life were quite far removed from what we would consider the bare needs of today. Then too, it must be remembered that the Greek citizen saved time by not having to travel to work and back home, that there were no conventional hours of work. Kitto has put it quite well:

> Again, the daily round was ordered not by the clock but by the sun, since there was no effective artificial light. Activity began at dawn. We envy, perhaps, ordinary Athenians who seem able to spend a couple of hours in the afternoon at the baths or a gymnasium (a spacious athletic and cultural centre provided by the public for itself). The Greek got up as soon as it was light, shook out the blanket in which he had slept, draped it elegantly around himself as a suit, had a beard and no breakfast, and was ready to face the world in five minutes. The afternoon, in fact, was not the middle of his day, but very near the end of it.[21]

---

[20] H. D. F. Kitto, *The Greeks*, revised edition (London: Penguin Books Ltd., 1957), p. 174. Copyright 1951, 1957 by H. D. F. Kitto. Reprinted by permission of Penguin Books Ltd.

[21] Ibid., pp. 134-135.

It is significant to note that such leisure as the Athenian had was directed to contemplative study of philosophy, civic service, rhetoric, and artistic creativity. Leisure to the Greeks, especially to the Athenians, was not conceived as many of us see it today. Leisure was a period to be put to practical use in learning (education), or in public participation of government. It was free time that was used to benefit the society in which the Greek citizen, that is, the nonslave lived.

How different is our conception of leisure. Many think of it in any terms but those of practical or educational usage. Many consider it, in its usual connotation, as the antithesis of work, labor, or study; as a time for loafing rather than living. The Greeks took their leisure seriously and spent it wisely in the pursuit of knowledge for living. People of our modern civilization take their leisure and use it to no purpose. We spend our time by letting it pass, "killing" it, so to speak, with no thought of what we can make with it. The Greek concept of leisure was one of participation, stimulation, learning, and living. Our concept of leisure is a time for doing nothing or, at best, watching someone else do what we either will not or are not skillful enough to do. This might be considered too sweeping a condemnation of our leisure practices, but it is indicative of what our culture does with its free time.

The purpose of this book is not to indict or condemn people's leisure pursuits. In fact, it is believed that leisure activities may be one phase of possible recreational acts. But it is the purpose of this section of the study to show Greek educational philosophy as the taproot for modern recreation thought.

Because leisure was a basic ingredient that produced one of the world's greatest cultures, it was natural that it was used in educating the young. The word *schola*, from which we derive the word school, is Greek for leisure.

> Of course, reasoned the Greek, given leisure, a man will employ it in thinking and finding out about things. Leisure and the pursuit of knowledge, the connection was inevitable—to a Greek.[22]

The love of play and the desire for freeing men for the most important aspects of their lives, namely participation in government, artistic works, and the never-ending search for knowledge impelled the Greeks to use leisure as a time for creative activity. Edith Hamilton put it in a slightly different way:

---

[22] Edith Hamilton, *The Greek Way* (New York: W. W. Norton & Company, Inc., 1930, 1942), pp. 31-32.

> The Greeks were the first people in the world to play, and they played
> on a great scale. If we had no other knowledge of what the Greeks
> were like, if nothing were left of Greek art and literature, the fact
> that they were in love with play and played magnificently would be
> proof enough of how they lived and how they looked at life. They had
> physical vigor and high spirits and time, too, for fun.[23]

The Greek concept of education is joined with freedom and their concept of freedom is tied up with leisure. On the combination of these two factors, freedom and education, in conjunction with árété or excellence, a philosophy of leisure can be based. These separate facets of a single whole form what to the Greeks was completeness and what can be thought of as the unification of the human mind and body to produce the complete person—at peace with self and the environment. All the person's faculties are in harmony, and there is no awareness of tension, strain, or discord. Such a person is truly re-created.

THE ROMANS

Traditionally, Rome is supposed to have been founded by the Trojan Aeneas somewhere about 1200 B.C. Many myths describe in minute detail the construction and development of Rome by Romulus. However, these stories, for such they are, do not stand the test of critical evaluation and are merely part of the elaborate heritage of folklore to which the uneducated masses subscribed in the days of ancient Rome.

The Neolithic Italian culture existed before 3000 B.C. For 500 years thereafter there was little change in that stagnant society. When foreign migrations started in 2500 B.C., progress in social culture was made. During the Chalcolithic age metalworkers from beyond the Alps began to move into the region of the Po Valley, and it is basically from these emigrants that Italy was to gain its first knowledge of civilized life.

While the people of the Italian boot were adopting themselves to Chalcolithic culture (about 1700 B.C.), a new wave of invasions began in central Europe. The Achaeans moved into the Greek peninsula, and ripples of migrant pressure were felt throughout the northern Mediterranean region. One of these groups left a deep impression upon the peninsula Italians—the "Terramara people."

---

[23] Hamilton, *Greek Way*, pp. 21-22.

Through profound contact with the Terramara people, great advances in both material and cultural institutions were made.

Some six centuries after the initiation of the Chalcolithic culture into Italy, a new flood of migrations brought violent repercussions to the lands lying along the Mediterranean Sea. One result was the Dorian invasion of Greece, another was the drive southward by the then inhabitants of the Po Valley to new locations in the central region of the peninsula.

About 800 B.C., Italian culture underwent another remarkable change for the better when invaders from Asia Minor, the Etruscans, overran much of western Italy. They rapidly transformed the land they conquered. They taught the Italic natives how to drain the swamps, log the forests, and introduced grape and olive agriculture into the country. The local iron, tin, and copper mines were successfully worked, and the practical trades of smithing, stone masonry, carpentry, and weaving soon appeared. Timber was transformed into ships, which were soon plying the trade routes between Italy, Sicily, Sardinia, and Corsica.

Once their initial landings and position had been consolidated, the Etruscan aristocrats began to enlarge their sphere of influence. They went south and invaded Latium and Campania, thus, probably founding Rome. The Greeks, too, had colonized parts of the Italian peninsula and when the Etruscans headed south, it was only a matter of time before the two would clash. From the sixth century on, the two peoples were almost continuously occupied by war. It was not until 535 B.C., that an alliance between Carthage and Etruria combined to expel the Greek colonists from Corsica. By 500 B.C., however, the tide in Campania and Latium had turned against the Etruscans, and after repeated revolutions on the part of the native populations, the Etruscan empire toppled. The growing power of Rome was an important factor in this decline of the Etruscans. Between 500 B.C. and 265 B.C., Rome first became the dominant power and then engulfed and united all of Italy into one state.

LIFE AND CULTURE IN EARLY ROME

Life was simple and somewhat crude during the third century B.C. The weakening of class distinctions and the lack of a very wealthy or very poor class mitigated against a heterogeneous culture. The economy was based on agriculture. People lived by traditions, and family unity was strong. There was little of the aesthetic quality about these Romans, and they cared little for the niceties of civilization.

Under such conditions, work, rather than leisure, was the central theme. Thus, everyone in the family worked hard and lived simply. Yet even in these times of simplicity and frugality people had leisure and the diversions that free time usually spawns. Religious holidays were numerous. Citizens were still obliged to attend public hearings and pass on laws in Rome. Markets or fairs were held every ninth day in and about the capital as well as in the rural areas.

Slaves in early Rome were usually captives of war. In this simple society they were used mainly as agricultural laborers. There were so few slaves during this period that they contributed little to the leisure of their owners. It was not until much later that large numbers of captives from Asia, Greece, and central Europe were introduced and cruelly exploited by their owners for purposes of luxury and vice, thus making slavery the abomination it became. As might be expected, the early Romans, having to cope with harsh environmental conditions, both human and natural, did little in terms of cultural achievement, i.e., the fine arts and literature. However, in the eminently practical arts of architecture and road and aqueduct building, they were unsurpassed.

LIFE AND CULTURE AFTER THE ROMAN CONQUEST

From 265 B.C. Rome began to dominate the western Mediterranean world. During Rome's consolidation of the Italian peninsula, its wars seemed largely defensive. However, as Rome continued to win, it had to protect new frontiers. This led to increased expansion. Inevitably, its sphere of influence clashed with that of Carthage, which, up to that time, controlled much of the western Mediterranean area. The conflicts resulted in the Punic Wars. Rome emerged victorious and by 200 B.C. was well on the way to imperial overlordship of the Mediterranean world.

With Carthage defeated, Rome became the strongest military power in the civilized world. Again, new frontiers led to new antagonisms with attendant wars, both of defense and of aggression. The stage was set for Rome's assumption of power over the eastern Mediterranean. Up to about 200 B.C., Rome's foreign policies had been based on opportunism and had had little contact with the Hellenistic states. Now it came into direct contact with them and was involved in an endless series of wars. As a result of these wars, Rome emerged, in 167 B.C., as the dominant power in the eastern

Mediterranean as well as the western. From that time until the decline of the Roman Republic in 79 B.C., Rome engaged in a series of major and minor wars that subjugated all of the former kingdoms and empires of the ancient Near East as well as Asia Minor, Greece, Spain, and the Danube region.

One of the unfortunate results of this imperial expansion was the decadence of the society. A salient effect of the increased wealth and might of the Roman people was a marked inequality in economic status between the rich and the poor. Slave labor replaced free labor, and depressed wages were the consequence. The well-to-do no longer performed the manual labor or lived the simple life to which their ancestors had adhered. A new leisure class arose—the aristocratic rich.

Public festivals and amusements became more numerous and varied both for rich and poor. From Campania came the gladiatorial combats, initially held in Rome in 264 B.C. This custom did not gain popular support until after 200 B.C. Theatrical performances, horse racing, and acrobatics were some of the events held to entertain the public. By 50 B.C. the aristocracy, by virtue of its reliance upon slave-worked agriculture and other commercial enterprises, lived a leisured existence on a scale hitherto unknown. As Van Sickle states:

> Indeed, many of the richer members and the spendthrifts who strove to imitate them at times adopted gaudy splendor and coarse luxury which was the scandal of their own later times. Eating, drinking, flashy clothes, expensive furniture, handsome slaves, and gambling cost these worthies enormous sums, and they went to the most absurd and revolting lengths to procure the objects of their desire.[24]

Yet, for all this apparent depravity and shocking activity, there is abundant proof of a rich cultural development during this period. The Romans were very creative and found means of self-expression in both the fine arts and literature. Architecture, sculpture, and painting flourished. History, poetry, oratory, and the didactic essay were integral parts of Roman literature. Roman architecture formed a style of its own. An age that had leisure produced Virgil, Horace, Livy, and fine arts that cannot be denied acclamation.

The years of the Republic's decline and abandonment, caused by the corruption and degradation of senatorial power and the illegal office holding of some men during emergencies, cannot be laid on

[24] C. E. Van Sickle, *A Political and Cultural History of the Ancient World From Prehistoric Times to the Dissolution of the Roman Empire in the West* (New York: Houghton Mifflin Company, 1948), pp. 341-342.

any single person. When the first Tribune of the people was murdered, the basic sanctions were lifted, and one consequence was the rise of a variety of warlords who hastened the decline of the Republic. After the Triumvirate and subsequent rise of Gaius Julius Caesar as a general and statesman, the fate of the Roman Republic was sealed. Civil war between Caesar and Pompey, proscription of enemies, dictatorship, assassination, and the war of succession heralded the Augustan Principate.

EARLY IMPERIAL SOCIETY

The aristocracy stood at the top of Roman society. It included the wealthy few who, through ownership of estates and shares in commercial ventures, or by corrupt methods in politics, had gathered the economic means to pursue a life of luxury. Estates were cultivated by tenants and slaves. With abundant leisure and, therefore, opportunities for education, the aristocracy followed cultural pursuits that were denied to the great masses of the people. The urban middle class, or curials, also enjoyed excellent educational opportunities. Through wise investments, a strong sense of civic duty, and other reasonable factors, they served Rome diligently until they were financially ruined by sustaining the cost of imperial government in the third century A.D. In the fourth and fifth centuries, its surviving members were no more than slaves of the state.

The urban proletariat was a composite of hard working, frugal freemen, hired laborers, and slaves. Because of slave competition, wages were very low and most workers lived a life of squalor and bare existence. In Rome, the emperors had to take over the task of feeding and amusing the populace, and these people shared in the free entertainment, public baths, food distribution, and other doles that the local ruling class saw fit to present. Much more numerous than the city masses were the peasants who cultivated the soil. Although slavery was never the principal ingredient used for agricultural production, some slaves were utilized along with free peasants. Agricultural implements were primative at best, and the peasants worked hard for a small return and little leisure.

Generally, the peasants' lives were hard and bitter. They had to pay their rent and taxes and face forced labor drafts and other imperial levies. They had little or no part in the brilliant, if wasteful, urban life that produced the appearance of great prosperity for the

Empire in the second century A.D., and educational prospects did not exist. Culturally, peasants were backward and their freedom, such as it was, became a farce at the end of the third century.

For the 250 years after Augustus' death, the Greco-Roman culture of the Empire was sustained by the intellectual and aesthetic traditions of its past, but the decay of classical culture had already begun. During the first century of this era much that was valuable was produced. Then routine and stagnation set in, and for the next century a rapid decline in taste and artistic form is noted. Van Sickle states:

> Literature succumbed to a taste for showy rhetoric and to blind worship of the past, and of the arts only architecture was producing anything which was destined to win the approval of later ages. Science and philosophy lingered a little longer, but before the accession of Diocletian they, too, had succumbed to the forces which were bringing the classical world to an end. The decline of economic prosperity, the breakdown of political absolutism, and a caste-ridden social order-all contributed to create an environment in which none of the distinctive products of earlier ages could flourish. Hence, they withered away . . . .[25]

LATE IMPERIAL SOCIETY

The decadent fourth and fifth centuries witnessed the fall of the classical tradition in the Roman empire, as well as the destruction of orderly government, sophisticated urban life, the economy, art, literature, science, and philosophy. This was closely followed by an almost complete lack of artistic activity. In the harassed and regulated cities of the fourth and fifth centuries, survival, rather than leisure, and the wealth to indulge in free time experiences, were the controlling interests. Economic support was no longer sufficient for building programs, and artistic creativity was displaced in communities continuously under attack by invading barbarians as well as supposedly protecting soldiers and rapacious bureaucrats.

The general view of society at this time is one of conformity, complicity, and stagnation. The urban middle class had been crushed and no longer existed. The wealth, leisure, and consequently the culture of the late Empire was to be found only in the possession of the great senatorial landlords who lived in seclusion on their vast

----

[25] Ibid., p. 523.

estates. Their wealth was drawn from the land and was created as a result of slavery

The Empire was doomed to destruction. Many factors influenced its inevitable decline, though it is not known just what specific conditions contributed to the final dissolution of Imperial Rome. The splendors of the classic era were routinized and strangled by an effete aristocracy or ignorant peasantry. The indulgences of the senatorial aristocracy amid the ruination of the other classes were scandalous. In every period of ancient and the later Roman Empire, there are traces of degeneracy. For sheer waste and brutality, the gladiatorial contests and orgiastic or sybaritic ways of living cast a pall that the ensuing Dark Ages could not dispel. There is little wonder at the condemnation of leisure by members of the various Christian sects during the following 1,400 years. A final commentary on the social conditions of Imperial Rome is offered by Johan Huizinga:

> Rome grew to a World Empire and a World Emporium. To it there fell the legacy of the Old World that had gone before, the inheritance of Egypt and Hellenism and half the Orient. Its culture was fed on the overflow of a dozen other cultures. Government and law, road-building and the art of war reached a state of perfection such as the world had never seen; . . . The Roman Empire . . . was spongy and sterile in its social and economic structure . . . .
>
> Rome in its later days . . . was slowly degenerating and being suffocated under a system of State slavery, extortion, graft and nepotism, circuses and amphitheaters for bloody and barbarous games, a dissolute stage, baths for a cult of the body more enervating than invigorating—none of this makes for a solid and lasting civilization. Most of it served for show, amusement and futile glory.[26]

The grandeur that was Rome was copied to a large extent from the Hellenistic culture. The Romans adopted the leisure style of the Greeks but added certain refinements and debasements. Thus, the gladiatorial schools for slaughter were developed as well as daredevil competitive events. In the period of the Empire, leisure excesses were so prevalent and leisure so demeaned that a negative reaction was formulated against all things recreational. The disapproval of most leisure activity or seemingly purposeless experiences has remained in one form or another in most Western cultures since the

---

[26] Huizinga, *Homo Ludens*, pp. 174-176.

early Christian Church denounced frivolous conduct, particularly after Saint Augustine wrote against sensuousness in human affairs. One might see this tendency in contemporary society in terms of the 1961 U. S. Supreme Court ruling that upheld the legal propriety of the blue laws.

SELECTED REFERENCES

Aristotle. *The Basic Works of Aristotle.* Edited by Richard McKeon. New York: Random House, Inc., 1941.

Baddeley, St. Clair, and Gordon, L. D. *Rome and Its Story.* New York: Gordon Press, Publishers, 1977.

Bosanquet, Bernard. *The Education of the Young in the Republic of Plato.* New York: The Macmillan Company, 1907.

Burney, C. A. *The Ancient Near East.* Ithaca, N. Y.: Cornell University Press, 1977.

Hamilton, Edith. *The Greek Way to Western Civilization.* New York: W. W. Norton & Company, 1930.

Jaeger, Werner. *Paideia: The Ideals of Greek Culture.* Translated by Gilbert Highet. 3 vols. New York: Oxford University Press, 1939-1944.

Kinzl, K. H., ed. *Greece and the Eastern Mediterranean in Ancient History and Prehistory.* Hawthorne, N. Y.: Walter De Gruyter, Inc., 1977.

Kramer, Samuel N. *History Begins At Sumer.* New York: Doubleday & Company, Inc., 1959.

Lloyd, Seton. *Archaeology of Mesopotamia: From the Old Stone Age to the Persian Conquest.* New York: Thames & Hudson, 1978.

Magnusson, M. *Archaeology of the Bible.* New York: Simon & Schuster, Inc., 1978.

Sayce, A. H. *Babylonians and Assyrians, Life and Customs.* New York: Charles Scribner's Sons, 1900.

White, J. Manchip. *Ancient Egypt: Its Culture and History.* New York: Dover Publications, Inc., 1970.

Woolley, C. L. *The Development of Sumerian Art.* New York: Charles Scribner's Sons, 1935.

Chapter 3

Leisure after the Fall

The thousand years between the fall of the Roman Empire and the Renaissance have typically been called the age in the middle or the medieval years. During this period national cultures grew; Western civilization solidified to a point where its character would determine the shape of succeeding eras. There was only one church—the Church of Rome. The downfall of the Roman Empire in the West brought the scourge of barbarism to Europe. The Hunnish invasions caused the fierce tribes of the north to migrate. In the process the Franks, Visigoths, Ostrogoths, Jutes, Angles, Saxons, and others overran the boundaries of the Roman Empire and finally brought its government down. With the destruction of Rome the great illumination of classical civilization went out. The ensuing 500 years were, with good reason, called the Dark Ages. During this period of alternating chaos and torpor, cities declined to towns and villages became mere cross-roads. Farms were left to rot, roads decayed, isolated fortified places existed, wild animals roamed where herds of domestic animals used to pasture.

The 500 years of this epoch were filled with fear, hunger, and disease. Survival constantly prodded people to seek out the protection of stronger neighbors. Looting and raiding by enemies were continual threats. An individual's real hope of protection lay in local chiefs strong enough to retaliate or stand off the raider. This fact was soon evident in the European countryside. The early medieval community was a clutch of huts set in close proximity to the manor house in which the local lord dwelt. But for survival, the free peasantry of

Europe paid an enormous price—freedom. For the protection offered by the lord of the manor, many peasants gave up their freedom for serfdom, which bound them to the manor for life. There were, of course, degrees of serfdom. At the bottom of the heap were the cotters, who were given three or four acres to farm but also did menial work at the manor. The villeins were given up to 40 acres of land to farm, but had to labor a certain number of days each week on the lord's farm and supply him with produce from their own small holdings.

Agriculture was the basis for all economy, and it proved to be a precarious enterprise, especially in the northern climates. Famine was endemic. The high aristocracy moved from place to place as provisions in one manor gave out. The king's court might be perpetually on the move throughout the realm. Unhappily the burdens of this destitute society fell most heavily on the serf. The load was severe and the requirements exacting. From every serf on the manor two kinds of labor were performed: fieldwork and handwork. Ditch-digging, manure-carting, tree-cutting, road repairing—all of the tasks normally associated with the term "handyman" were required. In addition, the serf also had to plow, seed, and harvest the manorial acres. As if this weren't enough, serfs also had to show gratitude for the lord's protection by supplying even more labor—boon work—over and above all of the other chores that were exacted from them.

WORK AND LEISURE IN MEDIEVAL EUROPE

In his *Colloquium*, Aelfric recites a dialogue between a serf and a visitor:

M. What do you say, plaoughman, how do you do your work?

P. Oh, sir, I work very hard. I go out at dawn, driving the oxen to the field, and I yoke them to the plaough; however hard the winter I dare not stay at home for fear of my master; but, having yoked the oxen and made the plaough-share and coulter fast to the plough, every day I have to plough a whole acre or more.

M. Have you any companion?

P. I have a boy who drives the oxen with the goad, and he is even now hoarse with cold and shouting.

M. What more do you do in the day?

P. A good deal more, to be sure. I have to fill the oxen's cribs with hay, and give them water, and carry the dung outside.

M. Oh, oh, it is hard work.

P. Yes, it is hard work, because I am not a free man.[1]

Hard toil, little surcease, and heavy penalties were the serf's expectations. Taxes came in many forms. The lord could impose a head tax, an income tax, and fees or charges for using the lord's mill, oven, or wine press. It was not unusual for a male serf to have to pay for the right to marry and, where the practice occurred, to yield his bride's virginity to the lord on the marriage night if called upon to do so. The serf did not escape even when he died, because the lord might confiscate the contents of his cottage. It was possible to flee from serfdom. Serfs who could make their way to a town and remain there for a year and a day, paying the town's taxes, were freed from bondage. Infrequently freedom could be purchased directly from the manor. If willing to work even harder than normal, on feast days as well as a few hours before dawn or after dusk, serfs might eventually amass enough money from the surplus produced to buy their own liberty.

Typically, however, holidays provided an all too infrequent break for the serf. Holidays afforded the free time necessary to rest and recuperate from the unceasing toil that feudal society demanded. It was a time for raucous activities, for letting go, for singing indecent love songs, dancing around a flowery maypole, and watching a traveling show with its mumming, masques, and dancing animals. These respites were brief; but the peasants deemed themselves lucky if they survived, and asked no more than the security they received from their masters. A medieval rhyme suggests that the human order was determined by God and one should not attempt to change the system. There were three castes—nobles, clergy, and aristocracy, and the function of the peasantry was to serve the latter.

The duty of the peasant to support the ruling classes brought with it certain reciprocal responsibilities. The serf served the lord of the manor, the clergy ministered to the spiritual needs of both serf and aristocrat, and the noble had to govern and to provide security. Within the aristocracy itself, there existed a complex mutuality of privileges and responsibilities; the concept of *noblesse oblige* was the foundation upon which medieval society rested.[2] The relationship

---

[1] George G. Coulton, *Medieval Village, Manor, and Monastery* (New York: Harper & Row, Publishers, 1960), p. 307.

[2] Carl Stephenson, *Medieval Feudalism* (Ithaca, N. Y.: Cornell University Press, 1942), pp. 18-38.

between noble and serf was based upon the manor, and called manorialism; that between noble and noble was called feudalism. The term feudalism stems from the Latin word *feudum,* or fief—a grant of land by a superior to a lesser lord, or vassal, in return for services performed and homage received. The rise of feudalism may be attributed to the kind of economy and insecurity that resulted from the barbarian invasions of the Roman Empire in the west. Constant harassment led to the demise of earlier clans as families began to die out. Geographic proximity assumed a greater importance than blood relationships. Landowners became more closely bound to neighbors whose lands adjoined theirs. By joining forces, they were often able to withstand threats of incursion or actual attack. Since the economy was essentially based on bartering, the exchange of services seemed a logical extension and quickly followed.

The feudal relationship cemented a bond between two individuals, both responsible for and accountable for their actions. Conditioned by the religiosity of the times, there being only one church, vows assumed a sanctity and meaning that have seldom been repeated in the course of history. The feudatory act was sealed by a formal pledge of homage in which the vassal placed his hands between those of the overlord and was kissed in return. The superior not only gave the fief and the assurance of his protection against all enemies, but also provided a court for the settlement of disputes that might arise.

The hierarchical scheme of medieval nobility required that vassals could have their own vassals and be subject to several overlords. Whoever was at the top of the pyramid—whether king, emperor or Pope—numbered hundreds or thousands of the aristocracy as inferior vassals. The services rendered by a vassal to a lord included a combination of civil, monetary, and military activities. The vassal might be called upon to administer justice in the fief, through various payments, to supply lodging if the overlord came through the fief, and to supply military service in times of need. This could mean castle guard duty and combat. When summoned, vassals had to appear with whatever retinue they were called upon to provide. This might mean a mounted regiment made up of their own vassals, who in turn provided their military services in much the same way. Feudal armies came to be based upon the mounted man or knight. From this term, *chevalier,* French for knight, the future system of chivalry was founded.[3]

---

[3] Edgar Prestage, ed., *Chivalry* (New York: Alfred A. Knopf, 1928), pp. 37-55.

Warfare was common in medieval Europe. Invasions by Arab Moslems bent on converting all to Islam were a constant threat after 660 A.D. Sweeping out of Africa after the vision of Mohammed, the Moslems threatened western Europe many times. The structure of the feudal system slowly developed after the great seven-day battle at Poitiers, in southern France, in October 732. The Christianized Franks defeated the Moslems and warfare was now to be based upon the cavalry rather than infantry. Charles Martel, ruler of the Franks, decreed that to receive his protection, his vassals would have to provide themselves with horse, armour, and whatever supplies were necessary. Poitiers proved to be the high water mark of Moslem incursions in the West. Never again would the armies of Islam advance so deeply into Europe. While they would continue to harass the fringes of Europe, particularly dominating Spain, southern Italy, and the Mediterranean islands, they would never again menace the European heartland.

The reign of the Martel family was brought to its peak by his grandson, Charlemagne. He became king of the Franks in 768. His entire life was dedicated to the restoration of Roman imperial power. In this regard he succeeded brilliantly. In St. Peter's Cathedral on Christmas Day, 800, the Pope crowned him emperor of the Roman Empire in the West. All of western Europe, except England, Scandinavia, and the Islamic territories in Spain and Italy, were under his control. Charlemagne's acquisition to the crown launched an era of tension and continual conflict with the Church. The struggle for supremacy between Church and state was to go on for another 600 years. Although Charlemagne's heirs would lose the empire within 150 years after his death, it was revived by the great German King, Otto I, as the Holy Roman Empire, this time minus France, but including Germany and northern Italy. This imperial power would exist until the 13th century, and its remnants would still be observed by the Hapsburg emperors of Austria until 1918.

Charlemagne's empire was a monumental legacy to later generations, despite the political and religious disputes that he left unresolved. Under Charlemagne, educational advancement was pursued as never before. Charlemagne became the patron of learning in Europe, and the schools he founded encouraged the spread of literacy and scholarship. His promotion of education eventuated in the establishment of the universities on which secular life depended for their administrators, doctors, lawyers, bankers, and men of commerce. The Carolingian Renaissance anticipated the wave of aesthetic achievement immortalized in Romanesque and Gothic architecture, sculpture, and manuscript illumination.[4] During his reign Charlemagne is thought to have sponsored new methods of agriculture that increased food production. His reign actually broke the sinister tide of medieval life, although this was slow to be realized. After the emperor's death in 814, Europe had to defend itself against the savage raids of the Vikings and other Norsemen. Towns had to be newly fortified, and Europe gradually took on the form which is still associated with the word "medieval."[5]

Towns and monasteries constructed thick walls around them. Many medieval towns grew up alongside a burg or fortress usually situated at a strategic high point, river, seacoast, or overlooking a pass. Here their merchant founders were conveniently based for trade and relatively secure from raiders. Some burgs were small castles, others were citadels. Outside the burg, the traders built a market and their homes enclosed by a surrounding wall. The inhabitants of such new burgs soon had a definitive name to distinguish them from old burg dwellers such as knights, clerics, and serfs. The residents of the new towns were called *bürgers* by the Germans, Burgesses in England, and *bourgeois* in French. Although all economic levels were included initially, the term soon came to denote middle-class affluence. The German *Berg* and burg passed into the venacular and really denoted the successful assimilation of the way of life generally associated with medieval Europe.[6]

Even as medieval towns were growing and a new middle class was beginning to appear, life was still brutish. Every castle, however small, had a dungeon. Punishments were extraordinarily cruel and debasing. Malfactors were burned, branded, mutilated, and eventually killed. Torture was typical. Justice was determined under the most primitive and superstitious manner possible. For example, the accused was guilty, if when thrown into water, he or she floated. Carrying hot irons and engaging in trial by combat were habitual. Of course, there was one way an individual could refrain from the course of physical brutality—by joining the Church. As more and

---

[4] Jeffrey B. Russell, *Medieval Civilization* (New York: John Wiley & Sons, Inc., 1968), pp. 245-250.

[5] Henri Pirenne, *Medieval Cities* (Princeton: Princeton University Press, 1925), pp. 70, 73-77.

[6] John Ciardi, "Lesson Plan for Today: The Mother Tongue," *Saturday Review*, Vol. II, October 18, 1975, p. 6.

more men elected this decision, their collective impact became a tremendous force upon medieval Europe. Both as the greatest spiritual power and now as a temporal kingdom, the Church would have an enormous role to play.

DAYS OF TOIL AND HOLIDAYS

Only about 10 percent of all medieval people resided in towns; most of the rest were peasants dwelling on manorial farms. The aristocracy, i.e., landowners, amounted to less than two percent of the entire population and controlled all of the rest.[7] The average peasants had a small patch of land, a cottage with thatched roof and dirt floor, and were required to perform almost unceasingly. Their view of the world was contained by their village, the manorhouse, and its fields and woods. If one piece of equipment symbolized the peasant's life, it was the plow. Because they were farmers, they lived and were guided by the seasons.[8] Each autumn, the peasants sowed wheat and rye; each spring they planted other grains plus legumes; each summer both crops were harvested. Between these periods of back-breaking labor came many lesser chores with brief reprieves. The peasants' toil brought them mixed rewards, and it diminished their lifespans considerably. A peasant was old and used up by 30 years of age.

Spring on the manor began as soon as seasonal rains had softened the earth sufficiently for plowing. The peasants sowed their own plots as well as their lord's with the crops memorialized in the old song "Oats, peas, beans, and barley grow." In fact, peas and beans were a staple of the medieval diet for both serf and noble. The old English rhyme, which every school child knows, is chanted as: "Pease porridge hot, pease porridge cold, pease porridge in the pot, nine days old." In addition, each family had its own vegetable garden and its own livestock to put to pasture. In April, when the cows could be milked, the peasant wives would be kept busy making butter and

---

[7] Francis Oakley, *The Medieval Experience: Foundations of Western Culture Singularity* (New York: Charles Scribner's Sons, 1974), pp. 106-121.
Leopold Genicot, *Contour of the Middle Ages* (London: Routledge & Kegan Paul, 1967), pp. 30-31.

[8] Nellie Neilson, *Medieval Agrarian Economy* (New York: Henry Holt & Company, 1936), pp. 45-48.

cheese and setting aside the necessary eggs that were due the lord at Easter.

Spring planting was finished by Holy Week, and for a few weeks thereafter a welcomed respite was allowed. The peasants thronged to church for the impressive ceremonies heralding Easter. Not long after, they celebrated another, more pagan custom, the festival of May Day. At this time abandoned dancing, singing, and other licentious behaviors were enacted. Despite such free exercise of their limited leisure, the peasants knew that May was also a month of continuing labor. Houses had to be repaired. Barns required patching. There were always fences, hedgerows, and drainage ditches to be worked on. Flocks needed protection from marauding wolves, and the peasants had to stalk these predators in the surrounding woods.

The summer months brought even harder work as the days grew warmer. Early in June vinedressers in France and Germany had to see to their vines. English and Flemish herdsmen washed their sheep, and shearers, supervised by the lord's steward or bailif, clipped the wool. The fields had to be weeded. By Midsummer Day, June 24th, the hay harvest would begin. This dawn-to-dusk work required that all persons work; women as well as children labored alongside the men. Naturally, the lord's share was brought in before their own. Hay gathering had to be completed by August 1, because the two major crops, wheat and rye, were ready for harvest. Reaping the grain usually took all of August as the peasants fought heat and exhaustion to finish. It was not until late September that they could stop laboring and give thanks for the long-anticipated harvest-home supper.[9]

As always autumn was a time for food storage and husbanding supplies in preparation for winter. The peasants brought in vegetables from their own small gardens, picked fruit in the orchards, gathered firewood from the manor's woods, and collected acorns and other nuts to feed their pigs. Now it was time to thresh the harvested wheat—by hand. In October, the grapes of France were picked, trampled, and the juice was placed into fermenting casks. October was also a time for slaughtering those animals that would provide meat for the coming year. In November, Flemish peasants scutched dried stalks of flax to separate the pith from the fiber. Fodder was always in short supply, and this was a time for driving livestock to market.

---

[9] Dorothy G. Spicer, *The Book of Festivals* (New York: The Woman's Press, 1937), pp. 81, 90, 171, 221-222, 263-264.

December brought some respite to the men, but the women continued to work. The 12 days of Christmas brought the high point of the peasants' long holiday season of feasting, churchgoing, and folk festivities. The main meal on Christmas Day was traditionally served in the lord's manor, and all of the peasants were invited. Roast pig and blood pudding might constitute the repast and often the men were permitted to sit and drink after dinner. After the holidays, harsh weather generally stopped the men from doing outdoor work, but their wives had to cook, weave cloth, and make clothes. Sometimes they were required to wait upon the lord or his minions. Through January little could be done out of doors, but in February, the peasants began spreading the fields with manure and sharpening their plows for the toil of another year. Thus, the seasons passed, and the peasants' calendar of toil remained in effect. Life was short, hard, and unrewarding. Only the holidays provided the leisure for rest and recuperation before another round of intense manual labor was begun.

TOWN AIR IS FREE AND PROVIDES LEISURE

Medieval towns had little to commend them. They were little better than a hodgepodge of dwellings with stores or stalls for selling or trading goods and services, together with open sewers and rooting animals in the narrow and dark streets (alleyways). Sanitary facilities were almost unknown, and disease incubated by filth was rampant. Any person who walked through town was assailed by the putrid odor of feces, garbage, and swilling pigs. Space was a luxury few could command, and crowding was endemic. Except for the thrilling sight of a Gothic belfry or church spire, the townsperson had little to find inspiring in the noisesome and physically confining limitations of the town. There was, however, one absolute benefit to be derived from being a townsperson. The air might be odoriferous, but it was free.[10] Unlike the serfs on the manor, the town dwellers could drink as they pleased, work or not, and speak their minds on any issue that concerned them. Although the physical aspect of the town might be restrictive, the townspeople's emotions and intellect were given unrestricted reign. The hustle and bustle of urban life

[10] Neilson, *Medieval Agrarian Economy,* pp. 38-39. Cf. also, J. H. Mundy and P. Riesenberg, *The Medieval Town* (Princeton: D. Van Nostrand Company, Inc., 1967), p. 43.

produced the social, political, and economic alterations that would eventually change the Western world from medieval to modern.

Aside from the few cities that had survived the downfall of the Roman Empire, most towns of the Middle Ages were not founded before 1000 A.D. Reconstituted trade encouraged their evolution. Essentially, international rather than local trade tended to support commerce. At the hub of East-West trade lay Constantinople.[11] For western Europeans Constantinople beckoned to be taken. Christian military forces overcame Islamic strongholds on the northern borders of the western Mediterranean basin, and this encouraged the traders of Venice, Genoa, Marseilles, and Barcelona to build and equip ships for commercial enterprise with the Levant. The torpor of the early Middle Ages was now being shaken off. A new spirit of involvement came to be felt. People started to travel again, some on pilgrimages, others back to rural areas that could now be opened up for farming because of new agricultural procedures. With agricultural advances, prosperity was greater, and consequently population grew. People felt that life could have greater meaning than the day-to-day struggle for survival.[12]

In this salubrious climate the introduction of exotic goods from the East stimulated appetites for more. Although most of the wares were prohibitive, except to the rich, there were many items to which lesser persons could aspire—among them sugar, spices, dyes, and fabrics. In the beginning, Europe had only one manufactured item for export—cloth. Eventually, exports consisted of grain, fish, flax, salt, and wines. Later on, there were furs, timber, hemp, honey, and caviar. Out of the stimulating contacts and ideas developed in East-West trade came an expansion of local European trade and manufacture. The results of such commerce could be observed at the traditional fairs where the artistry and craftsmanship of native Europeans could compete with anything that originated in the East. As trading places the fairs were unique.[13] The feudal lords who sponsored them and obtained revenue through taxes on them guaranteed safe-conduct through their regions. Large fairs might draw traders from all over Europe and the Near East. International mone-

---

[11] Howard L. Adelson, *Medieval Commerce* (New York: D. Van Nostrand Co., Inc., 1962), pp. 28-29, 32-34, 55-58. Cf. also, Pirenne, *Medieval Cities*, p. 85.

[12] Philippe Wolff, *The Cultural Awakening* (New York: Pantheon Books, 1968), pp. 197-203.

[13] Frederick Heer, *The Medieval World: Europe Eleven Hundred to Thirteen Fifty* (London: Weidenfeld and Nicolson, 1961), pp. 59-60.

tary units changed hands through obliging money-changers; from this rude beginning the banking system developed. But for all of their advantages, the fairs could not really satisfy the need for trade. One had to travel to reach a fair, and travel was dangerous. Significantly, the fairs were seasonal. Increasingly, the merchant-traders required a stable place in which to buy and sell. Out of this need came the towns.

Situated at crossroads, on waterways, and in close proximity to fortified places, the towns grew. Inevitably towns attracted people other than traders, and before long towns were being populated by artisans and craftsmen seeking outlet for their skills, serfs fleeing bondage, itinerant workers, footloose soldiers (mercenaries), the younger sons of nobility who would not inherit anything, and others who then provided the town with amenities. In this way the fabric of urban life developed swiftly. As previously explained, the new towns began to build their own defensive walls.[14] As population grew and space became even more limited, towns would be enlarged. Old walls were torn down to be replaced by new enlarged walls. A town's progress toward maturity could be reckoned by the successive sites of the advancing walls. Between 1100 and 1250, the number of towns with charters that enumerated inhabitants' rights multiplied rapidly.

The growth of the towns stimulated a new concept, that of political control. Under the feudal system, the lands on which towns were built was owned by some noble or clergyman who could exact a number of obligations in return. As the towns prospered, fiscal exactions enriched the aristocracy. The urban population quickly perceived the healthy position they were in and began to bargain for the remission of political and social constraints. They felt no need to require the lord's permission to marry, to migrate, to own and dispose of property, to participate in military exercises, or other personal infringements. They wanted their own courts and their own laws that would be better able to administer business affairs. By joining together to press their demands, town inhabitants frequently negotiated successfully for these rights. The town's charter, which enumerated the citizen's duties, obligations, and privileges, became the basis for individual freedom and self-government.[15]

---

[14] Maude V. Clarke, *The Medieval City State* (New York: Barnes & Noble, Inc., 1928), pp. 1-18.

[15] Pirenne, *Medieval Cities*, pp. 175-220.

A double exercise in solidarity existed to assist townspeople in the gaining and retension of their charters and freedom. One was the commune, in which all town dwellers joined to obtain political liberties. The other was the guild, which furthered both economic and social welfare. Originally, there were two kinds of guilds—those of merchants and those emphasizing specific crafts. The guilds became the cornerstone of social and recreational life, such as it was. There were guildhall banquets, saint's-day celebrations, pageants, and processions. Guild members were visited by their fellows when they were sick and were financially sustained when out of work or too infirm to continue their trade. Guild funds provided a dowery for a member's daughter, cared for his soul through prayer when he died, paid for his funeral expenses, and supported his widow.[16]

The power of the middle class, made up of townspeople, grew increasingly formidable. Dependent as they were upon the bourgeois wealth for their own revenue, the aristocracy, particularly kings, gave the rich merchants places in their councils. The merchants supported centralized authority and encouraged the diminuation of the feudal system which was to be replaced by the nation-state. In whatever guise they assumed, whether as bankers, business tycoons, or masters of crafts, the bourgeoisie inexorably altered the social environment of Europe. Although the clergy remonstrated against its capitalistic competition and the nobles condescended to it as *nouveau riche,* the affluent middle class could not be kept out of the medieval spectrum. Having acquired surplus capital by its determined labor, the bourgeoisie now aspired to heights that belied its original low-born station. Its members built magnificent mansions, schools, and churches, clothed their wives in furs and silks, became patrons of the arts, collected manuscripts, commissioned musicians and painters, and benefitted posterity with the way they invested their wealth. They wanted to educate their sons in the new universities, to endow their communities with great cathedrals, fountains, public plazas, and sculpture. Medieval civilization flourished in consequence of the new town's middle class.

THE BURGER'S LEISURE

During the course of their daily rounds, the urban dwellers had sufficient leisure to dine on enormous meals, a custom still observed

---

[16] Georges Renard, *Guilds in the Middle Ages,* trans. Dorothy Terry (London: G. Bell and Sons, Ltd., 1919), pp. 42-45. Cf. also, George Unwin, *The Guilds & Companies of London* (London: George Allen and Unwin, Ltd., 1938), pp. 116-124, 176-215, 267-292.

by many business leaders who take clients to luncheons or dinners on an expense account. As a guild member, a man could drop in at the guildhall, gossip about prices, drink wine or ale, and then return home for his meals. Since there were several guilds in every town and each had a time for festivals, parties, and public processions, there must have been much free time to forsake the business rituals and participate in or be a spectator at these festivities. Naturally, the holidays were celebrated in the towns and other public or private occasions when townspeople could observe the enjoyment of social intercourse. Traditional May Day, saint's-days, weddings, funerals, or commemorative opportunities could be celebrated with song, dance, costumes, parades, drum and trumpet flourishes, and other decorative devices. Churchgoing was an obligation, but it was a joyful occurrence filled with the symbolism, chanting, and choral music.

Although the town dwellers preferred not to participate in military adventures, they did maintain a guard to watch from the city's walls and learned archery for defensive purposes. Shooting at archery butts, bear baiting, dog and cock fighting, some forms of dice playing, passion plays, and other entertainments were common. Between the various guilds some medieval towns had competitions that might include horse racing, flag throwing and catching, processionals, or other exhibits. Strolling singers, acrobats, jugglers, story-tellers, musicians, and masquers also provided entertainment when they passed through the community.[17]

The trade fair, primarily designed to introduce commerce beyond the local area, was also a time that permitted the establishment of lavish display booths, enabled merchants to visit beyond the confines of their own towns, and attracted all types of buyers and sellers intertwined in a mosaic of color and sound that could also serve as a recreational outlet. Dancing bears, wrestling contests, stage shows, mountebanks, and an occasional hanging or other form of public punishment contributed to the leisure amusement of the traveler. Although the earlier fairs preceded the towns, many of the finest and most enduring of them were held in the town whose name they bore. Today's Leipzig Trade Fair is a holdover from its medieval forerunner.

Town dwellers had free time because they were not subservient to a demanding lord and the vagaries of nature to which the serf

[17] Robert J. Blackham, *London's Livery Companies* (London: Sampson Low, Marston & Co., Ltd., 1940), pp. 40-41. Cf. also, Herbert F. Westlake, *The Parish Guilds of Medieval England* (New York: The Macmillan Company, 1919), pp. 49-59.

was subject. Since he was his own man, inhibited only by the regulations of the guild or community to which he belonged, a guildsman could do with his time as he saw fit. He engaged in the give-and-take of capitalistic enterprise either as craftsman, trader, or provider of amenities. When his daily work was completed, at his own discretion, he could do with his time as he wished. With leisure and accumulated wealth he desired a better life. That the middle classes succeeded in upholding the process of civilization may be attested to by the monuments in art, architecture, and learning which they left. The greatest Gothic cathedrals were lovingly supported by money made in the towns in which they stand. The role call is gorgeous and stands as part of the leisure life on which guildsmen and merchants lavishly spent their revenue. Chartres, Rheims, Amiens, Notre-Dame in Paris, Mount St. Michael, York, Canterbury, Strasbourg, Ulm, and Cologne are but a few of these grand structures that still inspire all who visit them.

ARISTOCRATIC LIFE AND LEISURE

At the top of the social system was the nobility. Growing out of the wreckage of the withered Roman Empire, the former barbarians developed ethnic ties and managed to form a new breed of people who would succeed the Romans. Ancient clan chiefs and their families formed the nucleus for the new aristocracy that came into being as *Pax Romana* was obliterated. Into the vacuum created by the vanquished Rome, northern tribes hurried to establish their claims. They too were pressed by migrating eastern hordes and needed some surcease from continuous fighting. At strategic locations clan chiefs and their families established fortified dwellings from which they could sally forth and invest other areas, defend their own holdings, or attend to the process of enlarging their own domains. As they consolidated their possessions, always in land, feudalism became the dominant social system. There was no such thing as a central government, although a few powerful kings or emperors attempted to centralize their rule. Individual feudatories ruled over western Europe during the Middle Ages.

Originally, the aristocracy spent much of its time subjugating surrounding territories, engaging in military adventures, or just plundering the regions through which they marched. Once established as the ruling class, the aristocracy quickly sought to gain advantage by imposing obligations on those who sought to live and work on

their lands. The manorial system served to maintain the relationship between aristocrats. With the clergy, the aristocracy literally controlled all life in the Middle Ages, at least during the initial stage. Later, the development of trading centers, towns, and the crusades to the East would forever change and finally bring down the feudal system.

By the 12th century, increasing security and increased trade had transformed the aristocracy from itinerent warriors into a stabilized rural nobility. As warfare became conducted as a set piece, governed by tradition and season rather than by strategy, the former roving knight could settle down to an hereditary fief and turn his attention to his own pleasures. As long as his overlord did not require his military presence, the knight could enjoy much leisure, land tenure, and a great deal of life's amenities. Many aristocrats rebuilt early wooden forts into elaborate stone establishments. Here with a continuous stream of visitors and servants, the nobles banqueted, danced, and gambled. They imported chess from India, and indulged in backgammon, dicing, and other board games which had been popularized when first brought back by returning Crusaders.[18]

But these zestful, willful men did not remain indoors during clement weather. They rode to the hounds, hunted stag and wild boar, engaged in falconry, archery, horse racing, and the knightly games-tournaments. When there was no occasion to hunt, there were always gymnastics, running races, and the practice with arms. As with older civilizations, sport replaced warfare as the activity of the nobles' leisure. For country aristocrats, a stream of visitors to the castles had to be fed and entertained. This could mean boating in a nearby river or lake, hunting parties, picnics, or, for the knights who no longer had to worry about war, there was the practice of courtly love. The knights of the twelfth century were absolute masters of their own castles and everything in them, including their wives. Male chauvanism was complete. But a new force entered the picture with the spread of courtly romance, whose praises were sung by the travelling troubadours. This cult assumed tremendous recreational significance and was one of the uses to which the gentry's leisure was put.[19]

---

[18] William E. Mead, *The English Medieval Feast* (New York: Houghton Mifflin Company, 1931), pp. 15-31.

[19] Edgar Prestage, ed., *Chivalry* (New York: Alfred A. Knopf, 1928), pp. 17-18. Cf. also, Frederic V. Grunfeld, "The Troubadours," *Horizon*, Vol. XII, Summer, 1970, pp. 16-26.

Courtly love encouraged the relationship of a knight to his chosen lady—which really meant any woman not his wife. There was an elaborate code of invitation, words, gestures, musical interludes, and, perhaps, assignations. According to formula, the romantic knight had to be happy, ardent, discreet, and courteous. No matter how long the suit took—weeks, months, or years—the knight had to continue his courtship. While much of knightly romance was platonic, it also encouraged extramarital affairs and infidelities. The mythic romance between Queen Guinevere and Lancelot typifies the secret ritual of romance and dalliance that occurred during the new leisure.[20]

Toward the end of the 14th century, the emergence of the nation-state was well on its way. Feudalism diminished as the various monarchies gained more control over the central administration of government and law. France and England were the leading exponents of this as early as 1066 when William, Duke of Normandy, overcame Harold Godwinson at the battle of Hastings. This was the initial stirring of centralized government. Over the next four centuries arose the concept of trial by jury, equal justice under the law, and although Magna Carta was a completely feudal doctrine, it nevertheless provided the basis for many of the rights which free people now assume naturally.[21] In France, during the same period, there was an attempt on the part of the French kings to enlarge their tiny strip of land, the Ile de France. Paris was, of course, the international marketplace of Europe, and taxes poured into the treasuries of Philip I and his successors Louis VI and Louis VII. These were the kings who consolidated the monarchy. France developed its national existence at the beginning of the 13th century under Philip II (Augustus). By 1314, Philip IV had created an assembly of all classes that would eventually be known as the *Etats-Generaux* (Estates-General), named for the three estates of the kingdom—nobles, clergy, and commoners.[22]

Centralized monarchy was slower to develop in other countries of Europe, but laws were written and representative government began to appear all over Europe. The pace of medieval life quickened with the advance of technology, trade, and the arts. During the

---

[20] Thomas Bulfinch, *The Age of Chivalry* (New York: Airmont Publishing Co., Inc., 1965), pp. 71-72.

[21] J. B. Russell, *Medieval Civilization* (New York: John Wiley & Sons, Inc., 1968), p. 438.

[22] Norman Zacour, *An Introduction to Medieval Institutions* (New York: St. Martin's Press, 1969), pp. 129-132.

Middle Ages the first of the great seats of learning was founded.[23]
Schools were built and supported by a newly enriched middle class
as well as by prelates and the nobility. Medieval people were fascin-
ated with the effects of color and light. Venetian glassware is a
product of that curiosity as are the magnificent stained glass windows
that permitted sunlight to illuminate the vast interiors of the Romanesque and Gothic cathedrals constructed at this time. Science and
medicine were beginning to advance, and by the 13th century the
scientific method was articulated by Roger Bacon.[24] As the practice
of medicine spread, the containment of disease and good health
became public concerns. The first hospitals were developed during
the Middle Ages. But to all of these fine advances there came a
concomitant development of catastrophe. Between 1350 and 1450
famine, war, plague, peasants' revolts, schism within the Church, and
other vexations would tend to disrupt European life. Many noble
families were economically wiped out, and bubonic plague killed
off from one-quarter to one-half of the population of Europe. The
social fabric was torn and many of the elements of its structure would
never be seen again. However, the horrors of war and plague passed
away and winds of change blew everywhere. Blocked from trading
with Constantinople when the Turks overran that city in 1453,
Europeans looked to the West for new territories and trading routes.
The Cape Verde Islands were discovered in 1456, and this encouraged
other sailors to think of the possibilities beyond the western horizon.

The dawn of the 14th century was the climax and the decline
of the Middle Ages. The results of medieval culture were everywhere
apparent. Politics, economy, technology, medicine, education, and
social services were expanding to meet the needs of all. Medieval
people had established institutions to govern, to adjudicate, and to
educate. They had political freedom and used it to enlarge their
minds and make their place in society. They had the leisure to
participate in both secular and religious activities that uplifted them,
renewed their spirit, and provided the fun and entertainment that
made life worth living. The Middle Ages had reached their zenith.
New methods of warfare, continued religious problems, and economic
reality required intellectual expansion and new methods for solving

---

[23] James J. Walsh, *High Points of Medieval Culture* (New York: Books for Libraries Press,
1969), pp. 83-99.

[24] Herman H. Horne, *The Democratic Philosophy of Education* (New York: The Macmillan
Company, 1960), p. 416.

problems. The people of the Middle Ages had done what they could; now it was another generation's turn.

THE INFLUENCE OF THE RENAISSANCE ON CULTURE AND LEISURE

The outburst of intellectual endeavor that attempted to model itself on the classical antiquities of ancient Rome was intensely humanistic. People were conscious of a changing world around them and reveled in the idea that they were part of this evolving condition. The old anchors of feudalism and dedication to other worldly efforts were slowly giving way to the emerging nation-states and the revival of interest in ancient Roman legal and literary studies. The center of this intellectual ferment boiled out of the Italian peninsular between 1350 and 1525 A.D. The Middle Ages just did not disappear suddenly; medieval life and civilization gradually waned for more than a century before the Renaissance burst out in full force in Italy.[25] Again, as in the past, the new urban culture required methods and knowledge that feudalism and theological study could not provide. The coastal and interior Italian towns, situated as they were in the center of the Mediterranean trade routes, served as both ports of entry for seaborne goods and as trade centers and transshipment markets on overland routes. The cities of Venice, Genoa, Rome, Florence, and Milan were admirably suited to carry on the trade to western Europe, which a closed-off East made necessary.

In 1305 the papacy left Rome for Avignon in France and did not return until 1375. This hiatus permitted the former papal territories to become secularized and governed by leading local families, who were thus enabled to found independent city-states. By 1315 the cities and independent states of Italy had achieved a political position that allowed them to consider themselves exclusively rather than have to depend upon the great monarchical powers to the north and west that had previously influenced them so heavily. Another unique condition was also produced concurrently. The larger Italian cities became immensely prosperous as a consequence of trade. This economic development heralded a power structure that was different from other regions. Rather than being manifesta-

---

[25] Robert Ergang, *The Renaissance* (Princeton, N. J.: D. Van Nostrand Company, Inc., 1967), pp. 74-95.

tions of the landed aristocracy, all economic and political power resided in the cities.

The Bubonic Plague, which devastated much of Europe in the 14th century, could not dampen the enthusiasm and patronage for great art, architecture, and education. The Renaissance required a utilitarian kind of education that could not be found within theological study. The demands of business necessitated the study of law. Scholars began to search for the original Roman codes and indexes, and this led them into the study of other classical works. From the diligent study of the classics for business purposes, there soon grew the desire to read for pleasure. This ambition to imitate and learn from long-dead Romans led to the exploration of historical treatises. Once engaged in the study of history, it was but a short step to indulge in the reading of those who made the laws and placed their personal stamp upon the culture of the time. The writings of Quintilian and Cicero, which emphasized the qualities of character and intellect that was most appropriate for a man to meet the challenges of the ancient world, were deemed suitable for the 15th century. One Ciceronian quality that probably endeared itself to the men of the Renaissance was that of the stoic-humanist. Here was the combination of the life of action and that of contemplation. For the humanists, a person is the measure of all things.[26] The men of the Renaissance felt obligated to serve the community as well as to learn as much as they could about the rational world. The virtues that Cicero taught offered a model that could be followed by the students of ancient Roman thought. Of the four virtues (wisdom, justice, fortitude, and temperance), justice was considered most important. It contained two elements, social cohesion and beneficence; the former was concerned with consistency and truthfulness, while the latter was the most human of all concerns. Beneficence was the spirit of public giving, but performed in such ways that the recipient's character would not be harmed. People would not be made to feel that they were beggers, but that they should be treated considerately. Nevertheless, beneficence also contains the guide that individual's primary responsibility is with themselves. In this way, the individuals are capable of sustaining themselves before they offer aid to others.

One typically Roman trait that became the hallmark of the

---

[26] Samuel Dresden, *Humanism in the Renaissance* (New York: McGraw Hill Book Company, 1968), pp. 12, 83-91.

Renaissance man was that of universality. It was emphasized that the complete man had competence or mastery over many facets of life. Perhaps the epitome of this ideal may be seen in the life of Leonardo da Vinci. He explored everything and excelled in almost everything to which he put his hand. He had so many diverse interests that even though he was one of the greatest artists in an age when many great artists lived, he had little time to paint. What he did paint ranks among the world's most sublime art. His curiosity and genius drove him to study and extend the range of knowledge about anatomy, botany, geology, mechanics, and astronomy. He was an engineer, inventor, hydrologist, cartographer, optician, and writer. He worked on every problem that caught his attention with the unlimited enthusiasm of a man who was in love with life and learning. In this way he was the embodiment of his age.[27] Other men might also typify the ideal. Certainly Michelangelo, Cellini, or Lorenzo de' Medici (Il Magnifico) would qualify for the role of Renaissance man.

THE SPIRIT OF LEISURE

The Renaissance was an age of spectacles, filled with the mock combat of festival sports, the pomp and circumstance of processions, the uproar of great citywide celebrations. Almost any occasion—a saint's day, the arrival of visiting nobility, the anniversary of a great battle, even the political reverses of some feared or hated prince—was reason enough to bring to the streets crowds that were full of revelry. When there was no opportunities, however meaningless, to celebrate, the joyousness of the age found outlet in hunts, ball games, horse races, boxing matches, snowball fights, racquet games, gambling, dancing, musical entertainments, banquets, and tableaux. These were some of the recreational experiences that could be enjoyed either actively or passively.

THE PEOPLES' LEISURE ACTIVITY

Every city had its trumpeter heralds. With flourishes and martial blare they would announce the town criers, accompany brides to

---

[27] Ladislav Reti, ed., *The Unknown Leonardo* (New York: McGraw Hill Book Company, 1974), passim.

church, enliven banquets, or precede nobles or town councilors through the streets. A Renaissance procession was a civic spectacle that can only rarely be duplicated in the modern era. It brought together in one munificant display the luxuriously robed nobles, magistrates in full regalia, leading citizens, military companies, contingents of clergymen, and hordes of musicians, acrobats, clowns, horsemen, and animal handlers. The entire community turned out for the event. Thousands marched while, from housetops, doorways, windows, and along the streets through which the procession passed, thousands more beheld the display. Processions commemorated a variety of circumstances. Each city-state had a patron saint whose feast day was celebrated with a processional. Each ward, represented by companies in colorful costumes and following a float symbolizing its emblematic animal, would march around the central town square amid the waving of banners and the brilliant sound of trumpets. After the procession there would be general feasting and, perhaps, games. (See, for example, "Procession of the Contrade," an oil painting done by Rustice Viricenzo in the second half of the six-teenth century, and now in the Soprintendenza alle Gallerie, Florence.)

The energy and enthusiasm of the Renaissance found expression in a wide variety of sports and games. Schoolmasters considered physical activity an essential part of the curriculum.[28] Forerunners to tennis, baseball, and bowling were very popular. Exercise was deemed a necessity for both young and old. Physical activity was both utilitarian and enjoyable. It provided for the sound body in which a sound mind could exist, and it was fun to participate in. Spectator sports played a significant role as well. The rough-and-tumble horse races, or *Palio* with which Florentines honored their patron saint, were played in streets and squares of all Renaissance cities. Each city had its traditional sports, and no festival was complete without the excitement of these events. Some places were famous for their bullfights, others for jousts. The gondola regattas of Venice were known throughout Italy. In Pisa, the most popular sport was a mock battle on a bridge, commemorating an historic defeat of the Saracens. Florence not only held its horse races, but espoused boxing and a variation of football as well. The *Palio* was run in Siena then and is still annual tradition today.[29] So important

---

[28] Walsh, *High Points*, pp. 139-145.

[29] Roy McMullen, "Italy's Other Eternal City Siena," *Horizon*, Vol. XV, Spring, 1973, pp. 16-31.

were some of these activities to the citizens that even during periods
when the city was threatened by invasion, gunpowder was actually
taken from military supplies to provide fireworks for the festival.

ARISTOCRATIC LEISURE AND RECREATIONAL EXPERIENCE

Renaissance society was steeped in pageantry. When musicians
played, they often wore masks and elaborate costumes. The tumbling
of acrobats enlivened the most formal of courtly gatherings. At
dinner parties the dinner courses were announced by herald trumpets.
When actors performed, the content of the play was less of concern
than the scenery and costumes. Fantastic spectacles were usually
staged between the acts. Leonardo da Vinci was employed by the
Duke of Milan to produce and stage elaborate displays to the delight
of the Duke's guests. The greater the effect, the more pleasure was
induced in the spectator. Each impresario tried to outdo the other in
inventing special events. It was an age of supreme sophistication in
the arts and superficial stimulation to titillate the senses.

The pageantry of a Renaissance country hunt was at least a match
for the spectacles of the city. The chase was a true pastime for the
nobility.[30] A supreme gift from one aristocrat to another was a
well-trained hunting falcon. The hunt was, in its own way, compara-
ble to the city pageant in that it required stores of wines and food
supplies, colorfully costumed hunters, teams of beaters, dog handlers,
stewards, and other servants who were always close at hand to do
the hard labor while the lords cantered easily and rode up for the
kill. This amusement is most vividly depicted in Paolo Ucello's painting of the hunt.

Physical activity was a mainstay for the aristocrat. No less a writer
than Castiglione pointed out that:

> Also it is a noble exercise, and meete for one living in Court to play at
> Tenise, where the disposition of the body, the quicknes and nimble-
> nesse of everie member is much perceived, and almost whatsoever a
> man can see in all other exercises. And I reckon vaulting of no less
> praise, which for all it is painefull and hard, maketh a man more
> light and quicker than any of the rest.[31]

---

[30] Baldassare Castiglione, *The Book of the Courtier*, trans. Sir Thomas Hoby (New York:
E. P. Dutton & Co., Inc., Everyman's Library, 1948), pp. 41-42.

[31] Ibid., p. 42.

Still, the Italian Renaissance produced its own catastrophic events. There were intermittant invasions as the monarchical states continued to cast covetous eyes upon Italy. Internicine warfare was endemic among the princely houses that ruled the various city-states that occupied the penninsular. The rise of the Borgias, Sforzas, and Medicis are well known. Political intrigue, attempted Church domination, schism within the Church, and the selling of indulgences were to be reaped within a short time. The religious revivalism that reached epic proportions in the pronouncements of the Dominican friar, Savonarola, was not isolated in Florence. Preachers had been speaking out for the previous two centuries about licentious behavior, vanity, and other improprieties. In the end, however, his political supporters and disciples fell away, and Savonarola was burned at the stake in Florence.

While leisure might now be available to the great mass of people, there was still the necessity for hard work in order to enjoy the free time. Except for public festivals and recreational activities that could be enjoyed during holidays or other memorial occasions, the proletariat struggled for the basic necessities. Life remained hard for the farmer, apprentice, or urban shopkeeper. The wealthy and hereditary nobility had the time and the talent to utilize leisure expertly. They became art patrons, school builders, hospital founders, and commissioned composers to write music for them.

This is what Huizinga has to say about Renaissance Italy:

If ever an elite, fully conscious of its own merits, sought to segregate itself from the vulgar herd and live life as a game of artistic perfection, that elite was the circle of choice Renaissance spirits. We must emphasize yet again that play does not exclude seriousness. The spirit of the Renaissance was very far from being frivolous. The game of living in imitation of Antiquity was pursued in holy earnest. Devotion to the ideals of the past in the matter of plastic creation and intellectual discovery was of a violence, depth, and purity surpassing anything we can imagine. We can scarcely conceive of minds more serious than Leonardo da Vinci and Michelangelo. And yet the whole mental attitude of the Renaissance was one of play. This striving, at once sophisticated and spontaneous, for beauty and nobility of form is an instance of culture at play. The splendours of the Renaissance are nothing but a gorgeous and solemn masquerade in the accoutrements of an idealized past.[32]

---

[32] Johan Huizinga, *Homo Ludens: A Study of the Play Element in Culture* (Boston: The Beacon Press, 1955), p. 180. Copyright © 1950 by Roy Publishers. Reprinted by permission of Beacon Press.

The high point of the Renaissance was reached in Florence. No other city in all Europe could match Florence for its dynamism and intellectual achievements. In the arts, sciences, diplomacy, literature, banking, trade, and manufacturing Florence soared above all the others—in poetry, Dante and Poliziano; in prose, Baccaccio and Machiavelli; in painting, Giotto, Masaccio, Ucello, Verrocchio, Fra Angelico, Fra Filippo Lippi, Botticelli, Leonardo da Vinci; in sculpture, Donatello, della Robbia, Ghiberti, Michelangelo, Cellini; in architecture, Brunelleschi, Battista Alberti, and the Sangallo brothers. The Medici were associated with banking; Florence produced its share of popes, cardinals, and saints. Of course, other cities had their share of greatness too.

The flood of peace and prosperity continued until 1494. In that year Italy was overrun by Charles VIII of France. In swift succession the Italian cities were stormed, taken, and sacked. The disasters that overtook Italy in 1494 did not destroy the Renaissance culture. For a century afterwards, various cities, such as Genoa, flourished. Smaller principalities remained independent, although overseas rule was common. Though they were defeated in battle, the Italians were not obliterated. Once the riots were over and peace settled in the peninsular, the shops reopened and life continued. The cultural rebirth that had long dominated Italy was now being exported to the north and western European countries. To suggest that these countries had been drifting and then suddenly began a culture that departed significantly from what had gone before would be inaccurate. All the European countries had a vital national culture throughout the Middle Ages. The great German cathedrals, the poetry of Francois Villon in France, and the allegorical tales of Geoffrey Chaucer in England attest to that. However, in the sixteenth century a cultural explosion developed that was markedly different in tone from that of the Middle Ages.

Italian humanism was exported to the northern countries by travelers and the returning soldiers of the numerous wars fought for the tempestuous rulers of France, Spain, and Germany. The Renaissance came to Germany first, but it was short-lived. The invention of printing and the fact that men like Erasmus of Rotterdam could disseminate the philosophy of humanism throughout Europe, but especially to the German speaking peoples, assisted its assimilation. The greatest name in German art, Albrecht Dürer, eagerly took up the new naturalism and popularized the classical revival in his homeland. From 1494 until the first years of the sixteenth century,

Germany was home to the Renaissance, after which it was lost in
the squabbles of the Reformation.

In France, the Renaissance covered the middle years of the
sixteenth century. In art it is associated with the Italian painters who
were employed by Francis I. No less a personage that Leonardo da
Vinci was commissioned by the French king, and the former died
near Amboise in the Chateau country of the Loire River. With the
publication of *Gargantua* by Rabelais, French literature came to
the fore during this period. In England, the dictatorial tendencies
of Henry VIII prevented the humanist creed from developing. It
was not until Elizabeth I that the English Renaissance came into
full flower. The names of Edmund Spencer, William Shakespeare,
Marlowe, and the earlier Sir Thomas More redound to this period.
Spain too reached toward the humanist impulse during the last part
of the sixteenth and early seventeenth centuries. The creative talents
of Cervantes, de Vega, and El Greco were not immediately accepted.
However, as Spain slowly educated itself into the new age, the
works of these men became beacons by which the Spanish Renaissance was measured.

As the concept of humanism spread throughout Europe, the
influence of the Italian Renaissance was taken very seriously by other
countries as they became ready to throw off their medieval role and
accept the fact that a new cultural epoch had arrived. Although
Italy did not affect the major course of political and economic
events, it did assist the entire modern world to become aware of the
intellectual ferment that naturalism inspired in the arts, politics,
music, literature, and science. Moreover, Italy sponsored an era of
knowing how to enjoy life that had been in danger of being squashed
by the insecurities and other worldliness that abounded in the
medieval occupations before the rebirth. Because the Italian Renaissance gave unparalled opportunities to ability and genius for more
than 250 years, a set of attitudes toward life and to the arts was
developed that encouraged others, when they felt capable, of
assimilating them as a stimulus to their own aspirations. In this way
the Renaissance made way for still further adaptations as time and
people espoused new ways of looking at life.

THE REFORMATION, CALVANISM, AND LEISURE

In the fifteenth century northern Europe was a troubled mass of
ignorance, blind faith in the Catholic Church of Rome, and a belief

in the afterlife that was more important than the harsh life imposed
by ceaseless toil upon the masses. Europe had fallen on difficult
time. England and France had participated in a series of conflicts
for more than 100 years. In England regicide was not unknown. The
peasants of Europe had revolted and been beaten down. The Black
Plague infested Europe. Trade recessed; fields lay fallow; hunger,
disease, and death lurked everywhere. The few advances made at
the height of the Middle Ages now fell into a state of decay at the
close of the medieval era. Fear was constant. Hellfire and damnation,
rather than eternal bliss, were the incentives to righteous living. But
now, the constant warfare was over; the Italian Renaissance had
begun to turn people's minds from a deferred paradise to the
pleasures of life on earth. Exploration of the uncharted seas had
begun; the invention of the printing press brought a flood of information to countries that had a growing literate population. This was
a time for new criticism, debate, and a desire for political independence.

THE MONK, THE CHURCH, AND SCHISM

Twenty-nine years after his birth, Martin Luther of Mansfield,
Germany, took his doctorate degree at the University of Wittenberg.
He was an Augustinian monk who would rock the Catholic Church
to its foundations and create an entirely new religion. The year was
1517.[33] The Augustinian friar had long since traveled to Rome, had
seen the indecent haste of the Masses being read so fast that little
comfort could have been taken from them, had witnessed the
theological inconsistencies and dubious legalisms practiced by Pope
Julius II in his desire to construct St. Peter's Cathedral. All of this,
plus his own intellectual questioning of basic Catholic doctrine, led
him to the north door of Elector Frederick's Castle Church, where
he nailed his concepts in the form of 95 theses for debate. The
public, which typically dismissed academic discussion among theologians as obscure and abstract, was electrified by the statement.
For the first time, someone had articulated and written about what
the masses had only dared to think.[34]

---

[33] Thomas M. Lindsay, *Luther and the German Reformation* (New York: Books for
Libraries Press, 1970), pp. 64-65.

[34] J. Lortz, *The Reformation in Germany*, trans. R. Walls (New York: Herder and Herder,
1968), pp. 259-283. Cf. also, G. Freytag, *Martin Luther*, trans. H. E. O. Heinemann
(Chicago: The Open Court Publishing Company, 1972), pp. 60-68.

As Luther's ideas gained popular support, he authored numerous treaties and pamphlets that spread his ideas even more rapidly. Now the Roman Curia began to take an interest, and Luther was summoned to have one of his statements judged by Italians; the Pope consented to Luther's being examined in Germany. In 1518, Luther traveled to Augsburg to confront Cardinal Cajetan, General of the Dominican Order. The discussion only produced more argument and additional charges of heresy. Luther was now ready to denounce the pontificate as a manmade fabrication that caused the perversion of the Christian faith.

The debate with the eminent theologian John Eck in 1519 was notable because Luther attacked not only the pontificate, but the Church Council as having been in error when it condemned Jan Hus to be burned at the stake 100 years before. Luther not only questioned the authority of the Church, but by 1520 he had published several new tracts which resulted in an irreconcilable break with Rome. Pope Leo X issued a bill condemning Luther's works, and his excommunication followed. Emperor Charles V convened an assembly, the Diet of Worms, to hear Luther on charges of heresy. Despite the fact that the people were overwhelmingly in support of Luther, the young emperor decided to brand him an outlaw. The Elector Frederick, concerned with Luther's safety, arranged for him to be taken to the Wartburg, a mountain fortress, where he remained in hiding for almost a year. Neither the Edict of Worms nor Luther's seclusion could stop the ferment that boiled over Germany. The Reformation had begun and would never be stopped.[35]

THE RISE OF CALVIN

Calvin was born in 1509 in Noyon, a cathedral city of Picardy in northern France, where his father was the diocesean notary. As a child, he was remarkable for his precision of mind and absorption with perfectionism. He imposed harsh demands upon others, no less than himself, but it is reported that his school friends liked him.

Calvin went to Paris because he expected to enter the priesthood, but his father decided that he should study law at Orleans. Although he never practiced law, its study and his appreciation of it were to shape his life. At Orleans he studied on some humanists, but the contemporary humanist position, that worldly pleasure was ethical

---

[35] John M. Todd, *Reformation* (New York: Doubleday & Co., Inc., 1971), pp. 154-239.

and desirable, appears to have had no impact upon him at all. What really impressed him in his study of the classics was Greek Stoicism, the philosophy that exalted discipline and preached impassivity in the face of pleasure or pain. This doctrine was to serve as Calvin's fundamental creed thereafter.

During this time, Calvin came into contact with the literature of reform and associated with reformers. Fearing arrest in consequence of his associations, Calvin left France and took up residence in Basel. Here he undertook the writing of a text that was to influence the Reformation significantly and lead to his installation in Geneva.[36] *The Institutes of the Christian Religion* was a defense of the reform movement and a textbook of instruction. It had more influence on the Reformation than any single work of Luther's and was the first complete and logical statement of reform beliefs. Its tone was far more funerial than the writings of Luther. Whereas Luther had envisioned God as merciful and fatherly, Calvin perceived God as a vengeful figure who zealously guarded His total sovereignty over everything. Drawing upon the Old Testament, the writings of St. Paul and Augustine, as well as the Scholastic theologians and the reformists Zwingli and Luther, Calvin collected the views of those who had preceded him and synthesized their concepts into a clear, systematic statement of reform beliefs.

The *Institutes* opens with an exposition of the Ten Commandments. It then goes on to deal with creed, affirming belief in a trinitarian God, the divinity of Christ, and resurrection after death. Calvin wrote that salvation is only for the elect, chosen of God. He also taught that original sin is passed on to all mankind and that no one could arise out of the state of disgrace without God's help. Finally, the *Institutes* deals with the relationship between church and state. Calvin stated that "man is the subject of two kinds of government," civil law and God's rule. "Civil government is designed ... to establish general peace and tranquility." "It is impossible to resist the magistrate without at the same time resisting God Himself."[37] After publication of the *Institutes,* Calvin set out for Strasbourg. He stopped en route at the city of Geneva, where he had intended to spend one night only, and stayed for the rest of his life.

[36] Williston Walker, *John Calvin: The Organizer of Reformed Protestantism* (New York: Schocken Books, 1969), p. 181.

[37] John Calvin, *On God and Political Duty* (New York: The Bobbs-Merrill Company, Inc., 1956), pp. 72-73.

In Geneva, the proud Swiss, who had recently thrown off the yoke of Savoy, submitted themselves to the man's theocratic rule and personal domination that patently shaded their former political fealty.

Calvin established an austere regime in Geneva, at the behest of the Genevese themselves. Adhering to his concept of strict discipline and stoic outlook, he required that gambling, drinking, singing, and dancing be abolished. Although not ready to maintain such a program, the city council exiled Calvin, but within a short time recalled him to improve the people's morals and uphold the reform movement. When Calvin returned, he persuaded the city council to appoint a commission, with himself as head, to draw up a legislative code that would henceforth guide the community. The *Ecclesiastical Ordinances* became the constitution for the Reformed Church, which was to be supported by the state. According to the ordinances the law was the Bible; the pastors were the interpreters of the law; and the civil government was required to enforce the law as the pastors interpreted it. The constitution also formed a Consistory or Presbytery which supervised worship, oversaw the moral conduct of every citizen of Geneva, and inspected every house each year. Calvin's rule extended into every phase of society. He introduced sanitary regulations, financed new industry, founded what later came to be the University of Geneva, and preached unceasingly. His was a rule based on discipline, and his doctrine of the elect flattered the Genevese into believing they were God's chosen people.

Calvin's view of leisure can be summed up by an inordinate emphasis upon leisure being idleness, which is equated with mischief and the devil's work. Calvin announced rules for the conduct of public inns. Among these were prohibitions on dancing, dice, or card games. These were considered dissolute pastimes and were therefore immoral activities. However, Calvin himself was not an ascetic and indulged in a variety of recreational activities.[38] In Calvin's view, recreational activity could be justified on the grounds that it permitted citizens to recuperate their powers so that they would be capable of going back to work. This was wholly consistent with Calvin's doctrine of the elect. Any individual who was successful in his work received the benediction of God. To sustain the physical and mental ability to work, there had to be some time for rejuvena-

---

[38] Geogia E. Harkness, *John Calvin: The Man and His Ethics* (New York: Henry Holt and Company, 1931), p. 163.

tion. But recreational activity was not to be confused with idleness. Recreational activity was necessary to promote the primary virtue, work. The fact that recreational activities could be enjoyable did not justify their exclusion. The only thing that was intolerable was idleness.

Because Calvin's creed was not colored by nationalism, as was Luther's, it was better able to surmount international borders. The Calvinistic doctrine spread throughout Europe, and by 1559 it had reached as far away as Scotland. The Calvinistic creed was taken up by John Knox, who based his theology on much that inspired Calvin. But to Calvinism, Knox added a Scottish flavoring that could only be termed more somber than that which infused the founder.[39] Much that was basic to the Calvinism of Knox found its way to the Colonies of Massachusetts Bay and Connecticut when they were incorporated in the early seventeenth century.

LEISURE ACTIVITIES OF THE MASSES IN THE 16TH CENTURY

Four out of five Europeans were still tied to an agrarian economy in 1500. While many had risen from serfdom to become free or tenant farmers, paid handymen, or village craftsmen, most remained heavily burdened by taxes and services to their lords. Only within the community, village, or town, could one find some companionship and relief from imposed service or heavy toil. Isolated, self-sufficient, and close-knit, the peasant village was united by its communal pleasures as well as by shared hardship. Among the artists who recorded the joys and sorrows of the peasant's life, none has ever matched Pieter Breughel in depicting the vigor, accuracy, and tone of the times. His paintings are notable for the depiction of sports, games, social activities, ceremonies, and the drudgery under which the peasants passed their lives. Peasants' lives were little different from what had always been their lot in earlier centuries. Now, however, winds of change were sweeping through Europe and slowly, but surely the results trickled down to this most depressed underclass. Eventually, there would be protests, petitions, and finally bloody revolt.

---

[39] Henry Cowan, *John Knox, The Hero of the Scottish Reformation* (New York: Anos Press, Inc., 1970), pp. 379-383. Cf. also, W. Stanford Reid, *Trumpeter of God* (New York: Charles Scribner's Sons, 1974), passim.

From Brueghel's pictures, such as "The Peasant's Wedding" (ca. 1568) and "Wedding Dance" (ca. 1566), one can see that a wide variety of leisure activities were indulged in. A free afternoon might be whiled away in an outside tavern. Drinking, squabbling, courting, and listening to the bagpipe might constitute a social occasion. A peasant wedding was an opportunity to really let go. Prosperous peasants celebrated the event with a lavishness that would be remembered for some time. On such occasions, manners were coarse, talk free, and drinking prodigious. Undernourished and overworked, peasants might consume a gallon of wine or beer each day; at weddings they drank even more. Village dancing was not uncommon, and the participants went through the expected reels and bobbings as the expected reels and bobbings as the bagpiper played.

Farm and church holidays were free days, and the peasant looked upon them as a respite from backbreaking toil. The clowning and foolery often alarmed the higher clergy, but the Church continued to create more holidays than ever. By the start of the sixteenth century, a score of saints' days were observed each year. This was a time for carnival festivities, and with an irreverence that worried Church fathers, the peasants flocked to a central field where costumes were judged, a variety of games were played, eating and drinking were plentiful, and music and dance were evident.

LEISURE ACTIVITIES OF THE ARISTOCRATS IN THE 16TH CENTURY

As always, the nobility enjoyed leisure far more than did the peasant and town dwelling masses. The aristocracy had access to wealth, which permitted them to live on a grand scale. Others could aspire to this estate and self-made merchants sometimes acquired such riches that even crowned heads of state held them in awe. Jacob Fugger of Augsburg was typical of the powerful financiers. To the extent that the nobility of Europe could dispose of their time as they saw fit, particularly when not engaged in the various wars, uprisings, or other annoying aspects of the times, they participated in recreational experiences that were gracious, envigorating, amusing, and educational.

The royal progresses of Elizabeth I can be looked upon as the apex of prerogative and leisure, but it was not considered extraordinary in an age where nine-tenths of the people labored to keep one-tenth in magnificent state. Two months out of every summer, Elizabeth

led her court from London for leisurely rides through the country.[40]
Provisioned by some 300 wagons and carts, the queen rode horseback
or in an open litter. When her retinue stopped at a castle, there was
a lavish display of presents, entertainment, music, dancing, pageants,
and other amusements to capture the queen's attention.

England was brightened by music during the Elizabethan reign.
Virtually every Briton, including the queen, could perform on a lute
or virginal. Every country inn rang with the sound of madrigals. To
the love of singing was joined a fondness for dancing. Common folk
might dance a jig or reel, but the queen performed in stately pavans
and graceful lavoltas. Nothing suited the queen more than a stag
hunt. She was an expert horsewoman and deadly with a crossbow.
In full cry the quarry would be chased and finally dispatched.

When royalty was entertained by an outdoor show, townspeople
also crowded around to see the sights. Such attractions usually
included jugglers, tumblers, trained animal acts, and very rough
sports such as logrolling or a forerunner of football. Bearbaiting by
fighting dogs, fireworks displays, and sumptuous banquets were
all part of the program. Gentlemen would run at a quintain, a modification of the ancient game of jousting. There was always some
danger of injury in these activities, when, for example, the target was
missed, swung around, and knocked the rider off his horse. Apparently the scent of danger with possible broken heads or maimed
bodies added to the thrill of the show.

Toward the end of the sixteenth century, Protestantism had
established itself throughout Europe. England had thrown off
Catholicism during the reign of Henry VIII and only tolerated a short
period of reaffirmation under Queen Mary. The development of
Puritanism, however, led to some disorders wherever this variant of
Calvinism flourished. The Puritans were repressed by both Elizabeth
I and her successor James I. It was during the latter's reign that the
most radical Puritans, unwilling to compromise with the Church of
England and frustrated in their desire to change the episcopal
hierarchy and elaborate ceremony, fled to the New World.

The Calvinists believed that a citizen demonstrated his fitness for
salvation by obeying the law and being industrious, sober, and frugal.
The Puritans started with Calvinist doctrine and grafted their own
brand of sobriety, individual responsibility, and unremitting work to
form a creed that would take root in the northern colonies. Escaping

---

[40] John Wood, "The World of Edmund Spencer," *Horizon*, Vol. XVII, Winter, 1974, p. 78.

from religious persecution, the Puritans, like all other reformers before them, rescinded the right of disagreement to all who opposed them. Their unbending zeal required that they leave their homelands. They would transmit this to the New World and force others to seek havens from their strict faith and domination. The American adventure was about to begin.

LEISURE IN COLONIAL AMERICA

Two essentially different settlements, guided by completely polar views of life and religion, were established on the American continent during the early years of the seventeenth century. The original settlement at Jamestown in Virginia was made up of aristocracy, once removed from the possibility of inheritance, gentlemen traders, and adventurers who looked upon the new colony as the foundation of new capital or the opportunity to claim uncharted lands and untold wealth. The settlers came to the south with a good English background of sports and games, love of threatre, good books, music, and physical exercise. They saw no reason to give up these pastimes simply because they had a colony to build. Yet as soon as they were able to understand the magnitude of their undertaking and the peril in which they lived, they soon found that they had no free time for participation in recreational activity. They faced starvation, malaria, Indian attack, and distant anxiety. Just staying alive was a full-time job. It came as no surprise then when the governors of Virginia passed strict ordinances against the frivolous waste of time in recreational activities. The authorities wanted the settlers to pay attention to the business of putting the colony on its feet, economically and physically. As soon thereafter as was possible, when the threat of disaster passed and conditions of daily life eased, restrictions against leisure pursuits were lifted. The colonists were free to participate in whatever their enlarging opportunities permitted them to do.

Life was similar for the original settlers at Plymouth Bay. They too faced an uncertain future and the same hardships that visited their southern brethren. The basic difference between the two regions was the religious view and the philosophy that provided a frame of reference. The era of settlement in America was to provide a seat of religious dogmatism as well as a hodgepodge of political and social colorings. The colonists of the seventeenth century were under the theological domination of Calvinistic thought. Particularly were the New England colonies under the pressure of Puritanism. Under the leadership of the clergy in association with the governing authorities, the Puritan ethic indicated specific taboos and restricted social gatherings. The Calvinistic teachings of predestination, frugality, and an intolerance for idleness profoundly influenced later modern social life. In New England, although not elsewhere, almost all forms of recreational experience were prohibited by law.

During the years immediately after the colonies were settled on the American continent, the attitude toward leisure and recreational participation was decidedly unfavorable, especially in the New England communities. This was a time of frontier settlement and terrible hardship. Survival was uppermost in people's minds. Consequently, productivity in the way of material goods and services became the measure by which people lived. The early Puritans, bringing with them as they did the orthodox preachings of the Reformation, limited atonement, and irresistibility of grace, sought to stamp out the human desires for pleasure and amusement by limiting and prohibiting what individuals might do in the daily process of living.

> In New England, where the stern rule of Calvinism condemned idleness and amusement for their own sake, the tradition that life should be wholly devoted to work ("that no idle drone bee permitted to live amongst us") held its ground more firmly. The magistrates attempted to surpress almost every form of recreation long after the practical justification for such unrelenting attitude had disappeared. The intolerance of Puritanism was superimposed upon economic necessity to confine life in New England within the narrowest possible grooves.[41]

The unproductivity of the land and the stunning experience of frontier living combined with the stark pessimism of Puritan life in forming a philosophy that valued frugality, hard work, self-discipline, and strict observance of civil and religious codes. Such an approach to life considered play to be the "devil's work," and any time not given to productive labor or worship was wasteful and therefore condemned. In such a society, where survival pressed the inhabitants daily, legislation surpressing activities of a recreational nature was readily accepted by the people. The magistrate was the law, the law was the literal interpretation of the Bible, the Bible was handed down from God, and God was to be obeyed.

---

[41] Foster Rhea Dulles, *A History of Recreation: America Learns to Play* (New York: Meredith Publishing Company, 1965), pp. 5-6.

Time passed, and the struggle for existence ceased to pervade all the waking hours of a person's life. The problem of meeting each day eased. Land was fenced off for common pasturage, protection, and tillage. A person now had time to talk of social issues with his neighbor. Meeting grounds, later to become parks, were established as the stress of emergency living seemed to be over. When the agricultural economy was firmly built, trade and commerce, first between colonies and then with foreign contacts, allowed a leisure class to develop. People still performed their daily work, but those with more financial security, those with land holdings, mineral rights, or other valuable assets, found others to carry on the more onerous, detailed, and time-consuming tasks which, in turn, provided certain blocks of unoccupied time for these privileged few. This wealthy minority constituted the ablest, best learned, and most highly positioned people, and sometimes the most astute, ruthless, and unprincipled people whose background and education made them long for the modes of living that had been left behind in England and on the European continent. People of such breeding reverted to the accustomed pleasurable pursuits, and soon bowling on the green, cricket, horse racing, fox hunting, card playing, dancing, musical concerts, theatrical entertainments, and the common sports became the recreational activities of the day.

As the vigorous and aggressive leadership receded from Calvinistic idealism, people tended to find replacement in other concepts whose outlooks were more pleasing to their new-found security. By 1700, the Dutch settlers of the eastern seaboard pursued many pleasures within the environs of public houses. In addition to drinking, games similar to modern golf, handball, skating, tennis, and sleighing in season, and the more indiscreet activities such as gambling and prostitution were carried on. These leisure activities spread throughout the colonies, despite denunciations from the pulpit, and by the time of the American Revolution (1775-1783), masques or theatre parties, balls, entertainments, extravagant dances, drinking, gambling, animal baiting, and other equally censured but nonetheless pleasurable activities were flourishing during leisure.

SELECTED REFERENCES

Bremer, Francis J. *Puritan Experiment: New England Society from Bradford to Edwards.* New York: St. Martin's Press, Inc., 1976.

Byington, Ezra H. *Puritan As a Colonist and Reformer.* New York: AMS Press, Inc., 1976.

Dickens, A. G., ed. *The Courts of Europe — 1400-1800.* New York: McGraw-Hill Book Company, Inc., 1977.

Geanakoplos, Deno J. *Medieval Civilization.* Boston: D. C. Heath & Company, 1978.

Grimm, Harold J. *The Reformation Era: 1500-1650.* 2d ed. New York: The Macmillan Company, 1973.

Hay, Denys. *Medieval Centuries.* New York: Harper & Row Publishers, Inc., 1977.

Matthew, Donald. *The Medieval European Community.* New York: St. Martin's Press, Inc., 1977.

Miskimin, Harry A., et al., eds. *The Medieval City.* New Haven, Ct.: Yale University Press, 1977.

Ritter, G. *Luther: His Life and Work.* Translated by John Riches. Westport, Ct.: Greenwood Press, Inc., 1978.

Stickelberger, E. *Calvin.* Translated by David Gelser. Greenwood, S. C.: Attic Press, 1977.

Tuchman, Barbara W. *A Distant Mirror: The Calamitous 14th Century.* New York: Alfred A. Knopf, 1978.

Chapter 4

The American Experiment

The colonial period saw an emerging secularization of thought. From the prevailing orthodoxy of theological conceptions based on religious sanctions, there developed an insistence that human reason rather than divine law, natural rights instead of supernaturalism, reliance upon scientific method rather than traditional truths, social contracts and personal liberty rather than authoritarian mandate, and a humanitarian and democratic belief rather than aristocratic preferment were to be practiced. This change or enlightenment, from the German word *Aufklärung*, gave the age its name. In the more than 150 years of the colonial period in America, an increasing shift away from religious and supernatural foundations towards those based on secular and human studies could be discerned. Utilitarianism gained in scope and significance as the practicalities of life were contemplated. Although the classics were still part of aristocratic tradition, there was also notable growth of the physical sciences, social sciences, and the vernacular literatures.

INVENTION AND HUMANISM

The most spectacular accomplishments were the development of applied sciences that produced technological progress. The mechanical and material sciences began to come into their own. The science of navigation required more accurate measuring devices that were forthcoming as compasses, telescopes, barometers, and the like were pressed into service. The study of heat, light, electricity, and mechanics led to the development of machines and procedures that revolutionized mining, farming, animal husbandry, manufacturing, communication, and transportation. The industrial and agricultural inventions of the eighteenth century in concert with political and social philosophy paved the way for a growing liberalism which eventuated in the desire of ordinary people for a larger share in conducting their own affairs. The privilege of aristocracy began to fade, and the emergence of popular government gained prominence.

By the time Americans were ready to declare their independence, a new technological era was being ushered in when James Watt offered the world his steam engine. Between 1701 and 1800 a number of inventions appeared that would herald a new industrialization. From Jethro Tull's seed-planting drill of 1701, iron smelting with coke in 1709, steam pump in 1712, threshing machine in 1732, flying shuttle in 1733, Sheffield silver plate in 1742, beet sugar extraction in 1747, Spinning Jenny in 1768, winnowing machine in 1777, mill-rolled iron in 1784, cotton gin in 1793, and the improved lathe in 1800, the individual was free to pursue whatever goals hard work, frugality, honesty, and perserverance would bring.

The world was changing, and the eighteenth century was being radicalized by the views of Hume, Smith, and Jeremy Bentham. Bentham's creed was "the greatest good for the greatest number." His influence brought about a number of reforms in English government. He is credited with contributing to the alleviation of the terrible criminal laws, the abolition of defects in the jury system, the erasure of imprisonment for debt, the removal of usury laws, the repeal of religious tests for public office, and the passage of public health laws. His enlightened vision extended to almost every aspect of life. What was happening in England was reflected in the colonies. The beginnings of social reform were evident, much of it originating from an awakening of social conscience and the predeliction to advance the lot of the poor and disadvantaged.

The egalitarianism furnished by humanistic impulses and the theory of the natural rights of man rejected the Puritanical concept of the stewardship of the elect and embraced the idea that each person was worthy of respect and equal in the sight of God. Secular leaders campaigned for more humane treatment of jailed offenders, the promotion of welfare agencies, and the support of the underprivileged. Humanitarian services developed from Rousseau's contention of the inherent goodness of human nature. American liberals, steeped in the tradition of German Romanticism, accepted the doctrine of the perfectability of human nature. This orientation conceived poverty and lack of opportunity as the result of environmental deprivation, not personal inadequacy. Social reforms were urged as a means for enhancing society so that people might achieve better conditions. The cause of common people was advocated by Jefferson, Paine, and Franklin. These thinkers helped to change the method of improvement from personal charity to the need for organized effort, even to such a radical dream as governmental administration to promote the general welfare and the tranquility of the people. This shift to natural rights as the basis of government was forever established in America when, in 1789, the Constitution of the United States was adopted with the preamble of "We the people of the United States."

LEISURE AND RECREATIONAL ACTIVITY AFTER THE REVOLUTION

The decades following the adoption of the Constitution were years of rapid expansion. Settlers began to migrate westward where they carved new lives out of the wilderness. Life in these newly settled regions was harsh. Remote from the usual security of the towns and cities of the coast, the agrarian family was dependent on itself for all of its supporting services. Almost everything that was necessary for the maintenance of life—food, clothing, shelter, and the utensils and tools to operate the farm—were made on the farm. Each member of the family shared in the struggle for existence. The family was the basic unit from which all social life was derived.

Again, as it had during the colonial settlement period, leisure concepts underwent a change after the War of Independence. Once despised and condemned, recreational activity now assumed a place in all parts of the American social scene. The eastern seaboard cities and towns had their social gatherings, but the back country farmers and frontiersmen, living on the edge of the wilderness, remained relatively untouched by the quest for diversion initiated by their urban cousins. Utilitarian recreational activities were most popular during the leisure of the rural dwellers. Cooperative group experiences and efforts, such as barn raising, sheep shearing, corn husking, crafts, church suppers, quilting bees, town meetings, turkey shoots, and community fairs, tended to draw the interest of the rural people who realized that many useful benefits accrued from voluntary cooperation in getting a particular job done. Although individualism of the independent family unit was the characteristic of this agricultural society, there are numerous examples of communal activity. The cooperative raising of a new dwelling on a voluntary basis is a familiar instance of the rural life of the period. Individuals participated of their own volition. Here was a society of free and equal families.

The migration of people seeking a new and better life on the western side of the Appalachian Plateau helped to spread the doctrine of equalitarianism, the natural rights of man, and humanitarian faith rather than aristocratic privilege. Politically, economically, and socially, frontier agricultural life exerted a profound influence on the mosaic of American democracy. It not only introduced the principles of freedom, equality, and individualism to the frontier, but had considerable effect on the older, more populated sections of the country. This is readily seen in terms of the impact that the small frontier farmers had on the struggles over suffrage in the seaboard states.

The westward movement was strengthened by the attraction that empty lands had for immigrants and the growing populations of the east. Life could be started again. If one had the cash, the courage, and the skill, homesteads could be obtained in the western territories. This migration to the west brought with it the isolation of the frontier and freedom from the conventional restraint associated with eastcoast living. The recreational activities centered in the home, and the family was the social world by which the individual was surrounded until that time of year when road or river travel permitted all the families of one district to meet for common feasting, dancing, marketing, or other such enterprise. Life was severe and short for the unwary settler, and the pleasurable pursuits of social intercourse and other leisure activity were few and far between.

In effect, then, the leisure activities of the rural and frontier regions mixed recreational experience with work. The natural elements as well as survival techniques were used. In the well-developed and settled areas of the east and later on in the west, as civilization inexorably pushed back the frontier, a leisure class grew, and its typical recreational activities were games of chance, extravaganzas, the more aesthetic entertainments, and other forms of individual and social activity.

INDUSTRIALIZATION AND SOCIAL ISSUES

The years between the Civil War and 1900 saw advancing forms of a mechanistic technology, the explosive effect of Darwin's biological theory of evolution, and a humanitarian appeal; all exerted pressure for a new approach to the latest discoveries of the day. The advances made in the physical and biological sciences produced such profound changes in people's world view, their relationship to the environment, and the possibilities for education, that not only was reappraisal necessary to reconcile these diverse concepts, but a radical change was obviously required if any practical use were to be made of these facts and new knowledge.

Education began to take rapid professional strides as labor, a newly awakened force in the economy of the United States, insistently demanded a place. There was a call for more education better suited to the demands of those who worked at the manual trades, and for their children upon whose shoulders their hopes for better living rode. As education progressed, it carried with it, albeit more slowly, the little known and as yet unestablished field of recreational service. Industrialization and mass production called for new techniques. The demand for more efficient methods in turning out goods and services throughout the manufacturing and heavy industrial world stressed advances in communications, transportation, metallurgy, scientific analysis, and chemical research necessary to produce more and cheaper goods.

With the new technology, advanced techniques in science and industry after 1865 turned the attention of educators and those connected with the economics of the country toward utilitarianism and materialistic philosophies of life. Businessmen wanted an education that would orient their workers to a useful type of practical knowledge. They were eager to underwrite institutions of learning that would produce an employee who could fit into their particular form of economic enterprise. Coupled with this outcry for a utilitarian education was the swift growth of the natural sciences. Science became the byword for industrial growth and development. The consequences of this rapid acceleration in an area of learning that had formerly reposed behind ivy-covered walls were the opening of new vistas to the intellectually minded. Where the natural sciences had languished under the eyes of the academicians of the classical idealism school, there now appeared a movement away from faculty psychology doctrines.

The conflicting forces unleashed by Darwin's evolutionary view in 1859 struck with smashing impact upon the classical humanities. Deeply penetrating investigations in the biological and physical sciences produced empirical evidence which, when opposed to the customary theological views of the time, caused widespread anguish and dismay among traditionalists. Still the faculty psychologists remained unconvinced. The philosophical absolutists refused to give ground to this evidence. Conservative faculties were disinclined to accept the evidence of natural science. The struggle for intellectual and academic supremacy between idealistic humanists and revolutionary scientists intensified in the decade after the publication of Darwin's *Origin of Species.* But the great weight of scientific matter and knowledge could not be denied. Encouraged by the demand for better ways of doing things through industrial crafts, which needed the sciences for operational inventions, the natural and physical sciences gained ascendancy over the humanities in institutions of higher learning, and a new round of philosophical thinking was inaugurated.

THE NEW LEISURE AND RECREATIONAL SERVICE

The increasingly important role played by recreational activity is due to a variety of causes beginning with those that gave rise to the industrial revolution. The age of discovery brought the age of invention; the age of invention brought the age of power; the age of power brought the age of leisure. As in the past, new technical processes have improved production methods to the extent that it has become practicable to reduce the hours of work with corresponding increasing returns to the workers. Accordingly, within the past 60 years, the hours of factory labor have been reduced in some industries from 60 per week to 35. State and federal legislation has imposed restrictions upon the number of hours that minors and women might be employed. Along with the curtailment of hours of manual labor have gone equal limitations upon white collar work and employment in the professions.

A shift in public health agencies' interest from curing gross environmental ailments to procedures that will extend life and physical effectiveness, so that the average person may contemplate from 12 to 20 years of life expectancy after retirement, should have considerable effect upon the activities of leisure. The science of medicine has done much to reduce poor health among the aging. As science pushes back the frontiers of the unknown, it will surely find remedies for the diseases that now account for most morbidity at advanced ages.[1] Consequent increase of leisure of older adults and proportionate growth of their interest in community recreational service programs must be anticipated.

That the American people have been extremely ingenious in devising ways to employ their leisure is apparent to everyone. The amusements, entertainments, and diversions designed to provide vicarious experience and activities organized to induce direct participation are literally inexhaustible. They partake of nearly all the innate capacities for feeling and action and are multiplied by the development that these capacities undergo in the experience of living. Their complexity is increased by inventive genius, and they are not limited by the requirements of utilitarianism but are conditioned only by their ability to give human satisfaction and enjoyment. Innumerable hobbies and group activities in literature, science, craftsmanship, games, sports, music, art, and clubs abound. There are reported to be 150 million aquatic enthusiasts, 25 million bowlers, 8 million tennis players, 6 million joggers, 4 million golfers, 30 million softball players, 30 million fishermen, and unnumbered archers, riders, hunters, walkers, boaters, collectors, birdwatchers, and faddists[2] of one kind or another, ad infinitum.

CREATIVITY AND LEISURE

Coincident with the decrease in hours of work has been people's increased dependence on leisure activities for full expression of their faculties. In the preindustrial era, workers found outlets for a wide range of their faculties in their vocation. Work was not highly competitive, but was performed leisurely. It was varied in the skills it employed. It not only gave opportunity for creative experience

---

[1] Jay S. Shivers, "Recreational Service for the Aging," *Journal of the Association for Physical and Mental Rehabilitation,* Vol. XIV, November-December, 1960, p. 170.

[2] "Wheel Crazy," *Time,* Vol. 106, October 27, 1975, p. 46.

and invention and for individuals to place the stamp of their own genius on the character of the product, but also provided opportunity for social intercourse in the productive processes. Work was life in the full.

Today work in the trades and professions alike is restrictive in its employment of workers' full potential. Their success is almost directly proportional to the degree of their specialization. In the factory, workers often use the accessory and not the large skeletal muscles. This does violence to their physiological and emotional balance, so they must find relief in the big muscle activity during leisure. In their recreational pursuits they discover opportunities to live creatively and to give expression to the wide assortment of human capabilities with which they are endowed, but which atrophy through disuse if not released and cultivated in leisure.

> Because the satisfaction of basic human needs was inherent in the work of our predecessors, they did not need as much time for recreational activity as we do today. Few of us, at the present, can see the completed result of our labors, and even if we do we cannot readily identify ourselves with a particular product since we may have performed only one of the thousands of operations required for its completion.[3]

The need for individuality and self-expression is necessary in an environment that restricts conduct and demands conformity. Creativity allows individuals to realize their known skills and talents. It is during leisure that the individual engages in experiences that are uniquely personal. Because freedom is the essence of recreational pursuit, individuals are free to select their leisure activities and participate to the limit of their being, affording them a chance to shake off the confines of routinized daily living and slip into the realm of highly personalized self-determination.

In no other activity are individuals free to be as uninhibited as they desire. However, recreational activity is *not* escape from life. What individuals do in their leisure inevitably affects the kind of people they are or will become. Because people do what they want to do when they want to do it during leisure, there is the chance

---

[3] James A. Baley and Jay S. Shivers, "Recreational Activity and Family Health," *The American Recreation Society Bulletin,* Vol. XII, February, 1960, pp. 8-9.

that they will seek creative activity in their free time to satisfy their basic needs for achievement.

THE ECONOMICS OF LEISURE

Fortunately the processes that changed the nature of work and reduced its hours created a greater national wealth. This made possible many improvements and commodities that were needed if leisure was to bring compensatory satisfactions and values. Much of this wealth has been reinvested and consumed in the processes of further production; much has been wasted in wars and other enterprises that produced no social values; and much of it has been expended on social betterment, education, and recreational activity.

Realization of the potential values of our leisure has been enhanced by the increased national wealth. Many leisure activities require materials and services that cannot be had without spending money. Whereas it is true that some of the activities that rank at the top of the recreational scale in terms of value are free gifts of nature, others are unquestionably denied to individuals who cannot purchase the requisite commodities or services incidental to their enjoyment. The benefits of leisure before World War II had never been as universal as they are today. This was due, in part, to the unequal distribution of wealth. Yet, an expression of monetary expenditures of America's free time would show that with very few exceptions almost every family spent some money for recreational services, materials, or activities this past year.[4] Even when individuals did not have the necessary economic means for providing themselves with certain recreational commodities, they were assisted by public and other community facilities open to all. These include not only those available through agencies specifically established for recreational services, such as parks, playgrounds, and beaches, but those that are offered by public schools, youth serving agencies, churches, libraries, and other community enterprises. These facilities are still not uniformly distributed, nor are they by any means adequate

---

[4] E. Culen, ed., "Leisure," *Road Maps of Industry*, No. 1815 (New York: The Conference Board, September,1977).

for existing needs, but they are increasing in number as demand is created for them.

URBAN AND SUBURBAN DEVELOPMENT FOSTERS RECREATIONAL SERVICE

Urbanization has provided a fertile soil for the growth of leisure activities. The reasons for the phenomenal increase of public recreational service agencies in cities rather than in rural communities may be explained by the traditional conservatism of rural populations against accepting new governmental functions. The disinclination of rural people to facilitate the establishment of leisure-oriented agencies probably stems from the distrust that most ruralities have for governmental enterprise of any kind. Added to this is the historical concept that rural living has espoused, of work being opposed to leisure activities. Urban dwellers, on the other hand, have tended to be liberal and progressive in their outlook and willing to accept many new governmental services. There appears to be an almost socialistic willingness to allow government the responsibility for establishing agencies that will serve people's needs. With rapid development of urban centers there was a corresponding growth of municipal recreational service departments. Unfortunately, however, public dissatisfaction with declining urban public recreational service is growing.[5]

The noticeable migration of farm families to cities each year is part of the urban-suburban movement that developed in the United States. Approximately one million farm families moved into cities between 1940 and 1945. The obvious attraction was wartime industry, which required a labor force and paid premium wages to obtain personnel. During the past 30 years there has been a continual migration of rural populations to metropolitan areas, although the trend has begun to reverse throughout the last decade. Some central cities have attracted poor rural populations because of welfare benefits that the indigents receive. Courts have consistently upheld the rights of indigent persons to receive welfare assistance without having to establish previous residency in the community. Thus, many urban giants have had the experience of receiving poor migrants while

[5] Stewart Dill McBride, "Gallup: Neighborhoods Vital to Americans," *The Christian Science Monitor*, December 23, 1977, p. 12.

simultaneously losing their more affluent citizens to the surrounding suburbs.

Today, more than 151 million people, or 73% of the nation's total population, reside in metropolitan areas. The populations of metropolitan and non-metropolitan areas are currently growing at the same rate. Since 1970 the population of central cities has decreased by approximately 2 percent, while the suburban population continues to increase. The decrease in city populations occurred chiefly in the central cities of more than one million. Between 1970 1970 and 1974, about 7.7 million white persons left central cities for suburbs, while 3.4 million white persons left their suburban residences for the cities. The net loss of cities to suburbs during this period was 4.6 million persons. The great significance of internally migrating populations for leisure and the subsequent growth of public recreational agencies is that the sharp line of distinction that once probably marked the difference between rural and urban living no longer exists. There is less distinction and more similarity between urban and rural life than there ever has been. With the rise of the suburbs the accent has been a movement away from the central city, but to areas close enough to use commercial and recreational facilities. Suburban living and rural dwelling have literally become the same thing because of the advent of television and the great mobility that improved methods of transportation, including the private automobile, provide. With technological improvements a decided interest in the provision of public recreational service has become apparent in rural and suburban areas. An increasing number of rural communities, with populations of from 800 to 2,000 people, have been very much concerned with providing their children, as well as adults, with the recreational facilities and activities they need. This is evident throughout the south as well as in many other rural regions of the country.

The development of full-time public recreational service departments is somewhat slow in the most highly countrified areas. The small populations that can afford to be taxed for the necessary professional leadership and facilities and the lessened need for creative satisfactions due to the self-sufficiency attained in agricultural processes had retarded this growth. However, rural communities are beginning to consolidate services by combining with several small towns within a given geographic area and obtaining professional personnel on a mutually shared basis. Two or more towns vote to support whatever personnel and facilities are required to obtain public recreational service. In this manner the benefits of publicly organized recreational services have spread to the most exurban of communities.

THE ACCEPTANCE OF LEISURE AND RECREATIONAL ACTIVITY

The growth of the field of recreational service has also been accelerated by the breakdown of traditional cultural prejudices and religious taboos. A philosophy more tolerant of leisure and recreational activities and one that recognizes their importance in terms of human and social value has gained general acceptance. It is a function of sectarian systems to prescribe the moral code by which it intends its membership to abide. This is particularly true of the universal axioms as the specific branch or ideology defines the truth. Its power is traditional and ritual. As time has passed, however, the clergy have seen their members increasingly affected and influenced by the consequences of a highly technological society. Time, in terms of value, utilization, and understanding, has been strongly affected by economic reorientations. As work has receded from the preeminent place it occupied in previous societies of Western culture, ecclesiastical revision has come about concerning the place of leisure in human life.

The church, by the very decrease of working time, has been forced to consider leisure as an incorporated element in systematic philosophy and theology.[6] Thus, the Calvinistic tradition, which views work as the antithesis of leisure, has been dispelled for the most part. The church has in many instances entered into the support of leisure and recreational activities, particularly and significantly adopting the techniques that have been developed by practitioners in the field of recreational service. In the pluralistic culture of America, it would be difficult for any one clerical system to suppress much recreational experience performed in the new leisure. Even the most fundamentalist sects are developing recreational aspects for use in their own churches. The attitude against recreational activity and leisure pursuits has assisted the great development of recreational service by public agencies and the new awareness of

---

[6] Josef Pieper, *Leisure, The Basis of Culture*, trans. A. Dru (New York: Pantheon Books, Inc., 1952), p. 26.

leisure by private groups and persons. Although laws still prohibit certain recreational activities on Sundays, and a minor academic prejudice against the applied arts exists, the tendency to ascribe an insignificant role to leisure activity is breaking down rapidly.[7]

The last quarter of the twentieth century in America has been an age of massive human leisure. In no epoch of the past has there ever been a hope, if not full realization, of free time available to nearly everyone, free from unremitting toil. In all cultures, past and present, some leisure has always been available, but in earlier times only a privileged few were able to enjoy it. Historically, only the aristocratic class could ever afford leisure. Whenever there were slaves in any society, leisure was a commodity, i.e., something to be purchased. The rise of leisure can be traced to the recapture of time from that devoted to the imperative needs to obtain food, clothing, and shelter. Development of civilization with organization, division of labor, mechanization, mass production, and automation brought leisure within the grasp of all. Whenever time could be gained through the institution of labor-saving devices, e.g., the wheel, better agricultural implements, irrigation methods, sailing vessels, steam, internal combustion engines, and atomic power, then and only then did leisure accrue and tend to become a universal possession.

From an historical view of human development and cultural achievement throughout the thousands of centuries since the first true human being had the time to think, leisure has been an element of life. Significant advances in culture have been largely due to the creative use of whatever leisure was available. Free time, used to increase one's knowledge or ability, or to provide benefits to a community and by extension to society as a whole, affords a matchless step forward in the progress of civilization. The American tradition for recreational activity began to develop during the eighteenth century. The inventions of that century laid the foundations for the industrialized nation of the nineteenth century and ensured the growth of mass leisure.

The innovative ways in which Americans have found outlets for their free time in recreational participation has been documented in all of its varied forms for the past 100 years. Increased leisure influenced the need for constructive experiences. Initially individual

---

[7] Agnes Durant Pylant, *Church Recreation* (Nashville, Tennessee: Convention Press, 1959), pp. 9-17.

striving, and then collective concern for the provision of recreational services for the masses of people who began to pour into the country in successive waves, made itself felt. Several social movements developed and had profound impact on the eventual provision of public recreational service. Farsighted men and women from disparate trades, vocations, and economic strata began to examine private organizational administration of recreational service and found it inadequate to serve the needs of such a diverse population. First, private philanthropic agencies and altruistic people came forward to minister to the recreational and leisure needs of people; then other organizations offered recreational assistance to induce new converts or to implement their specific doctrines. Finally, public-spirited individuals banded together and urged governmental action, and this brought about a movement that is even now coming to full maturity. Americans learned to use their leisure for personal satisfaction and in most cases coincidentally benefitted the communities in which they lived. During this period of growth and learning the recreational service movement was established.

SELECTED REFERENCES

Berkhofer, Robert F., ed. *American Revolution: The Critical Times.* Waltham, Mass.: Little, Brown & Co., 1971.

Carlson, Reynold E., et al., *Recreation and Leisure: The Changing Scene,* 3d ed. Belmont, Calif.: Wadsworth Publishing Company, Inc., 1978.

Dorson, Richard M., ed. *American Rebels: Personal Narratives of the American Revolution.* Westminster, Md.: Pantheon Books, 1976.

Dulles, Foster Rhea. *A History of Recreation,* 2d ed. New York: Appleton-Century-Crofts, Inc., 1965.

Gay, Peter. *Enlightenment: An Interpretation — The Science of Freedom,* Vol. 2. New York: W. W. Norton & Co., Inc., 1977.

May, Henry F. *Enlightenment in America.* New York: Oxford University Press, 1976.

Neumeyer, Martin H. and Esther S. Neumeyer. *Leisure and Recreation: A Study of Leisure and Recreation in Their Sociological Aspects.* New York: John Wiley and Sons, 1958.

Scheiber, Harry N. *American Economic History.* New York: Harper & Row, Publishers, Inc., 1976.

Shahan, Robert W. and Kenneth R. Merrill. *American Philosophy.* Norman, Ok.: University of Oklahoma Press, 1977.

Shivers, Jay S. *Essentials of Recreational Service.* Philadelphia: Lea & Febiger, 1978.

Warner, Sam B., Jr. *American Experiment: Perspectives on Two Hundred Years.* Boston: Houghton Mifflin Co., 1976.

Chapter 5

Reflections on Leisure

The literature dealing with leisure has had a long and varied record. Historically, there have been several attempts to explain leisure. Among the traditional and contemporary appreciations of leisure are the following: 1) leisure as recreation; 2) leisure as pleasure; 3) leisure as rejuvenation; 4) leisure as a state of being; 5) leisure as a function; 6) leisure as social stratification; and 7) leisure as time. All of the concepts have proponents, and some have gained widespread recognition and currency. A critical evaluation of these proposals should enable the student to make value judgments about them. This chapter is designed to examine the different outlooks on leisure and offer explanations for the views held.

LEISURE AS RECREATION

The basis for a leisure concept of recreation was laid in fifth century B.C. Greece had reached its fullest ideational flowering during the lives of Plato and Aristotle. However, the leisure of those Greeks had a different meaning from the leisure of contemporary society. It was a time set aside for creativity and learning. Sometime in the centuries that followed the decline of Greek civilization, leisure as the Greeks knew it also declined. From an exalted level that would befit a symbol for cultural achievement, educational betterment, and democratic ideology, leisure plummeted to depths of depravity during the late Roman Empire and might only now be recovering from 2,000 years of social misinterpretation. The early Christian fathers denounced the immorality of activities practiced during leisure, and the later reformation leaders added their own special orientation to further confound leisure with impiety. The Christian Church has had much influence on the way people understand leisure. If compulsive workers still feel a twinge of guilt during their leisure, it is an anachronistic attitude largely supported by a Calvinistic conception of leisure as idleness and idleness as moral depravity.

On every side one hears about the moral decay of American society because of its lack of wholesome use of leisure. Various acts of delinquency are cited as occurring during the leisure of individuals and such activities are held up for critical concern as further evidence of the immoral equation. Whether or not such criticism is valid does not lift the awesome burden that leisure carries. Many think leisure is to be used without thought of usefulness either to the individual or to the community. In many instances individuals who are not well prepared to function during leisure become bored. They seek, therefore, some form of excitement to pass the time. In so doing, they may gain pleasure at the expense of some part of the social fabric. This merely reinforces the ideas of those who remain convinced that leisure is a harmful product of an industrialized society.

It would be admirable to equate the Greek concept of leisure with recreation because that idea covered, almost completely, every phase of human activity in which the Greek participated; everything, that is, except narrow trade activities. One might almost say that the Greek concept of leisure included vocation, at least the vocation of governing and managing the affairs of the state. One used one's leisure in the duties of citizenship, which of course demanded freedom from the necessity to produce goods and services.

The Greeks looked upon ordinary work as drudgery fit only for slaves. To be sure, there were free artisans and craftsmen to create the sculpture and ornamental buildings that decorated cities, but the common labor of soil tillers, commercial carriers, sailors—anything that was viewed as non-aristocratic—was labeled as wearisome toil to be engaged in only by captives of war and other servants. It came to mean that everything the Greeks gloried in, enjoyed, or respected as aristocratic privilege was performed during leisure; everything else was relegated to the backs of slaves. There is small wonder that this concept seemed so attractive to later writers. The attraction stimulated these people to look upon leisure as recreation. Because leisure was antipodal to work, so was recreation. Each succeeding generation of writers read a little more of the leisure concept into the definition of recreation until the two became so merged that they were considered identical.

Those writers who equate leisure with recreation have generally followed the same line of reasoning, regardless of terminology. Probably the outstanding exponent of the leisure-recreation equation was G. Ott Romney. The very title of his popular book, *Off The Job Living,* suggests the path to follow to achieve recreation. The entire line of thought in Romney's book precludes any possibility of recreation outside of leisure. He rests his case by defining recreation as ". . . all those things the individual chooses to do on his own time off the job for the gratification of the doing."[1] Recreation is off the job living, off the job living is leisure, *ergo* recreation is leisure.

The following definitions are also examples of this type of thinking:

> For the individual, recreation may be any wholesome leisure experience engaged in solely for the satisfaction derived therefrom.[2]

> Functionally, recreation is the natural expression of human interests and needs seeking satisfaction during leisure.[3]

The most used definition of recreation during the past 35 years has been: "Recreation is the worthy use of leisure." All of these concepts attempt to equate leisure and recreation.

Although it may be true that leisure activity can be recreational, and indeed may potentially lead to recreation, this is not always the case. To make synonymous two such distinct terms as *leisure* and *recreation* immediately casts a pall over the validity of this definition. Leisure is time. Time may be viewed subjectively or objectively. If viewed subjectively, it exists only as long as the individual realizes that it is passing. In other words, there is no time outside of individual consciousness. If time is viewed as a continu-

---

[1] G. Ott Romney, *Off the Job Living* (New York: A. S. Barnes and Company, 1946), p. 16.

[2] Harold D. Mayer and Charles K. Brightbill, *Community Recreation* (Boston: D. C. Heath & Co., 1948), p. 28.

[3] Gerald Fitzgerald, *Leadership in Recreation* (New York: Ronald Press, 1951), p. 3

um or as a series of intervals, passing and spending regardless of individual awareness, then it is objective.

Recreation, however, has nothing to do with specific time, aside from being a particular behavior that takes place in time. An apt simile would be campers in the forest. Campers, as human beings, cannot be defined in terms of the forest, yet their actions occur within the forest. Recreation is to be considered as individual behavior. If recreation is behavior, it may or may not be a visible phenomenon, depending upon the individual receiving its impact from physical and psychological stimuli in an attempt to retain or achieve equilibrium within the organism.

Viewed from this perspective, one can discern with remarkable clarity how palpably incorrect it is to equate these two utterly dissimilar terms. It is like comparing an apple and an orange and calling them the same because both are round, both are fruit, and both grow on trees. It is obvious that they are different, so different that to explain them as identical is inconceivable. Yet this very mistake has been made in the case of recreation and leisure. Even by qualifying leisure and investing it with use and activity, it still comes no closer to being identical with recreation. Add both of these words to leisure and one has free time that is used; wholesomely used or not makes little difference. The phrase still does not explain what recreation is, far less what it entails. It surely does not describe leisure. Worst of all it completely eliminates and ignores the largest body of human activities—those that take place outside of leisure.

Other attempts at defining leisure have also been made. The elusive meaning of leisure lends itself to the superimposition of other descriptive words upon it, as though by supplying more and more qualifications, the final result would produce a workable definition.

LEISURE AS PLEASURE

More than ever, we are made aware of the distinct and pertinent heritage derived from the Grecian golden age of philosophical thought when we read Aristotle's *Politics*, the book in which he delivers this statement:

> . . . But leisure of itself gives pleasure and happiness and enjoyment
> of life, which are experienced, not by the busy man, but by those who

have leisure. For he who is occupied has in view some end which he
has not attained; but happiness is an end, since all men deem it to be
accompanied with pleasure and not with pain. This pleasure, however,
is regarded differently by different persons, and varies accordingly to
the habit of the individuals . . . .[4]

To Aristotle, the end of all human striving, achievement, and
drives to action was based on attaining a measure of happiness.
Happiness was the universally sought end, a natural inclination or
deep-seated instinct. In the Aristotelian sense of the word, happiness
is a product of the good life; that is, a way of living within moral
and ethical boundaries that enabled individuals to work and serve
to the best of their capabilities. Happiness was a product of the
golden mean—of action set in leisure because it included those
values that were innate in *schola:* health, virtuous conduct, self-realization, expression, and satisfaction. The combination and interaction
of these values created the whole person—cultured, educated, and
loved; in other words, happy. Even the modern world has to admit
that this epitomizes what would be called the well-rounded person.
The Aristotelian form of eudaemonism tells what a person ought
to do or should be. It is concerned with ethical discipline for human
conduct and should not be confused with typical hedonistic philosophy, which places all human motivation on the sensory level of
mere pleasure seeking. The Aristotelian concept states that happiness
is a product of a way of life, i.e., it can be achieved only through
ethical practice even though a person's central aim is to achieve this
state. This contrasts the commonly accepted hedonistic doctrine
that states that people should focus their living patterns to obtain
pleasure and avoid unpleasantness at all costs.
In the history of human thought, hedonistic views have played
a considerable role. However, Aristotle developed an ethical doctrine
that appears to negate much that has come to be understood as
hedonism. Hedonism *per se* can more nearly be ascribed to the
later Greek writer Aristippus, whose ideas of pleasure seeking
include both ethical and unethical behavior. Aristotelian eudaemonism, as an ethical statement of profound morality, may be read in
his *Nicomachean Ethics,* but the psychological hedonistic view has
appeared in the writings of John Locke, John Stewart Mill, and
Herbert Spencer, among others. Of the modern psychologists who

---

[4] *The Basic Works of Aristotle, Politics,* ed. R. McKeon (New York: Random House,
1941), VIII, 3, pp. 1307.

have been linked with the hedonistic doctrine, the most outstanding is Freud. Although he later disregarded this view, Freud nevertheless devoted one book—*Beyond the Pleasure Principle*— and several years to this particular idea. E. L. Thorndike, the connectionist, is another who worked with the hedonistic doctrine.

Psychological hedonism teaches that humans persist in activities that give pleasure and shun unpleasant ones. Individuals educate themselves to perform activities that bring pleasantness and reject those that produce unpleasantness. This whole concept of pleasure as a motivating force for activity has had a tremendous effect on the definitions and philosophies of leisure that use this doctrine to explain its role in human life.

It is also interesting to note the similarity between Aristotle's idea of impulse or instinct as the source of action that culminates in happiness and the Groos theory of play, which takes as its basis the instinctive urges, or what would today be called motivating drives, of individuals as expressions for the outlet of play.[5] The Aristotelian conception of the highest good, happiness, has been made synonymous with leisure and activities performed during leisure. Naturally, leisure is meant to be taken in the ancient Greek way.

The underlying factors of hedonism, which have provided leisure with its usual meaning and content, have been laid at Aristotle's door and are said to have issued from his expressions. However, such impressions are not necessarily true. Upon closer inspection and analysis one sees hedonism more as an unethical type of behavior whose realization has been promoted during more recent times, rather than as an ideal of the Aristotelian era. It might be better stated that Aristotle promoted a eudaemonistic system of philosophy that has been corrupted to hedonism.

Certainly activities generally performed during leisure are pleasurable. It seems foolish to believe that people will voluntarily undertake activities they know will be unpleasant. But leisure cannot be equated with activity. It is not leisure that affords happiness, since many people are unhappy despite their having leisure. What is done during leisure and how the individual pursues leisure are indications of whether or not the outcome will bring happiness. Although Aristotle stated that the outcome of leisure is pleasure,

---

[5] *The Works of Aristotle, Magna Moralia,* ed. W. D. Ross (Oxford: The Clarendon Press, 1915), Vol. 1, 1915), Vol. 1, p. 1187.

he really did not equate the two. Something had to occur during leisure for happiness to be produced. For Aristotle that something was the act of contemplation. He rejected almost all other experiences and determined that the only act worthy enough to be manifested during leisure was ideal concentration. For him contemplation was the ultimate happiness. To a thinker, thinking would be associated with the sublimity of life.

Equating leisure with pleasure does not explain leisure. Its nature is misconceived if it is made synonymous with pleasure, because many leisure activities produce pain or other equally unsatisfying results. Some individuals with much leisure succumb to boredom, enervating listlessness, or absolute terror at the unending hours that appear to stretch out forever. The chief reason for this is a lack of knowledge about the use to which leisure can be put. Leisure should be looked upon as a time of opportunity. The recreationally skilled person will inevitably find creative and satisfying outlets during leisure. This use of free time provides satisfaction and happiness, just as the absence of activity can result in ennui or inability to find oneself in an enjoyable situation. Those who synonymize leisure and pleasure in an attempt to define the word are inaccurate in their understanding and have no logical basis for such conceptualization.

LEISURE AS REJUVENATION

A predominantly Calvinistic orientation assumes an explicit differentiation between leisure and work, but makes the former subservient to the latter. The objective of leisure is to enable one to work more productively. One rests just enough to be capable of labor, and participates only in those leisure activities that will enable one to function again. This attitude was fundamentally espoused by Calvin and his followers, who looked upon leisure as necessary for the individual's restoration to optimum working efficiency. The rejuvenation concept reflects a bias toward labor as the most important function in which humans may participate. Work assumes such a significant place in life that it becomes an end in itself.

George B. Cutten has written, "Leisure comes as the antithesis to compulsory work . . . ."[6] American culture has obtained a leisure

---

[6] George B. Cutten, *The Threat of Leisure* (New Haven: Yale University Press, 1926), p. 15.

existence through the technological advances made possible by modern industrial methods. In an automated society leisure, i.e., time free from occupational demands, provides extended periods that may be given over to indiscriminate application of energy. Thus, Cutten states:

> To enjoy leisure is only one way to use it, and it is likely to lead one to its misuse. I am still old fashioned enough to think that leisure may yet give an opportunity for work. The laborer today has more leisure than his father had, yet I do not believe that he is happier. Work is still the divine opportunity rather than the cruel tyrant. I cannot think of happiness as the sole product of leisure, and misery as the complement of work. Success, not in industry or business or in professional life but in life-making, depends upon work and more than eight hours of it; and true happiness depends upon successful life-building.[7]

This attitude is typical of persons who look upon work as the only real expression of self and the primary method by which the individual can achieve self-realization. So deeply interested in the work ethic are they that they would continue to work compulsively, stopping only when sheer exhaustion forced them to quit. However, the human organism requires more than cessation from labor when physical or mental exhaustion threatens. The human being needs some change, however minor, from the constant attention lavished on work. Such diversion occurs during leisure, when activities other than work are indulged in. The precious time taken from the work life is justified on the basis that it rejuvenates the individual and makes that person more effective.

The work-centered person judges leisure only on the basis of its service to the efficiency of labor. Leisure is thus legitimatized by being made an integral part of work. Nevertheless, all associations of leisure as potential idleness are swept away by denying that leisure exists. Instead, leisure is looked upon as rejuvenation, a necessary physiological and psychological stimulant required by the organism. In this manner, any feelings of frivolity that might creep into the consciousness of the individual are assuaged. Leisure, or time away from work, is simply equated with the process of recuperation.

---

[7] Ibid., pp. 122-123.

LEISURE AS A STATE OF BEING

Of all the writers who conceptualize leisure today, de Grazia is foremost in defining leisure as a state of being. He objects to the idea that leisure is free time. Rather, he asserts that:

> ... free time refers to a special way of calculating a special kind of time. Leisure refers to a state of being, a condition of man, which few desire and fewer achieve.[8]

De Grazia rests his treatise on Hellenic tradition, or so he insists. However, an interesting discourse concerning Aristotle's concept of leisure has to be carried to extremes for de Grazia to make his point. Aristotle, contrary to de Grazia, defines leisure only as a time segment. True, he discusses the uses to which leisure may be put, particularly that it should be reserved for music and contemplation, but it is de Grazia who insists that Aristotle's "... freedom from the necessity of labor"[9] is the equivalent of a state of being. One may choose to concentrate on the word *freedom* and support a contention that freedom is a condition of nonrestraint and therefore a fact of existence. Contrariwise, the reader may understand the sentence as having control of the means that preclude work. Either the possessor is wealthy enough to ensure against having to be employed in some enterprise that produces monetary rewards, or the individual is socially prohibited from business occupations, as were ancient kings.[10] In the latter instance freedom from the necessity of labor provides free time for other uses.

Johan Huizinga interprets Aristotle's key statement in *Politics* (i.e., "... because nature herself, as has often been said, requires that we should be able, not only to work well, but to use leisure well; for as I must repeat once again, the first principle of all action is leisure")[11] as follows:

---

[8] Sebastian de Grazia, *Of Time, Work, and Leisure* (Garden City, New York: Doubleday & Company, Inc., 1964), p. 5. Copyright © 1962 by the Twentieth Century Fund, Inc.

[9] *The Basic Works of Aristotle, Politics,* ed. R. McKeon (New York: Random House, 1941), VIII, 3, p. 1306.

[10] Thorstein Veblen, *The Theory of the Leisure Class: An Economic Study of Institutions* (New York: Macmillan Company, 1899), pp. 36-43

[11] McKeon, ed., *Aristotle,* p. 1307.

This idleness or leisure is the *principle* of the universe, for Aristotle. It is preferable to work; indeed, it is the aim of all life. Such an inversion of the relations familiar to us must seem strange until we realize that in Greece the free man had no need to work for his living and thus had leisure to pursue his life's aim in noble occupations of an educative character. The question for him was how to employ his *schola* or free time. Not in playing, for then play would be the aim of life and that, for Aristotle, is impossible because *paideia* merely is child's play. Playing may serve as relaxation from work, as a sort of tonic inasmuch as it affords repose to the soul. Leisure, however, seems to contain in itself all the joy and delight of life. Now this happiness, i.e., the cessation of striving after that which one has not, is the *telos*. But all men do not find it in the same thing. It will, moreover, be best where those who enjoy are best and their aspirations are the noblest. Hence it is clear that we must educate ourselves to this *diagōge* and learn certain things—not, be it noted, for the sake of work but for their own sake. For this reason our forefathers reckoned music as *paideia*—education, culture; as something neither necessary nor useful, like reading and writing, but only serving to pass one's free time.[12]

Of course, Aristotle does write that happiness is experienced not by the busy individual, but only by those who have leisure. But what can Aristotle mean when he explains that leisure is not experienced by the busy person? It seems too obvious to say that he means precisely what he says. Those who work do not have leisure because work is the antithesis of leisure. Aristotle really indicates that those who have obligations, i.e., those who are engaged in routine work assignments or are required to complete some task or responsibility, are preoccupied with their performance. Aristotle equated leisure with fulfillment and satisfaction. It is time that frees the individual from the ongoing exertion of labor because labor is never completed. Individuals who must work do so to finish some task, but such intermediate steps only provoke continual striving after an elusive goal that can never be attained. Leisure, on the other hand, produces happiness because it does not require eternal seeking. For Aristotle, leisure is a time of fulfillment and therefore the end toward which humans strive. If one chooses to interpret the contemplative act as leisure, then there is every reason to equate leisure with a state of being. However, if leisure is perceived as a specific time, time in which no occupation (work) or

---

12 Johan Huizinga, *Homo Ludens* (Boston: The Beacon Press, 1955), p. 161. Copyright ©1950 by Roy Publishers. Reprinted by permission of Beacon Press.

obligation intrudes, then contemplation is only the experience one chooses *during* leisure. The act of contemplation (total absorption in thought dealing with a particular subject or idea) may have the element of concentration or an existence state, but this does not include the segment of time given over to the involvement. Leisure as free time may not be thought of as a state of being because of the activity in which an individual participates. Rather, it is the activity that must be defined as the state of being. What one does during leisure cannot define leisure.

In two of his books, L. P. Jacks has described his perception of the art of living. He calls it an indivisibility, something that cannot be divided into compartments. All facets of life that include "work and play, labor and leisure, mind and body, education and recreation, are governed by a single vision of excellence and a continuous passion for achieving it. . . ."[13] Jacks feels that all of these pairs of terms are synonymous. He states that there is no sharp distinction between labor and leisure, "because the labor occupation of one man is often the leisure occupation of another."[14] Whether this statement is true, and it is moot, is not the question. Simply because certain activities have different meanings for those who engage in them does not make them identical in kind. The work of one person may very well be the recreational activity of another. However, it is unreasonable to equate such experiences. Jacks tries to equate a behavioral act (labor) with something (leisure) that is not an act, but only a segment of time. Labor is an activity the individual performs as a result of some motivation; leisure is not an action, nothing compels it; it is outside the realm of human behavior. One cannot equate symbols of human behavior and terms representing concepts that are beyond the scope of human behavior.

H. Allen Overstreet's *A Guide to Civilized Leisure* is a most inclusive representation of the synonymity of work and leisure. Almost every page is devoted to activities that are termed leisure but are commonly thought of as recreational. The *Guide* tells what there is to do with leisure, how such time can be spent, where participation may be enjoyed, and why participation should be engaged in, and sums up with the statement: "Leisure that is worth the living must issue out of a work-life that is equally worth the

---

[13] L. P. Jacks, *Education Through Recreation* (New York: Harper and Brother, 1932), p. 1.

[14] Ibid., p. 98.

living."[15] If leisure grows out of work, then it must be a part of work, although this would appear inconsistent with current diction-ary definitions of leisure and with historical concepts of leisure as being in contrast to work.

Arthur N. Pack is another writer who has substituted leisure, as a period of free time, for a manifestation of human behavior. Pack asserts:

> . . . that the only essential difference between work and play is the presence or absence of the element of necessity, we must logically admit that practically any human occupation may become an ab-sorbing leisure time activity provided it is not pursued primarily for commercial reasons. In leisure the motive is the important thing.[16]

By stating that leisure can have a motive, Pack classifies it with behavior and therefore as a state of being. Not only is the basic assumption incorrect, but it is carried to an absurd conclusion. If Pack had been commenting on play or recreation, the above state-ment would more nearly mean what it intends to say.

The contemporary work that espouses leisure as a state-of-being concept is *The Psychology of Leisure.* In this text, John Neulinger sets the proposition that leisure is attitudinally formed and must be perceived as a state of freedom. For Neulinger, the basic assumption is that of human dissatifaction with life and work. There must be something that can fulfill unsatisfied longing for self-realization and actualization. That something is leisure. According to Neulinger a new definition of leisure is required. He offers the following response:

> *To Leisure* means to be engaged in an activity performed for its own sake, to do something which gives one pleasure and satisfaction, which involves one to the very core of one's being. To leisure means to be oneself, to express one's talent, one's capacities, one's potentials. How many people are fortunate enough these days to have a job that allows them to leisure?[17]

One must question Neulinger's basic assumption of human dis-satisfaction. Surely not everybody is dissatisfied, uninspired, and unable to obtain self-expression and creativity through work. If

[15] H. Allen Overstreet, *A Guide to Civilized Leisure* (New York: W. W. Norton & Com-pany, 1934), p. 19.

[16] Arthur N. Pack, *The Challenge of Leisure* (New York: The Macmillan Company, 1934), p. 59.

[17] John Neulinger, *The Psychology of Leisure* (Springfield, Ill.: Charles C Thomas, Pub-lisher, 1974), p. xi.

this were true, most of the people who hold jobs that do not offer these very rewards would surely seek change. The fact that there is no widespread and constant change refutes the primary contention Of course, there are bound to be persons who have not attained personal satisfaction and fulfillment in the kind of work they do. It is unfortunate, but hardly a discovery from which so sweeping a generality can be assumed.

Secondly, there is an etymological inconsistency in Neulinger's idea of *to leisure (sic)*. The word *leisure* is a noun, and nouns normally name a person, place, thing, quality, or idea. Nouns may also modify other nouns, but they are not verbs or adjectives. Adjectives modify nouns or pronouns. They describe or in some way make the meaning more precise. While adjectives can be made out of nouns, the meanings, as well as spellings, are modified. Thus, leisure (noun) becomes leisurely (adjective). In the latter case the meaning shifts quite radically. *Leisurely* has come to mean *deliberately*, *slowly*, i.e., in one's own good time. It does not carry the meaning of condition or activity. Verbs indicate action, condition, or process. *To leisure* is not only poor language usage; it is of questionable value. One either possesses, uses, or is at leisure, but there is no basis for "leisuring." One simply does not "do leisure."

Some nouns have been vernacularized as verbs, e.g., *taxied* for *taking a taxi*, but few of these words have received widespread popularity. For the most part they are considered anomalies of the language, and their use is discouraged.

Finally, leisure has never been considered as occurring during work. Work is the antithesis of leisure. Whether from a classical point of view or the most common appreciation of the term, leisure is perceived as opposed to work in any form. When a definition completely opposes the commonly understood meaning of the word, it is not a good definition. Neulinger's frame of reference distorts the conventional meaning of leisure. More significantly, the philosophical discourse is questionable. He seeks to convince the reader that leisure is a state of being and therefore one that can appear under any circumstances. Leisure should be defined in its own terms and not by activities performed.

LEISURE AS FUNCTION

The leading sociologist of leisure study in France is Joffre Dumazedier. In his numerous books and articles he has attempted to define leisure as:

... activity—apart from the obligations of work, family, and society—
to which the individual turns at will, for either relaxation, diversion,
or broadening his experiences and his spontaneous social participation,
the free exercise of his creative capacities.[18]

Leisure is therefore defined in terms of functions that are required
by individuals if they are to achieve satisfying lives. Analysis of
Dumazedier's definitions provides one with the elemental functions
of relaxation that nourishes recuperation from toil and other forms
of induced fatigue; diversion that permits escape from the routine of
daily living and defeats boredom; and social participation, which
means those voluntary associations through which individuals
humanize themselves. It concerns affiliations within the broad fabric
of the society to which the person belongs and can be observed insofar as family, business, club, spontaneous group, or other dynamic
interaction is concerned; finally, there is self-realization through
the development of whatever talent for innovation the individual
possesses.

Dumazedier's concept is further strengthened and expanded by
his statement detailing the function that leisure serves. He states:

Both in terms of accuracy and of operationality, I prefer to reserve
the word leisure for the time whose content is oriented towards self-
fulfillment as an ultimate end.[19]

But how does leisure satisfy self-fulfillment? According to Dumazedier leisure offers free choice in the sense that "leisure is freedom
from a certain number and from certain kinds of obligations."[20]
Thus he states that while a variety of obligations are laid upon the
individual by basic societal agencies—e.g., institutional components
such as the family, occupation, political, or religious units—those
that are voluntarily entered into and, presumably, just as easily
cancelled, are not looked upon as infringements of the individual's
leisure. Naturally, this brings up the entire question between leisure
and free time. Dumazedier implies that they are different. Free time
is an accretion of time that has occurred because of technological

---

[18] Joffre Dumazedier, *Toward A Society of Leisure* (New York: The Free Press, 1967),
pp. 16-17.

[19] Joffre Dumazedier, *Sociology of Leisure,* trans. M. A. McKenzie (New York: Elsevier,
1974), p. 71.

[20] Ibid., p. 73.

advances in industry or labor-saving devices in the home. However, such free time is not necessarily leisure. Time free of whatever obligatory labor the individual may be involved in may be consumed in other ways. Thus, the person may decide to take on another job, become active in politics, be more involved in family matters, or perform social "duties." For Dumazedier leisure is a specific time wherein the individual attains ". . . his own fulfillment and self-expression."[21]

Of course, it must be realized that Dumazedier is attempting to develop a sociological branch, the specialization of which is the study of leisure. To establish this special branch, he must banish inconsistencies within the discipline he has selected. This requires a frame of reference that can clearly distinguish between activities undertaken during free time, which could conceivably include everything, and those engaged in during *leisure.* To avoid the dilemma of hopeless confusion, Dumazedier neatly prunes all aspects of free time and delimits his subject only to those experiences that permit self-fulfillment or leisure.

Leisure has a variety of characteristics, among which are free choice; intrinsic worth, i.e., performance for its own sake; hedonism, i.e., satisfaction as an end in itself; and subjectivity, i.e., referral to highly personalized needs. But is this really a definition of leisure? To be sure, it is a concept, and one that will find favor among those who seek to equate leisure with activities and functions.

There are several inconsistencies within Dumazedier's statement. The idea of utilitarianism is cast aside, and rightly so, when it comes to the idea of remuneration for performance. However, many activities of value to the individual may have utilitarian overtones, i.e., be useful without being remunerative. Surely a window-shopping expedition without purchase could conceivably be as self-fulfilling to the person participating as a tour of a museum or art gallery. In fact, the very same properties, functions, and characteristics espoused by Dumazedier might be an integral part of such activity. It could also be utilitarian in motive. Does this make the activity any less leisure for the individual? Yes, according to Dumazedier. It is what he calls semi-leisure, although in this instance, the utilitarian motive produces the overlap rather than monetary remuneration or some other commitment.

---

[21] Ibid.

Furthermore, time plays an essential role in Dumazedier's leisure definition. It is not free time; that is too broad. It is leisure time, time in which leisure occurs. But what is that time? It must be a segment of free time because there is no other time. It is one of the activities that conform to the functions and characteristics that Dumazedier has established. If it is a part of free time, how is it differentiated from free time? Fundamentally, then, leisure is activity that displays specific functions, motives, and conditions. Actually, Dumazedier appears to be describing recreational activity. Almost everything that has been ascribed to leisure is also definitive of recreational experience. It may be that sociologists desirous of a more sophisticated term have advocated the use of *leisure* as the term that imparts profundity to their studies. Nevertheless, a close analysis of sociological statement regarding leisure, particularly Dumazedier's, indicates with unmistakable clarity that the term being defined is recreational activity, not leisure activity.

If one substitutes the word *recreational* for leisure in the Dumazedier lexicon, one finds absolute synonymity with every current definition and understanding of what recreational activity is. Here is an activity that occurs during free time and has the functions of recuperation, relaxation, social involvement, and self-expression. It contains the features of subjective need, is voluntary, is hedonistic, and is performed for its own sake, certainly not for monetary reward. For every sentence and description that Dumazedier employs in his attempt to define leisure, there is a stronger and stronger reason to understand his leisure concept as being recreational. One striking example is the following:

> This hedonistic character is so essential that when leisure fails to give the expected pleasure, when it is not enjoyed, it loses its intrinsic character: "it is not interesting," "it is not fun." Then leisure is no longer itself, it is impoverished.[22]

Nowhere is the similarity to recreational activity more pronounced than in that paragraph. And there are other corresponding ideas throughout every volume that Dumazedier has published. All of the material extols leisure, but in actuality the subject is recreational experience.

---

[22] Ibid., p. 76.

Using categories of activities to distinguish leisure from other forms of human experience is futile. This is not the way to determine what leisure is. One may question whether leisure *is*. If leisure were simply activity conforming to specific characteristics, there would be little argument. The great discussion does not revolve around leisure as activity; almost everybody is aware that there are leisure activities. Rather it is concerned with defining leisure so that it has universal application. Despite a profound admiration that Dumazedier arouses for his enlightened scholarship and persistent research dealing with leisure, there is much disagreement concerning his fundamental assumptions. There is still required a definition that will sharply denote the essence of leisure without qualifying it by an encrustation of activities. Such a definition would be universal and omit discrepancies that tend to creep into some modern analyses.

LEISURE AS SOCIAL STRATIFICATION

Thorstein Veblen wrote extensively on the concept of leisure as a product of social stratification. His outstanding work, *Theory of the Leisure Class*, shows a reversal of the trend toward considering leisure as the only time for creativity. The book, published in 1899, had almost instantaneous critical reaction. To many who read it, Veblen appeared to have written a satire against aristocracy everywhere. He was taken to task for having dared to question time-honored activities and customs of what he called "the leisure class." Veblen's polemic was conditioned by what he observed in the America of the late 1800s. He wrote a satire, or at least satire was used in his work, but it was not directed against an aristocratic class. It was pointed toward exposing the envy in which the aristocratic class was held by all other social levels.

Veblen produced some thought-provoking ideas concerning what he described as the unrestrained or conspicuous spending of one class to live up to its conception of all others. He described the leisure class as having evolved from a predatory stage to a quasi-predatory stage where, instead of using outright naked force to reduce all competitors to subservience, there is a reliance upon constituted authority to enforce customs of ownership. Veblen looked upon the ownership class as diametrically opposed to productive labor. The occupations of this class were institutionalized as religious order, government administration, warfare, education, and sports. In these occupations the leisured class could carry on its interest in pecuniary gain without crossing the line of producing gain through labor. This could be seen in the activities of those engaged in war or government, where gain is received by the honorable processes of annexation and naturalization. He also described the early differentiation out of which the distinction between a leisure and a laboring class developed as a dichotomy maintained by male and female work in the earliest stages of savagery—an invidious distinction out of which came industrial and nonindustrial occupations at the next highest level of culture.[23]

Veblen uses the term *leisure* to mean nonproductive use of time.

> Time is consumed non-productively (1) from a sense of the unworthiness of productive work, and (2) as an evidence of the pecuniary ability to afford a life of idleness.[24]

This show of pecuniary ability gives rise to vicarious leisure, that is, an exhibition by the possessor of goods, services, and other decorative but nonessential devices. This is manifested by the use of servants and the vicarious leisure of the wife as a symbol of the master's wealth and power. Conspicuous leisure from productive activities is by far the more classical and inclusive principle of the leisure class plan.

A striking concept that Veblen invested in his thesis is diametrically opposed to conspicuous waste and considers people as having an impulse or instinct for workmanship. This instinct, the court of last resort in the human organism, rationally lauds what is economically effective or productive in life and condemns economic waste or inutility.[25] This scale of economic worth is closely associated with the moral scale of behavior and the aesthetic scale of refinement. It is not an inclination towards effort, but a desire for accomplishment. Thus, intelligent persons want to believe they are useful, and they generally want to see others performing at some productive task or plan. This trait of workmanship leads to produc-

---

[23] Thorstein Veblen, *The Theory of the Leisure Class: An Economic Study of Institutions* (New York: The Macmillan Company, 1899), p. 4.

[24] Ibid., p. 43.

[25] Ibid., p. 93.

tive creativity, and leisure therefore becomes just another area of time set aside for certain activities having hedonistic qualities.

According to Veblen, recreation held a mediating position between the instinct of workmanship and the instinct of sportsmanship. The latter is an expression of an aversion to labor and is thus a part of the code of the leisure class.

> The leisure class canon demands strict and comprehensive futility; the instinct of workmanship demands purposeful action. The leisure class canon of decorum acts slowly and pervasively, by selective elimination of all substantially useful or purposeful modes of action from the accredited scheme of life; the instinct of workmanship acts impulsively and may be satisfied, provisionally, with a proximate purpose.[26]

Sports gives the individual an excuse to exercise skill and predatory actions. As long as people react to life with naive impulses, sports will compensate their instinct for workmanship. By satisfying the two prerequisites of conspicuous waste and proximate purposefulness, any given activity can maintain its position as an historic and accustomed form of proper recreational activity.[27]

> In the sense that other forms of recreation and exercise are morally impossible to persons of good breeding and delicate sensibilities, then, sports are the best available means of recreation under existing circumstances.[28]

The leisure class of Veblen's book contemplates a life devoted to pleasure based on a nonessential expending of wealth derived by manipulating industrial products or workers through ownership and/or exploitation. The meaning such a thesis has for the field of recreational service is recognizable by its implication of a new concept concerning social service that might more nearly equalize leisure expenditure for all groups of people to satisfy the desire of social classes in the American culture. Another pointed implication is an awareness of creativity performed in pursuits other than

---

[26] Ibid., p. 258.

[27] Ibid., p. 260.

[28] Ibid.

leisure. This unique concept challenges customary ideas on the worthiness or usefulness of acts performed in leisure as opposed to those performed in nonfree time.

Perhaps the most class-conscious group of those who study and write about leisure are the Soviets. Almost all of the articles and books that have appeared in the last decade are Marxist-oriented dialectical discussions of definitions, uses, economics, worker productivity, personal development, time-budget factors, and analyses of bourgeois errors that concentrate on the role of leisure in social development.[29] Typical of the Russian writings is that of B. A. Grushin, who attempts to analyze the structure of leisure. It is his contention that Soviet society has been able to modify and overturn the social position of different strata and groups. Through the universalization of labor and the "equalization of all members of society at work," an equalization of leisure has resulted.[30]

Some of the materials would be extremely helpful and capable of disclosing the sociological problems that researchers have in the development of concepts if the works were not as tainted as they are with Communistic ideology. A class system does exist in the Soviet Union, no matter what euphemism is used to rationalize it, and this is an open secret in Russian society. There is no real equality of either work or leisure. An elite governs and collects perquisities that the average Russian citizen would never dream existed. The leisure of the ruling body, whether in the scientific, cultural, military, or political field, is rigidly controlled by a system of organized, privileged consumption that extends to the furthest districts and and culminates within the restricted and rarified confines of the Soviet hierarchy in Moscow.[31]

Nevertheless, some very interesting information can be culled from the literary productions as the Russians attempt to define leisure and show the impact of free time on the social and cultural development of the average citizen. In Marxist ideology it is an article of faith that economic equalization will produce leisure, thereby freeing individuals for socially beneficial purposes as well

---

[29] V. N. Pimenova, "Sociology of Leisure Time and the Problem of Leisure Time," *Todays Marxist and Bourgeois Sociology* (Moscow, 1964), p. 448.

[30] B. A. Grushin, "Leisure Time and Current Problems," *Thought* (1967), pp. 75-80.

[31] Hedrick Smith, "How the Soviet Elite Lives, At Play in the Shadow of the Kremlin," *Atlantic Monthly*, December, 1975, pp. 39-51.

as personal betterment.[32] How this is translated into current Communist dialectic in light of ideological stress on work as the intrinsic force of human life is a most intricate process.[33]

LEISURE AS TIME

Much of the difficulty in identifying and classifying leisure disappears if it is defined as a particular segment of time. Leisure is discretionary time. If leisure is so defined, then many of the semantic difficulties disappear. It only remains to define free time, without having to qualify what the individual does with it, and many of the problems that have been brought about by adding usage and ethical practice are eliminated. If free time is that portion of time available at the discretion of the individual, then all time not required to maintain biological functions, economic worth, and sociocultural obligations may be termed leisure.

Insofar as biological functions are concerned, this would include time for basic survival needs, i.e., eating, sleeping, elimination. Economic worth refers to all undertakings for which monetary remuneration is obtained. Sociocultural obligations may incorporate a vast array of activities the individual participates in because of social forces that impinge, or in consequence of cultural conditioning that imposes, certain obligations upon a person. This may run the gamut from cutting one's front lawn because the neighbors expect it, to being a member of a religious congregation because the immediate family requires it, or caring for immature or aged family members because society demands it. All of these sociocultural forces impose upon the discretionary time that individuals have and further restrict the use of that time through the development of persuasive instruments that begin to act on the person from when he or she is able to receive parental guidance or nursery school training. In many subtle and not-so-subtle ways, the individual is brought up to believe that particular behaviors are considered correct or morally right, and others wrong. Even if parents, peers, and teachers do not develop

[32] K. M. Nikonov and F. T. Zinnurov, "Freedom of the Individual and Leisure Time," *Collection of Scientific Research, A. S. Serafimovicha Pedagogical Institute of Volgograd,* Vol. I, 1964, pp. 165-172.

[33] A. V. Myalkin, *The Individual and Building Communism* (Rostov: Rostov University Publications, 1971), pp. 10-40, 76-80.

socially approved behaviors, other elements in society add behavioral objectives that tend to constrain the individual. The law is a pervasive influence and so are the fundamental institutional forms of society. All of these forces play a vital role in shaping the individual's attitudes, biases, and ways in which behavior is manifested. The outcomes of these modifying pressures tend to restrain the individual from using leisure completely.

Much time is channeled away from the individual's discretion. Some time may be used for gainful secondary employment. This can no longer be looked upon as leisure. Some time is drained into activities requiring positive commitment on the part of the individual. If the individual reaches a point where that commitment proves onerous, but the person cannot break away because of guilt feelings that would arise or because one's personal commitment requires the fulfillment of the obligation, then that segment of time is no longer free and cannot be called leisure. It is only when individuals can enter or exit from participation at their own discretion, without any feeling of moral revulsion or self-denial, that leisure is present.

This does not mean that people cannot commit themselves to significant social activities from which they receive satisfaction. Commitment here simply refers to the entrance into some verbal or morally binding obligation which, if the psychic payment or personal satisfaction is not forthcoming, can be voluntarily voided without recrimination, pangs of guilt, or other socially imposed constraint. How an individual disposes of free time does not have to be questioned. There is, in fact, time available in which individuals may perform in whatever way they are capable or time in which to do nothing. One does not always have to do something and surely not something purposeful. Time may be spent without any purpose but still be leisure. It may be put to some socially beneficial use. It remains leisure. The only time that cannot be called leisure is that in which the individual has no discretion or the decision to leave or cease an activity is denied by cultural expectation or social stress that preempts personal choice.

Once leisure and free time are equated, it is possible to discuss how leisure can be used or misused; whether it is beneficial to society, the individual, or mutually worthwhile; and if it has developmental or demoralizing properties for the individual. Some societies would require that the individual's leisure be organized. This has typically been true in dictatorships of whatever 'ism' prevails. Other societies are so open that individuals may do whatever they please during free time—a form of anarchical view exists. Each of these orientations may be valuable and/or dangerous both for the society in question and the individual. If the individual has complete discretion, but does nothing to infringe upon the rights of others, then the constraint of law or some other behavioral contract is operating. If the individual is forced into some kind of mould by society, then spontaneity or choice is absent, and the entire concept of leisure is placed in abeyance.

The usual objection to equating free time with leisure is that there are obligatory engagements to which the individual submits. Thus, free time is consumed in a variety of ways ranging from second jobs, or "moonlighting," to volunteer efforts dealing with youth groups, hospitals, church, or other charitable, social, or cultural activities that tend to benefit others. All of this consumes free time. Additionally, there are certain social obligations on which others depend, e.g., the Wednesday night bridge game, the Saturday night bowling league, community theater group, and a host of other experiences. Each of these takes up the individual's leisure. Built into the routine of scheduled appointments or social occasions is the idea that others depend on the person who submits to the involvement. For most people, once they have agreed to participate in these social groups, they feel obligated to perform because others depend on them. This reliance may be for personal enjoyment, services rendered, or other satisfactions obtained by the individual's presence. Of course, it is at least understood that the person who volunteers for such arrangements does so with the expectation of receiving satisfaction and/or enjoyment in return.

What happens when such satisfaction is not reciprocated? Does this make the occasion any less leisure? All of these vexing questions and obfuscating problems can be dissolved by defining free time or leisure as purely discretionary. The individual has the option to participate or disengage at will. Thus, despite sociocultural pressures to the contrary, anyone who feels a lack of desire for participation is under no compulsion to remain. The option lies with the individual. To the extent that individuals defy conformity and are willing to express themselves, they need never experience the emotional trauma of guilt. Moreover, leisure should be observed as a time of opportunity for people to express themselves in ways that are satisfying and emotionally stimulating or through the absence of activities. The only criterion to be applied is whether or not the options for participation and withdrawal lie with the individual.

Under these circumstances, how or what the individual does with leisure no longer clouds the definition. Classification of activities, quantification of hours available, social approval, cultural traditions, and all other qualifications can be examined without inconsistencies. It is understood that people do not always use their leisure for their own benefit or for the benefit of society. Many instances of crime, immorality, incivility, delinquency, and other degenerative acts are performed during leisure. This does not make the time any less free. Activities of an antisocial nature may be universally deplored, but they exist. Such activities cannot be ruled out by definition. However, the fact that degrading or antisocial activities do occur during leisure is simply another way in which human behavior may be assessed. Negative activities are as much a part of free time as are positive ones. The only difference is tnat society or its representative analysts may now determine all of the experiences that take place during leisure.

With emphasis on discretionary time as the definitive mark of leisure, some of the formerly unanswered questions and puzzling contradictions may be resolved. There have always been questions concerning whether the work-leisure dichotomy existed or was an artificial orientation brought about by philosophical point of reference. It can now be determined that work is antithetical to leisure since, at least at certain times and in specific places, it is required if the individual is to survive. Those persons who do not work and are supported in whatever way they are, either by the state or through some form of pension, royalty, or other form of financial sustenance, still have leisure. Leisure is not tied solely to work. Even if there were no work, there would still be biological necessities to attend to, and this would infringe upon free time.

Some writers argue that enforced idleness is not leisure. Again, it is only a question of discretionary available time. Thus, people who are furloughed from their usual jobs, those who are ill and are required to be institutionalized, those who are retired or forced out of work by mandatory age-retirement rules, those who are too young to be a part of the labor market, all have free time. It makes no difference how one obtains leisure; the fact remains that leisure becomes available. The choice of activity or nonactivity is patently the prerogative of the person who has the free time.

Leisure should not be thought of in terms of work; it has nothing to do with work. In those situations where one must work to survive economically, work cannot be leisure. Even if one were wealthy and voluntarily accepted some position for which there was monetary exchange for services rendered, the commitment that abrogates free choice as to commencement or termination of employment would negate leisure. Leisure should not be thought of in terms of being antithetical, but rather in terms of providing opportunity.

One of the better analyses of leisure is by Stanley Parker. His interpretation of various leisure definitions and his handling of the troublesome concept of voluntary obligations during free time are thoughtful and well constructed. According to Parker:

> The position of leisure is rather special. It is clearly at the 'freedom' end of the constraint-freedom scale, but it need not be restricted to non-working time. We draw attention to this paradox when we say that someone else's way of choosing to spend leisure looks to us more like hard work. 'Work' and 'leisure in work' may consist of the same activity; the difference is that the latter is chosen for its own sake. Thus mountaineering is work for the guide but leisure in work for the amateur climber. Leisure and employment time cannot overlap, but there is no reason why some of the time that is sold as work should not be utilized by the seller (that is, the employee) for leisure-type activities, provided that the buyer (that is, the employer or his agent) has no objection, or is ignorant or cannot control the situation. In addition to such oases of leisure in the desert of working time, there remains the point that leisure means *choice*, and so time chosen to be spent as work activity—though not involving the constraint of employment—can be leisure just as much as more usual leisure activities.[34]

Parker does not confuse work and leisure. Rather, he is concerned with life space and those variable dimensions that occupy that space. It is possible, for example, to have two activities occupying the same time frame. Thus, an individual could be performing a vocational task while listening to the radio or be engaged in satisfying a physiological need, i.e., eating while reading, watching television, or conversing. The fact that both forms of activity occur simultaneously does not reduce the effectiveness nor minimize the value that each provides to the individual so engaged. This may be the most logical intermingling of work and leisure, but it certainly does not blur the distinction between the two.

---

[34] Stanley Parker, *The Future of Work and Leisure* (New York: Praeger Publishers, 1971), pp. 28-29.

SELECTED REFERENCES

De Grazia, Sebastian, *Of Time, Work, and Leisure.* New York: Doubleday and Company, 1964.

Dumazedier, Joffre. *The Sociology of Leisure.* Amsterdam: Elesevier, 1974.

Hartworth, J. T. and M. A. Smith, eds. *Work and Leisure.* Princeton, N. J.: Princeton Book Company, Publishers, 1975.

Ibrahim, Hilmi and B. G. Gunter, eds. *Leisure Behavior: A Psychological Approach.* Los Alamitos, Calif.: Hwong Publishing Company, 1979.

Kaplan, Max. *Leisure: Theory and Policy.* New York: John Wiley and Sons, 1975.

Larrabee, Eric and Rolf Meyersohn, eds. *Mass Leisure.* New York: The Free Press, 1958.

Murphy, James F. *Concepts of Leisure.* Englewood Cliffs, N. J.: Prentice-Hall, Inc., 1974.

Parker, Stanley. *The Future of Work and Leisure.* New York: Praeger Publishers, 1971.

——. *Sociology of Leisure.* New York: International Publications Service, 1976.

Pieper, Josef. *Leisure, the Basis of Culture,* rev. ed. New York: Pantheon Books, Inc,, 1964.

Veblen, Thorstein. *The Theory of the Leisure Class: An Economic Study of Institutions.* New York: The Macmillan Company, 1899.

II

Intellectual Forces That Shaped Recreation and Leisure

Chapter 6

Formation of an American Philosophy of Play and Recreation

Just as the altruistic views of social reformers became more clearly defined in the late nineteenth century, so too several philosophic formulations became more pronounced as the first practitioners and theoreticians of the young recreational service movement strove to define the need and explain the points of origin. No one competing philosophy attained an ascendent position during these early forays into the rationale for the budding movement. There were many possible ways to characterize the philosophical outlooks that prevailed. It is generally agreed that at least four distinct philosophies were significant, each with roots in previous eras. Among the four, idealism, realism, humanism, and experimentalism were the orientations from which the movement's thinkers drew for stimulation or guidance.

Henry Barnard could be classified as an idealist who prized the creative activity and interest of children above all else. Luther Gulick, on the other hand, would be seen as a realist who considered the necessity for preserving and transmitting fundamental values of society through organized recreational activities. To the extent that he believed in the benefits of discipline, truth, and tradition that could be fostered by such media as the Campfire Girls and the Folk Dance Movement, his realism was evident. Later William James and John Dewey would influence generations of students with the concepts of experimentalism and pragmatism. All of these intellectual functions assisted in shaping the view of play and recreation.

HENRY BARNARD'S VIEW OF PLAY

In distinguishing between play and labor, Barnard subscribed to this statement: "Labor performs the prescribed task. Play prescribes for itself."[1] In effect, his concept of play was inbued with freedom. Play meant deliberate choice-making and spontaneity on the player's part. Barnard felt that play was an instinctive, natural process designed to prepare the child for adulthood. In fact, he was convinced that in play the child used what he called the *instinct of imitation,* which produced imaginative acts so immersing the child that representation became reality. He also thought that play was aimless and needed direction in order that the child use what would otherwise be expended to no avail—intellectual curiosity.

Barnard viewed play as so absorbing the player's mind that all other interests would be blotted out. But as the psychology of his day had not developed to the point where cause and effect relationships elicited any great concern, his overview of play led him to believe that its ultimate purpose was to produce tolerance, fairness, and social grace in the child.

Whether play does create these moral and ethical behaviors is not under question here, but it should be noted that Barnard's concept was a forerunner of modern recreational objectives for the prevention of antisocial activities. What is more important is Barnard's appreciation of the interest that play had for the individual and his awareness and perception that a behavioral act that could exclude all thought of other actions from the participant's mind would be the one all-consuming activity, play.

Although he devoted precise detail to the freedom and spontaneity involved in play as the bulwark of his definition, he nevertheless recognized the phenomenon of intensity inherent in play and any other manifestation in which the play element is involved. An example of this type of other activity would be work. Work intensely absorbs the individual only when it elicits the play spirit in the worker. If work produces in the worker an emotion commonly found in play, then both experiences are the same and the difference between them is more one of semantics than reality.

---

[1] William T. Harris, "Kindergarten in the Public School System," *American Journal of Education,* Vol. XXX, July, 1880, pp. 527-528.

LUTHER HALSEY GULICK ON PLAY AND RECREATION

It was not until after Gulick's death that his book *A Philosophy of Play* was published. The student must turn to this book to obtain the essence of Gulick's thought on the subject of play. He tells the reader that a 20-year effort of constant study, experimentation, sifting, and compilation was required before he was satisfied that what he had to say would be pertinent and complete. What he produced certainly was pertinent, for his day.

At least four principal sections are discernible in Gulick's philosophy of play. For one thing, he felt that play and recreation were not the same, although they may have been two sides of the same coin. Secondly, he considered play as nature's preparation for adulthood, i.e., play for the child was a preparation for adult life. Thirdly, he felt that play was a recapitulation of the stages in the human epoch. Finally, he was convinced that the "play attitude" was found in all human activities, regardless of their functions.

In deciding that play and recreation were essentially different in structure, function, and meaning, Gulick provided his contemporaries and those who followed with the idea that play is for children and recreation is for adults. He was further impelled to say:

> There is a real difference also between play and recreation. The function of play in the life of the individual, and the function of recreation, are problems that must be solved before undertaking provision for these needs. The boy who is playing football with intensity needs recreation as much as does the inventor who is working intensely at his invention. Play may be more exhausting than work because one can play much harder than one can work. If there is any difference of intensity between play and work, the difference is in favor of play. Play is the result of desire; for that reason it is often carried on with more vigor than is work.
>
> Recreation is different in character. It consists for the adult, in reversion to the simpler fundamental activities acquired during childhood. It means relaxation in contrast to the child's outlet of energy. The intense adult plays may be as exhausting as the intense plays of children. For the adult who is working strenuously in his business, it is not sufficient that he shall be strenuous in his play. He has another and quite different need, the need for recreation.[2]

---

[2] Luther Halsey Gulick, *A Philosophy of Play* (New York: Charles Scribner's Sons, 1920), pp. 124-125.

Gulick looked upon play as a feeling, attitude, or desire that permeated an activity and thus determined its acceptance by the individual. No compulsion was attached to the activity; it had to be decided upon freely by the individual. No economic restraint or advantage could accrue from its participation, or this would destroy its fundamental meaning. It was a self-activated experience carrying with it its own motivation.

That play could be engaged in intensely was not questioned, but to Gulick such intensity by and of itself needed further sublimation, and that was to be found in recreational activity. Thus the ultimate purpose of recreational experience was in the restorative and recuperative powers that it had for the tired individual. He said that play is:

> . . . a series of activities as wide as the scope of human action, when those activities are performed not from external compulsion, but as an expression of the self, as a result of desire. In this sense the problem of play is the problem of a rich free life; the problem of recreation is only one of its phases.[3]

In the second aspect of his philosophy, Gulick seemed quite sure that the child was prepared for later life through the educative function of play. He went as far as stating:

> Play is nature's preparation for the business of later life. It finds its roots in the remote past when men lived by hunting and climbing and fighting; . . . It is life itself in miniature . . . the broad, simple, diversified life of a more primitive humanity.[4]

In this instance he combined two opposed play theories, those of Karl Groos and G. Stanley Hall. The former professed the practice theory of play that had the child developing himself for adult life through play. The latter created the recapitulation theory of play in which the child relived the epochal development of humanity through all the primitive stages to a higher mental level. Whether this combination evolved because of Gulick's belief in the Groos theory and the fact that Hall was a close friend whose influence was strong, or because Gulick reconciled these theories incidentally in

---

[3] Ibid., pp. 126-127.

[4] Ibid., p. 169.

his regard for the play instinct, is not known. One can only surmise that this reconciliation was Gulick's answer to the problem of defining and interpreting the play problem in the psychological and physiological terms of his day. The fact remains that Gulick tied himself to a play-instinct theory and set about proving it.

Gulick believed that instinctive reactions to physical changes of the maturing individual cause the child to play. From his observations of the learning process, he concluded that because children learn the manipulative skills more easily as they grow older, or are able to grasp mental problems and understand their meaning when they proceed at their own pace, rather than be forced to perform at an earlier age without lasting results, then it must also follow that the type of play in which children become interested is based on instinctive urges that change as individuals mature. He also wrote:

> There is, however, a force other than mere instinct feeling which guides the choice of the child in play. Play traditions furnish the form in which the instinct feeling finds expression.[5]

The play traditions he referred to were the activities children observed and imitated. However, his idea that the play instinct embodies a recapitulation of the epochal stages of mankind is explained by the natural outgrowth of inherited tendencies, so he claimed, to react at various age levels in ways that signified primitive conduct. These activities could take the form of hunting and fighting, running, climbing, throwing, building, home-making, and group experiences, each suggestive of a stage in the development of the human race.

Proceeding from this concept was the idea of play as the natural instrument for providing skills that would otherwise be forgotten in the machine age. Gulick went so far as to say:

> Play is the only equivalent that can replace the inheritance which the child has lost. It is the whole of the child that is called into action here: muscle, imagination, and moral force.[6]

In Gulick's view, play allows the child to attain a neuromuscular and mental growth through hedonistic forms of self-expression.

---

[5] Ibid., p. 178.

[6] Ibid., p. 78.

Everything depended on the pleasure evoked from participation in play if the child were to mature in a coordinated fashion. This thinking reflected the then attractive opinion that without play children would not develop into healthy, normal, adults. Certainly Groos gave impetus to this thinking in his book *The Play of Man.* A further point to note is Gulick's conviction that a spirit or attitude of play is found in all human activities, regardless of the peculiar function of any activity. For Gulick, play was a process through which joy or pleasure was derived. In this way, any activity that gave rise to this same pleasurable feeling could be construed as play. "The distinction is one of mental attitude, not of actual activities."[7]

He cited statements of such men as Mark Twain (Samuel Clemens), who felt that the tasks of their lives were play rather than what was commonly referred to as work. For them, as well as for Gulick, play was where one found it. It depended upon a mental attitude that looked for pleasurable experience in activity. Incidentally, Gulick also hit upon the fascination of play in the pleasure process. Indeed, he linked the entire derivative to the element of fascination that play has for the individual.

Gulick expressed the consummatory effect of play better than any of his contemporaries. In his concept, the play attitude was the culminating factor by which the consummatory experience was brought about. Individuals' willingness to find play in whatever task they perform served as a vehicle that supported this behavior. The extremely interesting feature here is the closeness to which Gulick came to stating that play was any absorbing activity. He did not make this statement, but he approximated it.

The last chapter of his book *The Philosophy of Play* is replete with implications that point to this type of definition. Time and again Gulick approached the point from which the next logical step should have been a new definition of play involving the consummatory experience, but he stopped just short of this conclusion. Yet there is no question that he believed that play was an all-absorbing activity. When all other qualifying hindrances were brushed aside, he could say that the pursuit of an ideal was in the spirit of play.

This more nearly approaches a definition of play in the consummatory vein. However, this proximity does not reach the actual mark. Contradistinctions and contradictions are still involved. If

---

[7] Ibid., p. 125.

Gulick had been ready to forego his distinction of play levels—e.g., child play versus adult recreation, or his insistence upon maintaining a difference between play and recreation, or the qualifying barriers that the word *freedom* brings to this concept—he might have concluded that the absorptive feature of play is the condition that distinguishes play from all other behavioral manifestations.

Any comparison of play concepts between Henry Barnard and Luther Gulick will show striking similarities. Of the two, the specialized approach of Gulick is of more immediate importance to the field of recreational service, but Barnard's greater insight and his diligent and scholarly profundity in understanding human behavior almost equalize their material significance.

The two men studied Froebelian play concepts, and both were quick to discern areas that were out of plumb. Both rejected the indirectness and symbolism they found and called for inductive contemplation of children's play if such activity was to be self-motivated and have use for kindergarten education. Each returned to the spontaneous, free choice, and self-activated content of play. Each held that for an activity to be considered play, it had to contain its own motivating force. The minor differences in the theories of these two men were reconciled in their major agreements.

Both considered play an educative device; each thought it was nature's instrument by which the child could learn the neuromuscular coordination needed for later life. Play was also conceived as a moral force that could shape the ethical character and personality of the individual. Each stated that what the child did for play reflected the child's maturing characteristics, and that without play there was little likelihood for the child to attain a well-rounded personality or a well-adjusted life pattern. The two men also recognized the intense interest or absorption that play had for the player. However, it was Luther Gulick who more nearly defined play in terms of consummatory experience.

The remarkable similarity here is that both extemporized on the spirit of play. Barnard and Gulick came to see play as an attitude of mind, a state brought about on the individual's own terms. They consistently wrote along the same lines, although they felt that the ultimate purpose of play was different: Barnard perceived in play the path to cultured adulthood; Gulick felt that play objectives were neuromuscular as well as moral. The differences thus expressed were not considerable and could easily be reconciled.

It is not known whether Gulick used Barnard, the elder educator and writer, as his model, but there is the possibility that he realized the worth and quality of Barnard's writing and further developed this thinking to cover a more specialized aspect of play. This would account for the striking similarities of thought found in these two men's works.

An aspect of Gulick's theory that appears at variance with his knowledge of human physiology and endurance is his use of the term *recreation* as recuperation. If he conceived of recreation as a rebuilding of physical strength through rest rather than activity, this idea would be valid. However, Gulick used the term recreation to denote some form of activity invested with the spirit of play. According to his views, if one plays to the limit of physical strength, recuperation through recreation is the antidote. Activity is piled upon activity. It is the modern view that when an individual plays to exhaustion, the recuperative process takes place either in sleep or by cessation of all activity, until such time as the organism regains the physical strength to continue.

His apparent view of play as the overall activity with recreation as one phase of it also presents a problem for interpretation. Generally, though not necessarily, people's recreational activities are intense and exhausting. To call recreation a phase of play seems incorrect. Although Gulick may have been accurate in his view of play as a mental attitude rather than energy output, his description of recreation as a "reversion to the simpler fundamental activities of early childhood"[8] in the adult leaves much to be desired. Thus, the adult is said to regress for relaxation. Possibly what Gulick had in mind was the carry-over value that various athletic activities have for the adult, the residue of past achievements. But even if this were true, recreational activity is not to be confined to activities and skills acquired during early childhood. Recreation is much wider in scope, embracing, potentially, all the activities in which humans engage. In this respect it is very much like the definition Gulick gave for play. And why not define the two synonymously?

There is more to the confused light in which Gulick placed recreation. Is there any reason why individuals' achievement of recreation must be opposed to their work? They might still receive recreational value from whatever activities they participate in, whether through using intellect or muscular action. The type of

---

[8] Ibid., p. 124.

vocation should have little or no effect on the form of recreational activity the individual indulges in, i.e., the activity that may be considered recreational by the individual concerned. A banker might like to work out double acrostics or add figures for recreational leisure, and participate in strenuous physical exercise or neither of these. The day laborer may lift weights, compose verse, or do any number of things for recreational activity. Recreation is not necessarily opposed to work or similar to it, yet work in and of itself may have some recreational value for the worker.

Recreation may or may not be recuperative. It does not necessarily have to be of the neuromuscular variety, but probably a matter of mind-body relativity. This mind-body relationship can be explained through the principle of homeostasis, or the restoration of psychological and physiological equilibrium in the individual.

As far as any criticism of Gulick's instinct appreciation of play is concerned (it must also be pointed out that Barnard considered play to be instinctive), the psychology of Gulick's day deemed such a theory valid. In the light of today's psychology, such a concept would be open to question. As yet no one has discovered the answer to the instinct question as it pertains to play. However, much material has been gathered that might refute any claim by play theorists that there is a play instinct.

The common factor in the play concepts of these two educational writers can be summarized as follows: play is a self-activated, spontaneous experience interesting the individual in such a way that all other activities become insignificant beside it. It generates satisfaction and pleasure through self-expression produced in the process. Such feelings evoked by play are to be found whenever the individual wishes to produce them regardless of the activity engaged in and therefore constitute a state of mind rather than a physical state.

It should be noted that whereas Barnard subscribed to the hedonistic doctrine, Gulick did not so subscribe. For Gulick, pleasure was an ingredient, that is an effect or by-product, of play; it was not the cause or motivating force. Although Gulick never did explain the motivating force of play other than to say it was self-activated and carried its own drive, he nevertheless approached play with enough scientific understanding to fabricate a concept that approximated a new definition of play. Unfortunately he never refined his ideas to the point where it broke away from every other definition. He did not bring himself to the place where the synonymity of play and recreation was identified; in this respect he remained with his predecessors and those who followed.

PHILOSOPHICAL AND PSYCHOLOGICAL ADVANCES IN THEORY OF LEARNING

By the 1880s, there had been collected enough systematic and logical findings in the biological and physical sciences to enable more adventurous thinkers to question and challenge the psychological facts of that era. Among the first to capitalize on the explorations opened by the evolutionary discoveries of his century was William James. At first he was content to criticize the idealist philosophy popular in his day, but soon he struck out on his own to examine the possibilities implicit in the findings of the natural and physical sciences.

WILLIAM JAMES ON PLAY

Working at Harvard College during the last decade of the nineteenth century, James initiated a new approach to psychology by investing it with empirical concepts formulated by an evolutionary, and thus a biological, basis. More than anyone else, he transformed psychology from its dependence on the scholasticism of philosophy to a science based on naturalism or physiological evolution. His views of the conscious mind, as operational behavior attempting to achieve some sort of equilibrium in an atmosphere that presented constant variety, was a direct challenge to faculty psychology, which insisted that compartmentalized faculties were the essential features of the mind.

James' monumental *Principles of Psychology* not only helped to destroy the myth of faculty psychology but also did much to supplant the then current philosophy of idealism. Up until the 1890s only Charles S. Pierce had started to combat the core tendencies of the idealist school of philosophy, based upon the classical German concepts of Kant and Hegel. Idealism postulates that there is an ultimate or absolute truth or good. It is a known value that is immutable and perfectly represents all facts and affiliations. It is the complete harmony between natural and supernatural thought. Human beings and the material world are expressions in the mind of the absolute, or God. Although the material and physical structures of the world appear to exist, they are in fact an expression of God's mind. The essential form of a person is the soul or spirit, and all morality revolves around spiritual and mental factors.

James had the ability to dramatize a new type of thinking which held that:

> True ideas are those that we can assimilate, validate, corroborate, and verify. False ideas are those we cannot. That is the practical difference it makes to us to have true ideas; that, therefore is the meaning of truth, for it is all that truth is known as.[9]

This statement of the pragmatic view was eagerly followed by physiologists. James paved the way for a pragmatic approach to many of the social sciences, especially for the field of education. His ability to state his position and work within the definition that he set up attracted a good deal of attention, both favorable and antagonistic, to this new philosophy. As Butts and Cremin explain:

> James was also influential because of his insight into the application of the pragmatic method of all realms of life, not merely to the abstraction of philosophy. His great achievement was the effort to apply philosophy to the practical affairs of men, in ethics and conduct, in religious experience, in art and science, in law and government. In all these realms our inherited ideas should be critically examined, should be tested to see what effects they produce in practice, and should be revised or changed until they produce the results deemed desirable.

> James was thus a wide-ranging and stimulating thinker whose influence fanned out in several directions. His biological conception of mind influenced Thorndike's objective psychology; his criticism of the idealists and his challenges to the realists stimulated them to dig deeper; and his pragmatism prompted John Dewey to go on to develop his theories of experimentalism.[10]

James's preoccupation with the development and refinement of a philosophical expression, pragmatism, his investigations into the various social sciences of human activity, and his work in scientific

---

[9] William James, *The Philosophy of William James Selected From His Chief Works* (New York: The Modern Library, 1925), p. 165.

[10] R. Freeman Butts and Lawrence A. Cremin, *A History of Education in the American Culture* (New York: Holt, Rinehart and Winston, 1953), p. 343.

psychology also led him to write on the theory of play. With all his tremendous insight into human behavior and learning, it is difficult to understand why he propounded the instinctivist view of play. However, in 1890, when he wrote his book on psychology, the term *instinct* had not yet fallen into the disrepute in which it is held today. The psychology of his day had not advanced to the point where motivational impulses of behavior could be described in anything but instinctual terms. In applying his theory to play, James said:

> The impulse to play in special ways is certainly instinctive . . . . All simple active games are attempts to gain excitement yielded by certain primitive instincts, through feigning that the occasions for their exercises are there. They involve imitation, hunting, fighting, rivalry, acquisitiveness, and construction, combined in several ways; their special rules are habits, discovered by accident, selected by intelligence, and propagated by tradition; but unless they were founded in automatic impulses, games would lose most of their zest.[11]

Aside from this he related another type of human play, that of higher feeling, to instinct. In this type of play there was a universal sensibility for ceremonies and rites stimulated by the emotional pleasure derived from group interaction. This particular form of play he ascribed to the "emotion of pursuit."[12] He continued to express instinct motivation for play, even in the face of Lazarus' definition and denial of play as instinct. He disallowed Lazarus' explanation of play as noninstinctive on the grounds that the particular forms that play takes and the direct "excito-motor" stimulations engendered by games must be founded on instinctual motivation.[13]

In an essay titled "The Moral Equivalent of War," James presented an interesting study of sublimated activities as part of the process of catharsis. Throughout this work he continuously makes reference to the fact that ". . . war's irrationality and horror . . . has no effect on modern man because he . . . inherits all the innate pugnacity and all the love and glory of his ancestors."[14] He stated

---

[11] William James, *Principles of Psychology*, 2 vols. (New York: Henry Holt and Company, 1890), 2:427.

[12] Ibid., pp. 428-429.

[13] Ibid.

[14] William James, "The Moral Equivalent of War," *Essays on Faith and Morals* (New York: Longmans, Green and Company, 1943), p. 323.

that war is fascinating, that it implies complete obsession for the individual. However, he decried war in all of its forms and pleaded for activities that would allow a working out of these innate hostilities without bloodshed and naked aggression.

> Patriotic pride and ambition in their military form are, after all, only specifications of a more general competitive passion. They are its first form, but that is no reason for suggesting them to be its last form.[15]

Here again one is made aware of a connection between the acting out process of Aristotelianism and an implication for sublimated reactions to environmental and internal stimuli. Probably James's strongest emphasis on this type of thinking is seen in the statement, "We should be *owned,* as soldiers are by the army, and our pride would rise accordingly."[16] One recognizes the impelling meaning that this has for James. By this he sums up his feeling concerning the need for a compensatory activity for war that could provide a possessed state for the individual without actual recourse to bloody violence. An astute reader may understand why some people have a compelling desire to participate in vigorous activity; for them it produces a spirit or feeling of heroic power.

JOHN DEWEY'S CONSUMMATORY CONCEPT

From the 1880s to the 1930s, the most eminent American philosopher-educator was John Dewey. Through his writings the philosophies of pragmatism and educational experimentalism reached their fullest development. As the outstanding spokesman for the dynamic and evolutionary approach to education, he advocated a biosociological concept of the human organism as a product of environmental influences.

Dewey conceived of human intelligence as emerging through an evolutionary process.[17] Intelligence is behavior that is a natural consequence of social interaction; it evolves in connection with communication, i.e., language. The existence of intelligence is coincidental with the life force. In Dewey's view, intelligence emerged

---

[15] Ibid., pp. 323-324.

[16] Ibid., p. 326.

[17] John Dewey, "The Reflex Arc Concept in Psychology," *The University of Chicago Contributions to Philosophy,* Vol. I, January, 1896, pp. 39-52.

by means of an adjustment mechanism to preserve the organization or equilibrium of the organism in a hostile environment. Outside pressures of social intercourse as well as environmental obstacles produced the need for language communication. Intelligence grew and was nurtured by meeting and solving problematic situations whenever they arose. With this type of background to dwell upon, one can understand Dewey's reason for looking upon psychology as essentially social. It was through environmental or social pressure that mind evolved; the individual organism was a product of this interacting pressure. It seems only natural that social psychology should be the basis upon which Dewey built his philosophical and educational concepts.

Dewey looked upon the philosophy of pragmatism as an instrument for testing ideas in action. It was an objective frame of reference in which any idea could be placed and tested experimentally. As a pragmatist, he found truth as an execution of process, i.e., an idea is true if it performs according to the plan that it implies.[18] Truth is verifiable through experience, and ideas are judged by the consequences of effects to which they lean.

Included in his outlook of instrumentalism, the combination of Pierce's logic with James's psychology and morality, Dewey always had a deep and abiding concern for ethics and integrity and the human comprehension of both. This interest in the social dimensions of morality became a first step in his regard for democratic principle as the heart of meeting and solving problems on a society-wide basis. He conceived of experimentalism as a method by which problem-solving could be accomplished, and he looked upon the social sciences, particularly the discipline of education, as the area in which ideas were to be examined in the light of need where intelligent self-direction based upon individual self-respect could be tested by experience.

JOHN DEWEY'S CONCEPT OF PLAY

Perhaps the most widely quoted excerpt from Dewey's works, in relation to play or recreation, has been:

---

18 John Dewey, "What Pragmatism Means by Practical," *Journal of Philosophy, Psychology and Scientific Method*, Vol. V, February 13, 1908, pp. 85-99.

Play—a name given to the activities which are not consciously performed for the sake of any result beyond themselves; activities which are enjoyable in their own execution without reference to ulterior purpose.[19]

The initial wording of this article became a basis for the ideas of many later theorists. Apparently Dewey had such a profound influence on these writers that they never looked further for his views concerning definitions of play. How unfortunate that these same writers did not bother to discover Dewey's more pertinent and important subsequent discussion of play which appeared in his books during the 1920s. In the article cited, Dewey stressed the fact that play, being born of action, precedes work:

But as action involving the idea of an end grows naturally out of a spontaneous activity, so work in this psychological sense is inevitably preceded by play and grows insensibly out of it.[20]

His concept of the relation between play and work, suggesting that any difference between the two is founded upon a misconception put forward by those who confuse work with drudgery, may be read in the following:

Play and work cannot, therefore, be distinguished from one another according to the presence or absence of direct interest in what is doing.[21]

This viewpoint may be more fully explained with this example:

A child engaged in making something with tools, say, a boat, may be just as immediately interested in what he is doing as if he were sailing the boat. He is not doing what he does for the mere sake of sailing it later. The thought of the finished product and the use to which it is put may come to his mind, but so as to enhance his immediate activity of construction. In this case his interest is free. He has a play motive;

---

[19] John Dewey, "Play," *A Cyclopedia of Education*, ed. Paul Monroe (New York: The Macmillan Company, 1913), Vol. IV, p. 725.

[20] Ibid., p. 726.

[21] John Dewey, *Interest and Effort in Education* (Cambridge, Mass.: Houghton Mifflin Company, The Riverside Press, 1913), p. 78. (See also Volume 7, *The Middle Works of John Dewey, 1989-1924.* Quoted with permission of the Center for Dewey Studies, Southern Illinois University at Carbondale.)

his activity is essentially artistic in principle. What differentiates it
from more spontaneous play is an intellectual *quality;* a remoter end
in time serves to suggest and regulate a series of acts.[22]

In this instance one may be aware of a future or anticipated satisfaction, but the activity itself is performed for the interest it generates
in and of itself. This same concept was reiterated in *Democracy and
Education* with a more profound explanation of play in relation to
work. Here the problem of timespan was brought out as it influences
the consequences of direction. According to Dewey, play has a
direct interest, i.e., it is ". . . its own end, instead of having an ulterior result."[23] He did not consider this to mean that play is a
momentary proposition; he saw it as an interest for action. Play is
a combination of activity initiated by physiological necessity with
logical determinants or subsequent imaginative involvement.

> . . . play has an end in the sense of a directing idea which gives point
> to the successive acts. Persons who play are not just doing something
> (pure physical movement); they are *trying* to do or effect something,
> an attitude that involves anticipatory forecasts which stimulate their
> present responses. The anticipated result, however, is rather a subse-
> quent action than the production of a specific change in things.[24]

Dewey also defined recreation as a recuperation of energy. He thus
used the traditional idea of recreation as a rejuvenating force. He
did this to express the idea that education has a task to perform in
the preparation of people for wholesome recreational activity, not
antisocial in nature, but some sort of constructive activity to be
performed in leisure. He did not say that recreational activity could
occur only in leisure, but he spoke of recreational leisure in this
context.

Dewey's concept of play in relation to work, which he restated
in *Democracy and Education,* was bitterly attacked by reactionaries
who represented the idealist and realist schools of thought in education. He early showed himself interested in play as an educational
tool. In an article written for the *Elementary School Record* in

---

22 Ibid., p. 79.

23 John Dewey, *Democracy and Education* (New York: The Macmillan Company, 1916),
p. 238.

24 Ibid.

1900, he spoke of play as an activity that could lift the child to greater power in his own actions. It would enable the child to learn control of self for enlightened growth.[25]

Most important of Dewey's earlier writing was his consummatory concept of play. Although it was not until his book *Art As Experience* was published that a complete and detailed analysis was given to this idea, its first manifestations were propounded in an article written in 1900. In this article he ascribed to play the power of total absorption.

> Play . . . is typical of what writers call spontaneous attention, or, as some say, nonvoluntary attention. The child is simply absorbed in what he is doing; the occupation in which he is engaged lays complete hold upon him. He gives himself without reserve. Hence, while the child is intent, to the point of engrossment, there is no conscious intention.[26]

At this point in his development, Dewey was still steeped in the traditional views of his contemporaries, G. Stanley Hall, George E. Johnson, and Luther Halsey Gulick. He used their work in executing the article on play for *A Cyclopedia of Education* (1913), so it is little wonder that he held views that were similar to theirs in 1900. However, it is to his later work that one must turn to fully appreciate his deep understanding of the effect of consummatory activity on the human organism.

Dewey consistently treated art and play with the same respect due any of the activities by which human beings strive and grow. He linked play with art by their common bond of spontaneity and morality. Just as play implies certain rules that must be adhered to, even in fantasy, so too does art imply a morality of harmony in its line and form. In *Democracy and Education*, Dewey ends a striking paragraph that deals with the creativeness of play, with the remark that art may also have the capacity to release individuals from tension and uplift them in the cycle of growth.

In another work, *Human Nature and Conduct*, he wrote:

---

[25] John Dewey, "Froebel's Educational Principles," *Elementary School Record*, Vol. I, June, 1900, p. 145.

[26] John Dewey, "Reflective Attention," *Elementary School Record*, Vol. I, May, 1900, p. 111. Quoted with permission of the Center for Dewey Studies, Southern Illinois University at Carbondale.

Relief from continuous moral activity—in the conventional sense of moral—is itself a moral necessity. The service of art and play is to engage and release impulses in ways quite different from those in which they are employed in ordinary activities. Their function is to forestall and remedy the usual exaggeration and deficits of activity, even of 'moral' activity and to prevent a stereotyping of attention. ... whatever deprives play and art of their own careless rapture thereby deprives them of their moral function. Art then becomes poorer as art as a matter of course, but it also becomes in the same measure less effectual in its pertinent moral office. It tries to do what other things can do better, and it fails to do what nothing but itself can do for human nature, softening rigidities, relaxing strains, allaying bitterness, dispelling moroseness, and breaking down the narrowness consequent upon specialized tasks.[27]

Thus Dewey moulded a pattern which sought to show the integration of play and art. The discussion of the 'art as play' theory was taken up in more detail in his *Art As Experience*, where he stated:

The truth in the play theory of art is its emphasis upon the unconstrained character of aesthetic experience, not in its intimation of an objectively unregulated quality in activity. . . .[28]

Play remains as an attitude of freedom from subordination to an end imposed by external necessity, as opposed, that is, to labor; but it is transformed into work in that activity is subordinated to *production* of an objective result. No one has ever watched a child intent in his play without being made aware of the complete merging of playfulness with seriousness.[29]

Although Dewey did not confuse art with play, i.e., define objective with unconscious objective, he nevertheless stated that play, as an attitude of mind, attains direct interest as it undergoes transformation through maturing experiences. He held that there is no contrast between work and play; he deemed this an invention of adulthood which calls certain acts recreational because they stand in opposition to grinding or necessitated attention.

---

[27] John Dewey, *Human Nature and Conduct* (New York: Henry Holt, 1922), pp. 161-162.

[28] John Dewey, *Art As Experience* (New York: Minton, Balch & Company, 1934), p. 279.

[29] Ibid.

One characteristic of play is the spontaneity of activity in the individual. Dewey also saw this spontaneity in art, not as release, though well it might be, but as absorptive for the person undergoing this experience. The aesthetic experience is consummatory and its content is reserved for the player. Play is taken in its broadest sense to include plastic art forms as well as mental images.

Dewey posits the basis upon which the consummatory experience rests as a biological adjustment known as homeostasis, or equilibrium seeking. Realizing that the human organism experiences an unending series of tensions brought about by internal and external pressures which influence survival, Dewey was quick to point out that activity is the essence of all human life. The motivating factors of behavior therefore could be explained in terms of psychological homeostasis or equilibrium seeking by the organism.[30] Inner harmony, then, comes about whenever equilibrium is attained. This state of grace (not theological in nature) represents total integration or unity. It is a feeling of ease, an unawareness of stress, which pervades the entire being.

> Inner harmony is attained when, by some means, terms are made with the environment. When it occurs on any other than an objective basis, it is illusory—in extreme cases to the point of insanity. Fortunately for variety in experience, terms are made in many ways—ways ultimately decided by selective interest . . . . But happiness and delight are a different sort of thing. They come to be through a fulfillment that reaches to the depths of our being—one that is an adjustment of our whole being with the conditions of existence. In the process of living, attainment of a period of equilibrium is at the same time the initiation of a new relation to the environment, one that with it potency of new adjustments to be made through struggle. The time of consummation is also one of beginning anew.[31]

This 'beginning anew' concept inevitably leads one to connect consummation with recreation. In the real sense of the word, recreation is the re-creation of renewal or the human organism—perhaps both mentally and physically, but assuredly the former. It is relativistic, i.e., it occurs at intervals rather than in a single outburst. It arises from the restoration of equilibrium within the organism and because that also occurs at varying intervals, so too, its product

---

[30] Ibid., p. 14.

[31] Ibid., p. 17.

and process, recreation, can occur only at intervals. Consummation is a phase of growth, recurring, being lost, and recovered again. Recreation must also be a phase of growth. As such it is immediately responsive to behavioral motivation.

The outstanding features of Dewey's concept of play may be enumerated in the following ways:

1. Play is construed as a method by which growth, and thereby education, may be attained. It may take the form of mental or physical reaction stimulated by the organism's attempts to maintain survival balance.

2. Play is serious. Play is a conscious attempt to effect a change in future actions, which in turn excites present reactions. It is a continuous activity, i.e., it is not an activity of the moment without thought for further pursuit.

3. Play is a basis of work. It involves the ideas of an end in view even though it may be spontaneous.

4. Play is deeply absorptive. It is a consummatory experience based on the need for equilibrium. This need, the origin of human motivation, occurs spasmodically. It rarely occurs rhythmically and usually puncutates an otherwise highly tensed organism with a feeling of calm and well-being lasting for short periods of time, depending on the individual's capacity.

5. Play, like art, demands intelligent, consciously determined action to satisfy the individual. Play without purpose is mere physical activity or a careless expenditure of energy that does not bring consummation; such could be better termed diversion.

6. The spontaneity of play is not to be construed as a spur-of-the-moment type of activity; it is, rather, a lack of constraint on the individual who is attempting to communicate a feeling of self or who is creating an atmosphere in which one seeks to dream. The end in view, whether consciously desired or not, is to effect a change from what the individual is to what he would like to be.

REACTIONS TO DEWEY'S IDEAS

That section of philosophical discipline known as realism had proponents who were quick to find fault with Dewey's concept of play as related to education. The splinter group, known as essentialists, took issue with the concept that play and work could be indistinguishable or that work might normally grow out of play.

Essentialism as an educational philosophy conceives of education` as a reestablishment of traditional authority. Its advocates hold the view that conservatism in education is the best method by which the individual will be taught. Philosophers who profess this respect for the social and physical sciences as providing the requirements for all knowledge fall back on the absolutes of accepted truths and values. They insist that the validity of knowledge is readily available and its stability of fact attested to by traditional dependence upon it. Because this is the case, a fairly constant body of knowledge, valid and stable, should be the prerequisite for those who must learn about and live in the contemporary society. Theodore Brameld has described the philosophic views associated with essentialism in this way:

> ... it views the established beliefs and institutions of our modern heritage as not only real but true, and not only true, but good. It recognizes, of course, that this heritage is marred by flaws—by war, disease, and poverty—but it insists that these are usually, if not al- ways, the results of mistakes in human judgment not evils inherent in the universe or in men. "Ignorance," in other words, is simply a term for misjudging the underlying rightness and order of the uni- verse and "understanding" a term for accurately judging their right- ness and order.[32]

One of the leading essentialist philosophers, William C. Bagley, in attacking the progressives in American education, was much troubled and concerned over their "confusion of work and play."[33] In his argument against such thinking he stated that play "is the primitive, spontaneous, purposeless activity of the immature."[34] Work, on the other hand, "is purposeful and effortful."[35] It is the "controlled activity through which ... volitional maturity is achieved."[36] By "volitional maturity," Bagley referred to ". . . the

---

[32] Theodore Brameld, *Philosophies of Education in Cultural Perspective* (New York: Holt, Rinehart and Winston, 1955), p. 204.

[33] William C. Bagley, *Education, Crime, and Social Progress* (New York: The Macmillan Company, 1931), p. 89.

[34] William C. Bagley, *Education and Emergent Man* (New York: Thomas Nelson and Sons, 1934), p. 65.

[35] Ibid.

[36] Ibid.

capacity to sustain and control effort even if the effort is not pleasurable."[37] In effect, what Bagley expressed was his belief that education should follow the hard and fast rules laid down by tradition.[38] Knowledge is validated on the assumed existence of absolute laws that must be acquired if the student is to achieve any idea of the society of which he is a part. Such knowledge is prescribed as "hard work," not something with which to fool around or play. The mastery of subject matter is reached through authority and discipline, not coddling. The whole idea of individual learning through and by one's own interests is rejected.

Bagley's concept of play is questionable. By stating that play is primitive, purposeless, and the activity of the immature, he overlooks the vast body of knowledge handed down from the Platonic era to modern educators and psychologists who use play as an educative and therapeutic device. If he means that the play act is itself purposeless, then he overlooks the anthropological significance of play as a form of cultural development. If he means that play has no meaning beyond itself, then he misjudges the physiological and psychological necessity expressed in the human organism's struggle to maintain organization. When he writes that play is primitive, he forgets that aesthetic achievements derived from play are all the arts. When he says that play is an activity of the immature, he tacitly assumes that play must be a regressive outlet of the adult, or else he overlooks all the adults who play. Bagley thus construed play in its narrowest sense and apparently did not see nor understand how really broad is this aspect of human behavior.

Realism, as a reaction against the theological basis of idealism, attempts to base its world view on the premise that people have the ability to understand, i.e., they are rational and are able to assimilate truth and knowledge through experience in the world in which they live. Realism gives priority to and evaluates the real objects as measured by the physical sciences. External objects can be measured by empirical methods, and the existence of such physical things do not depend on human knowledge or experience. The realist process of education is the attainment of validated

---

[37] Ibid.

[38] William C. Bagley, "Just What Is the Crux of the Conflict Between the Progressives and the Essentialists?" *Educational Administration and Supervision,* Vol. XXVI, January, 1940, pp. 508-511.

knowledge and the compatability of learners with the physical properties of their environment.

The educational theory of the realist philosopher Bertrand Russell brought him to a point where he had to criticize the position of the progressives led by Dewey. In discoursing upon his educational outlook, Russell wrote on play and the implications it had for the good life. Taking the stand that play was a preparation for the child in achieving the practice necessary for later life, he said:

> There seems no reason to doubt the most widely accepted theory that in play the young of any species rehearse and practice the activities which they will have to perform in earnest later on.[39]

Like most realists, Russell invoked the hedonistic theory of play when he wrote, "In real play, amusement is the governing purpose."[40] He felt that children are fundamentally aware of making believe when they play and that they are not actually living with a real situation.

> It is commonly said that children do not distinguish between pretense and reality, but I see very little reason to believe this .... His games do not take up time which might be more profitably spent in other ways; if all his hours were given over to serious pursuits, he would soon become a nervous wreck.[41]

The statement concerning play as a departure from serious life needs immediate clarification. Russell speaks of childplay in this context, and nothing could be further from being accurate. If Russell was commenting on play for the adult, which seems unlikely according to the text of his book, then the entire output up to this point has been falsely based on an immature individual—the child.

According to historian Johan Huizinga:

---

[39] Bertrand Russell, *Education and the Good Life* (New York: Horace Liveright, 1926), p. 124.

[40] Ibid., p. 127.

[41] Ibid., p. 129.

Every child knows perfectly well that he is 'only pretending,' or that it was 'only for fun' . . . . This 'only pretending' quality of play betrays a consciousness of the inferiority of play compared with 'seriousness,' a feeling that seems to be something as primary as play itself. Nevertheless, as we have already pointed out, the consciousness of play being 'only a pretend' does not by any means prevent it from proceeding with the utmost seriousness, with an absorption, a devotion that passes into rapture, and temporarily at least, completely abolishes that troublesome 'only' feeling. Any game can at any time wholly run away with the players. The contrast between play and seriousness is always fluid. The inferiority of play is continually being offset by the corresponding superiority of its seriousness. Play turns to seriousness and seriousness to play.[42]

Russell further revealed his play concept by stating:

At first a child's play is solitary . . . . But collective play, as soon as it becomes possible, is so much more delightful that pleasure in playing alone quickly ceases.[43]

Thus he ran the gamut of signifying that play is an imitation for later life, that it has no purpose except for pleasure, that it represents a departure from serious life, i.e., profitable pursuits, and that solitary play is not only less desirable than group play, but that the former is never referred to once the latter is practically established. This view appears to follow the Groos, or practice, theory of play. The basis for this theory was instinct in which motivational urges to play were based on the satisfaction of a need to grow. Later psychologists discounted this theory as a motivational cause for play or any other human behavior.

Although it might be true that at first a child's play may be solitary, it does not follow that collective play, when practical, will completely shut off the existence of solitary play, especially in the child. All children need and want some moments alone, when they can commiserate with themselves and perhaps talk to an imaginary playmate, notwithstanding the fact that there are real live playmates just waiting for their call. No one questions that a human being is a gregarious animal, but at times even the most gregarious want a

---

[42] Johan Huizinga, *Homo Ludens* (Boston: The Beacon Press, 1950), p. 8. Copyright © 1950 by Roy Publishers. Reprinted by permission of Beacon Press.

[43] Russell, *Education and the Good Life*, p. 132.

little solitude to "play with an idea," or just to perform by themselves rather than with a group. That is why there will always be the individual camper, hunter, artist, collector, hobbyist, or philosopher. The play of these individuals will always be more delightful to them when performed in solitary fashion. As for the play of the child, all children may like to be with someone, attain the center of attention from a group; nonetheless, there comes a time when it is more delightful, to use the words of Russell, to go off in a corner and let their small hoard of wonderful objects, irreplaceable treasures trickle through their fingers for no one else to see or enjoy.[44]

Although vibrations of the impact between psychological and philosophical concepts reverberated throughout the educational world, the field of recreational service and its own infant philosophy were no longer dormant. With the faculty psychologists and idealist academicians opposed to evolutionary biologists and connectionist psychologists, new theories of play were explained, and this aspect of human behavior was finally given serious consideration by many outstanding educators. In the late nineteenth and early twentieth centuries, the groundswell of a recreational service movement was clearly discernible.

The establishment of a discipline for the field of recreational service depends on its relationship to concepts that are traceable to early Greek philosophy, Renaissance explorations, Enlightenment humanism, and contemporary philosophies of the American culture. With these ideas upon which to build, a discipline of learning set in the framework of rational value judgments that have reference to ethics in human development and behavior has been indicated.

Students can point to the various meanings given for recreation and discover just where in the formulative period they arose. They can point to Locke as the originator of the rest and refreshment idea; to Rousseau as the libertarian; to Goethe as the formulator of work and play having a common denominator; to Schiller as representing the creative doctrine of play; and to Froebel as the activist.

Of all the writings thus far examined, few approached a point whereby a new or more valid definition of recreation could be developed. If a careful analysis of the works on education and play is made, then only John Dewey's concept of the consummatory experience as a factor in equilibrium seeking is compelling enough

---

[44] Clyde Kluckhorn and H. A. Murray, *Personality in Nature, Society and Culture*, 2nd ed. (New York: Alfred A. Knopf, 1953), p. 213.

to warrant expansion. As a manifestation of behavior based on the motivation of homeostasis within the human organism, this theory affords the best foundation upon which to build subsequent views of recreation.

SELECTED REFERENCES

Barnard, Henry. *Kindergarten and Child Culture Papers, Papers on Froebel's Kindergarten, with Suggestions on Principles and Methods of Child Culture in Different Countries.* Hartford, Ct.: F. C. Brownell, 1890.

Brameld, Theodore. *Philosophies of Education in Cultural Perspective.* New York: The Dryden Press, 1955.

Butts, R. Freeman and Lawrence A. Cremin. *A History of Education in the American Culture.* New York: Henry Holt and Company, 1953.

Dewey, John. *Art As Experience.* New York: Minton, Balch & Company, 1934.

Gulick, Luther H. *A Philosophy of Play.* New York: Charles Scribner's Sons, 1920.

James, William. *The Philosophy of William James Selected from His Chief Works.* New York: The Modern Library, 1925.

———. *Pragmatism: A New Name for Some Old Ways of Thinking.* F. Burkhart, *et al.*, eds. Cambridge, Mass.: Harvard University Press, 1976.

Kallen, Horace M. and Sidney Hook, eds. *American Philosophy Today and Tomorrow.* New York: Arno Press, 1968.

Riley, Isaac W. *American Philosophy: The Early Schools.* Tampa, Fla.: Russell Publications, 1958.

Shahan, Robert W. and Kenneth R. Merrill. *American Philosophy.* Norman, Ok.: University of Oklahoma Press, 1977.

Chapter 7

An Analysis of Play and Recreation Theories

Total, conscious intellectual absorption is necessary for an individual to achieve recreation. This state, which is an integral part of human behavior, is neither qualified nor affected by time, place, activity, or will. It is completely subjective and beneficial to the individual, and can never be construed as debilitating.

For the reader to grasp more fully what this statement embodies, a complete discussion of the philosophical development of the term *recreation* is included. Basically, this chapter presents an analysis of a variety of theories of play and recreation to arrive at a meaningful and understandable definition that can be applied to human behavior.

Why do people play? Do they have to be motivated for recreation? If recreation is a human need, what is its essence? It is presumed that the answers depend on the definition of motivation and its components. For purposes of this discussion, recreation and play will be treated synonymously. Recreation is defined as a nondebilitating, consummatory experience.

Recreation, like any other word, is an abstract symbol, having many meanings that depend on context. Although the word *recreation* suggests leisure activities or other experiences of relaxation, pleasure, or satisfaction, it does not reveal precisely what is meant by the single term. Recreation in and of itself means nothing; it has no form, nature, or function until the human mental process develops a rationale and places the word within a given situation. When this is done, recreation is traditionally seen as a consciously performed act. It is that, but it contains a more inclusive meaning as well.

INSTINCT AS MOTIVATION

For many modern recreationists and writers, *instinct* is the rallying point around and on which they base motivation for activity. Throughout the literature of this field, many theories deal with instinct as motivation for human behavior of all kinds. Generally, instinct definitions have taken the form of mind mastery or stimuli, i.e., the controlling of external pressure through reactions of response to these stimuli. Environmental processes, which incite the mental apparatus, are a continuous source of these stimuli. Internal stimuli, those of the somatic field, the neuro-chemico-muscular variations in the body organs that impel response, have been called instincts. The basic difference between internal or somatic stimuli and environmental or external stimuli is that individuals cannot withdraw from the somatic as they can from environmental stimuli.

Instinct is conceived as the mental messenger of a perpetually active force initiated within the organism and traveling to the mind from the physical body; it is a mental movement that arises from bodily origins, a borderline symbol relating to mind and body. It acts as a constitutional spur in the mind, as a continually changing item. In the psychoanalytic sense, the word *instinct* was used to link psychology with biology and thus negate the artificial separation of psyche from soma, or mind from body.

Instinct has been represented in several ways. An eclectic overview would show that four factors are found in different theories: the drive, the aim, the object, and the source. Drive is the dynamic energy causing action or reaction. The aim of an instinct is to remove tension. The object is environmental, i.e., outside of the somatic field. The source of an instinct is in a body organ, the incitement of which is reflected in the mind.

In some instances instinct has been thought of as consciously performed acts as opposed to reflex acts, which are unconsciously performed. Instinctive acts are similarly performed by all members of the same restricted group of animals, but are subject to variation and subsequent modification under the guidance of individual experience. Only on their initial performance are acts purely instinctive; all subsequent performances are in some degree modified by the experience afforded by previous behavior of like nature and the results it achieves.

> The characteristic feature of the instinctive act is itself instinctive because at the presentation to sight or hearing it calls forth a mode of behavior of like nature to, or producing like results to, that which affords the stimulus.[1]

What is spoken of in terms of instinct tendency is, in any species, the expression of a considerable number of particular responses, each of which is congenitally linked with a specific presentation of stimulus. The traditional instincts included one that was termed *play.* Whether instinct was a reflex action or unlearned purposive behavior, play was a part of it. In separating the two components of instinct, reflex movement from unlearned purposive reaction, a leading reference of the day printed this statement:

> On biological grounds a distinction can be made ... from this point of view, the instinctive movement unlike the reflex, is that which involves the whole organism. The animal crouches in fear, advances in anger, disports itself in play.[2]

Thus, the instincts in human beings, though developed to a lesser degree than those found in insects, are quite numerous but probably less powerful because of the molding capability of the human nervous system. Instincts are supposed to include actions that are similar to reflexes, i.e., sneezing, smiling, coughing, crying. However, there are reactions called *large general tendencies.*

> The tendency which makes us take the world of perception as a world of real things; the empathetic tendency, which makes us humanize our surroundings; the tendencies to imitate, to believe, to dichotomize. Certain movement complexes expressive of the emotions must also be considered instinctive.[3]

---

[1] "Instincts," *Encyclopedia Britannica,* Vol. XIV (Cambridge, Eng.: The University Press, 1910), p. 650.

[2] "Instinct," *New International Encyclopedia,* Vol. XII (2nd ed.), (New York: Dodd Mead and Company, 1928), p. 228.

[3] Ibid.

This then has been the expressed reasoning contained in instinct motivation for play or recreation. The instinctivists say that recreation is instinctive in human beings just as play is instinctive in the lower animals. The instinctivist argument follows the line of reasoning that although the instinct to play or recreate has been surpressed to a great extent in children, and even more so in adults, it is never completely abolished. Whereas there is no empirical method by which to determine whether play is an instinct in human beings, there is nothing to prove that it is not. There are, on the other hand, more logical explanations of the play phenomenon in human beings than instinct affords.

Play is recognized in animals below the human level as instinctive. This assumes that animals do not reason logically but survive through instinctive patterns of behavior. When the same activity is observed in human infants or young children, it is called something else, e.g., random movements or imitation. How can it be known that such activity is not play? The older child, left completely alone, will not sit still, but will move about, talk, construct make-believe images, or indulge in day dreams, all quite unlearned and not imitative. This line of thought supposedly shows instinctive action. Perhaps, however, the mental pictures that the child summons during this period are already familiar through prior experience. The physical activities have presumably been learned during the developmental or large muscle stage of the child's physiological growth.

Recreation or play is considered a response to stimuli and situations that have not been learned through prior experience; thus it is considered instinctive. Going one step further, the carrying point for this doctrine emphasizes that people instinctively turn to recreation or play to satisfy a felt need. Because they do not experience or receive the unifying force of recreation in other activities, they satisfy this instinctive craving through leisure diversions. The instinctivists believe that recreation is a universal need, not because of its possible values to the individual, such as refreshment or mental stimulation, but because it is instinctive to the human animal, and experiencing certain stimuli compels this need to be filled.

INSTINCT THEORIES OF PLAY OR RECREATION

The two earliest play theories based on instinct as motivation were the Kamesian relaxation theory and a similar theory by the German educator Johann Gutsmuths. In essence, both these theories stressed the recuperative powers in play and the instinctive seeking-after of such activity as a method of relaxation from the labors of the day by the human or lower animal. Gutsmuths was under the impression that instinct for activity creates the impulse or stimulus to play and that boring or prolonged sieges of dull activity afford another permissive situation in which people were stimulated to play.[4] In this theory the hedonistic doctrine expressed the main play objectives. Gutsmuths also presented, as incidental, the view of play as a preparation for later life, a concept that was seized upon and expanded to its greatest extent by Karl Groos. Thus, the earliest play theories accepted as instinctive those motivations for activity now termed play or recreation.

Other play theorists accepted and added to this type of thinking. G. T. W. Patrick published *The Psychology of Relaxation,* in which he upheld the relaxation theories and stated that children must play because of inherited patterns or tendencies that impel them to act. He based this motivation on what he called "the great multitude of old racial habits" and "deep seated human instincts."[5] A much more detailed description of Patrick's theory is presented in Mitchell and Mason's *Theory of Play* and in Lehman and Witty's *The Psychology of Play,* and is therefore not elaborated upon here.

Of all the instinct theories of play or recreation motivation, the views of Herbert Spencer have affected theoretical considerations more than any other, perhaps because he wrote one of the earlier works attempting to define the nature, meaning, and function of play. Eminent writers have cited Spencer's theory of "surplus energy," sometimes miscalled the Schiller-Spencer theory of play, as a major contribution to the knowledge of play more often than almost any other work. Surplus energy is expressed in sensory motor activity above that energy needed to satisfy basic biophysical needs. This theory served as a basis for the writing of Karl Groos and his successors, and can be found in almost every book dealing with play theory.

Spencer viewed play as a gratification of an instinct, usually of a survival type of action.[6] He felt that play was a result of impulses

---

[4] J. C. F. Gutsmuths, *Spiel zur Uebung und Erholung des Korpers und Geistes fur die Jugend* (Erzhier zu Schnepfenthal, 1796), pp. 38-44.

[5] G. T. W. Patrick, *The Psychology of Relaxation* (New York: Houghton Mifflin Company, 1916), pp. 34, 65.

[6] Herbert Spencer, *The Principles of Psychology* (New York: D. Appleton and Company, 1873), Vol. II, p. 631.

received from continuously active stimuli originating within the physical organism and streaming into the mind from the somatic field.[7] Thus, in his chapter on the development of the human nervous system, he laid the foundation for the theory of surplus energy. He realized that play was so broad in scope that it could not be explained by one manifestation alone. He therefore adopted Schiller's views on art and play, not to the same extent, or even with all of the implications found in Schiller's concept, but with enough of the original aesthetic principle to avoid the pitfall of using one absolute base as a definition.

Karl Groos, the German philosopher, published two important works concerning play theory. One, on the play of animals, became the groundwork for his subsequent treatment involving the play motive in humans. His basic understanding of play is " . . that it is, in short, preparatory for the tasks of life."[8] Groos concurred with Spencer's surplus energy theory of play, but he felt that it was not complete. In accordance with that belief he expanded Spencer's line of reasoning to include practice for adult life.

Although Spencer himself felt that such a practice theory would not answer the motivation question in play, Groos turned this idea around because he did not feel that the surplus energy concept alone was the correct motivational representation. Groos further presented the recreation or relaxation theory of play and the surplus energy theory of play as being diametrically opposed.[9] Groos' attempt to use the surplus energy theory of Spencer materialized in his concept of play as a cathartic agent. Play, in his view, represented a built-in control activated by an instinctive urge for expression. Although he stated that the carthartic value of play was of minor importance compared with the self-development aspect, he nevertheless thought it important enough to devote several articles to it.[10] He expressed his attitudes about play as catharsis in terms of emotional reactions to painful stimuli; in other words, he assumed that in play harmful impulses as a reaction to instinctive tendencies would be avoided.[11]

---

[7] Ibid., pp. 647-648.

[8] Karl Groos, *The Play of Man* (New York: D. Appleton & Co., 1908), p. 361.

[9] Ibid., pp. 365-366.

[10] Karl Groos, *Der Lebenswert Des Spiels* (Jena: Gustav Fischer, 1910), pp. 20-21.

[11] Karl Groos, "Das Spiel als Katharsis," *Zeitschrift fur Padagogishe Psychologie*, Vol. XII, 1911, pp. 353-367.

Throughout his entire treatment of play, Groos maintained an unvarying approach and attitude. He consistently reiterated, whether discussing what he called the psychological, biological, physiological, aesthetic, sociological, or pedagogical views of play, that it was nothing more or less than "... the agency employed to develop crude powers and prepare them for life's uses ...."[12]

The criticisms of Groos' theory seem to have been well founded, but he had his adherents as well. One of these writers, taking the Groos theory as his basis and continuing to discuss, interpret, and point out the value of "our best of Germans and chief teacher in this matter" was Joseph Lee. A contemporary of Luther H. Gulick and a student of child development, Lee did much to enhance the prestige of the recreational service movement during its formative years early in the twentieth century. His enthusastic interest in play as an educative device for the child was fully brought out in his book *Play in Education*.[13] In this work he extolled the virtues of Groos and detailed his own ideas of play in human life. Although Lee was neither an innovator nor a particularly profound scholar, he nevertheless performed a distinct service to the entire recreational service movement as a speaker, writer, and demonstrator of the value of play and recreational activity.

Lee predicated his whole philosophy on play as growth and on its readying the individual for future activities as an adult. Throughout his writings, his educational views were colored by a faculty psychology approach. For Lee, the only explanation of play motivation was instinct.

> Man's cardinal qualities, the activities through which he is to make
> and hold a place in the world's competition, are given in his leading
> instincts; and these instincts take charge of him in plastic infancy
> and mould him to their ends.[14]

Lee defined *play* as "all pursuits that justify themselves." How this coincides with his idea that the play instinct leans towards an ideal seems difficult to understand, unless one interprets his statement to mean that play is an end in itself and that all motivation for play is play.

---

[12] Groos, *The Play of Man*, p. 375.

[13] Joseph Lee, *Play in Education* (New York: The Macmillan Company, 1916), pp. 3, 6-7.

[14] Ibid., p. 10.

Lee seems to deal in contradictions. He conceives of play as growth, i.e., having value because it prepares the individual for life. At another time he makes a complete turnabout and states that play "... represents the non-utilitarian motive," by which he implies that play serves no other end than itself.[15] He is as positive on one side as the other. Yet for all his seeming nonuniformity of thought, Lee expressed a position worthy of more profound masters. Aside from his dependence on the practice-instinct theory of play and his acceptance, partial though it may have been, of the surplus energy theory, he formulated an idea, the implications of which should assure him a permanent place in recreation philosophy; he rejected the hedonistic doctrine as a play motive.[16]

He was aware of an even more important facet of play, its consummatory quality, although he never elaborated it to a satisfactory conclusion. It is reasonable to assume that the psychology and educational theories of his day would not logically have led him to such a radical interpretation of the consummatory qualities of play. He did recognize that play captivated the player to the extent that:

> In successful play a child does not know that he is having a good time; he does not know that he is having a time at all; time, in fact, has ceased to exist along with self-consciousness.[17]

However, he tenaciously clung to instinctual motivation, and there is no indication that he ever fully realized the content and the opportunity offered to him. In the last chapter of his book he described play for adults as recuperative, thus identifying himself with others who made the same claim. Whether recreation or play is recuperative or relaxing is not a consideration here, inasmuch as such attributes do not explain the meaning or nature of play or recreation.

The play instinct, covering as it does groups of instincts, stimulates several interests or brings about an interest in a different set of objects or focus of attention. This is clearly before the onset of

---

[15] Ibid., p. 55.

[16] Ibid., p. 255.

[17] Ibid.

puberty. It would appear necessary, therefore, that recreationists be made aware of the psychological and biological factors during their professional learning experiences. Such education, along with technical preparation, would enable the recreationist to choose the most favorable moment when the individual is instinctively interested in a group of objects to encourage proper modes of reacting to these objects.[18, 19]

Opposing the practice theory of play was G. Stanley Hall, whose monumental work on child development and education culminated in his recapitulation theory. In essence, this theory maintains that the key to present behavior lies in the past. Hall thought of play as motor habits whose best index ". . . is found in the instinctive, untaught, and non-imitative plays of children which are most spontaneous and exact expressions of their motor needs."[20] He always stated that play motivation was instinctive and that these instincts were of an epochal nature. In play the human organism relives each stage in its development on earth. Such explanations of the nature of play have largely been found invalid. Although heredity may have a part in the formation of attitudes towards objects and actions, how much a part, if any at all, is unknown.

Among the followers of Hall's theory was George E. Johnson, one of the first recreationists in the United States. Johnson felt that although Groos' practice theory was acceptable, and whereas surplus energy contributed to a favorable climate for play, it was nonetheless a basic reliving of cultural stages in human development that really defined play as an instinctive motivating force.[21]

Notwithstanding the fact that many writers have credited something they call the play instinct (perhaps for want of something better) as the motivating force of human play, other experts, who are also instinctivists, discount play as one of the instincts. Probably the most comprehensive and lucid treatment of this view is L. L. Bernard's work on instincts in which he has categorically denied the existence of a play instinct. He stated in part:

---

[18] Ibid., pp. 38, 62-67.

[19] Joseph Lee, "Leadership," *The Normal Course in Play* (New York: Playground and Recreation Association of America, 1925), p. 111.

[20] G. Stanley Hall, *Adolescence* (New York: D. Appleton and Company, 1906), p. 74.

[21] George E. Johnson, *Education By Play and Games* (Boston: Ginn and Company, 1907), p. 13.

... we shall be compelled to repeat out former statement that play
represents no concrete describable and definable unitary or structural
fact, unless it connotes a concrete method of playing. Play is a word,
an abstraction, ... It is a synthetic concept, a word image, symbolizing
all or more than one of the concrete ways of playing. The word play,
when signifying an instinct either represents structurally all the ways
of playing or it represents less than all. If it represents less than all,
it should be described in terms of those activities and structures which
it does represent and not in terms of the general word play.[22]

A scholar in the field of anthropology, Leo Frobenius, in his
book *The Cultural History of Africa,* was adamant in protesting
against the instinctive theory of play. He conceived of play as something other than instinct and devoted much consideration to a
consummatory view of play. He contended that:

Instincts are an invention of helplessness when compared with the
sense of reality. Science discovers the play drive as an appearance
which is noteworthy because it already appears in the child naturally
so without having anything to do with education.[23]

To some, this appearance, unlearned in form, meant instinct. To
Frobenius, it decidedly meant a mental process of permutation
and creative imagination.

HEDONISM AS MOTIVATION

Many recreation and play definitions have considered pleasure
seeking the source of motivation and the factor that operates as
the stimulus for continuing such activity. The doctrine of eudaemonism, is contrasted to hedonism because the former concepts were
based upon value judgments, i.e., the good life and the attainment
of happiness were considered an aim rather than the cause or
motivation. The *summum bonum* of Aristotle involved the moral
values of ethics and principle. It was said that people should seek
happiness, that they ought to try for the highest good. Such a
doctrine was not concerned with happiness as motivation, nor did

---

[22] L. L. Bernard, *Instinct: A Study in Social Psychology* (New York: Henry Holt and
Company, 1924), pp. 343-344.

[23] Leo Frobenius, *Kulturgeschichte Afrikas, Prolegomena zu einer historischen Gestaltlehre:
Schicksalskunde im Sinne des Kulturwerdens* (Zurich: Phaidon Verlag, Inc., 1954), p. 24.

it state that people act for pleasure. The latter view presents a much different philosophy. Hedonism is predicated on the principle that people act in search of pleasure; pleasure is the motivational force that drives them to perform certain acts or to behave in a particular way.

Sigmund Freud's earlier writings abound in the expressions of the hedonistic doctrine, better known as the pleasure principle. Infants, according to this principle, begin life with an intense desire for pleasure; all their activities are carried on with the intent of deriving pleasure from them. If some prior activity has given them pleasure, they seek to re-create that pleasurable circumstance.

Another psychologist committed to the hedonic concept was L. T. Troland, who devoted several chapters of his book on human motivation to this belief. He felt that past experiences, whether favorable or unfavorable, pleasant or unpleasant, modify neural patterns. Through such change behavior becomes regulated by emotion.[24] Hedonism teaches that individuals tend to continue activity that elicits pleasure and avoid situations or behavior that evoke unpleasantness. This has been widely accepted as a theory of human motivation. E. L. Thorndike contributed to this idea when he wrote that the strengthening of neural bonds is achieved by repetition in accordance with the laws of effect, frequency, and recency. The law of effect is based on the premise that an appropriate successful act that leads to satisfaction survives, or is "stamped in," and thereby takes precedence over unsuccessful or frustrating ones which are "stamped out."[25] Under this law, the satisfying situation is sought or maintained, whereas annoying situations are avoided as much as possible. Thus the organism seeks the pleasurable and learns to avoid the unpleasurable.

The pros and cons of the law of effect fill many pages of psychological literature, and many errors have been committed in the name of Thorndike's theory. He very clearly differentiated between satisfaction and pleasure, but several writers have tended to ignore this distinction. Although no empirical study on human beings has yet been made that clearly defines the experience under study, the delimitations of the conditions, the facet of behavior to

---

[24] L. T. Troland, *The Fundamentals of Human Motivation* (New York: D. Van Nostrand, 1926), pp. 278-279, 290-306.

[25] E. L. Thorndike, *The Fundamentals of Learning* (New York: Columbia University Press, 1932), p. 183.

be considered, or the neural pattern of the individual under investigation, many readers assume, wrongly, that pleasure and satisfaction are synonymous, contrary to Thorndike's implications.

The hedonistic principle is consistently referred to as an explanation for recreational activities. Nearly every person will answer in the same way when asked the reason for engaging or participating in what is termed play or recreational experience. The response will usually be: "Because I like it" or "Because it's fun and I receive pleasure from it" or "Because it pleases me." Thus, it is taken for granted that pleasure is the prime motive that influences the individual toward performing or engaging in so-called recreational activities.

The following definitions of play and recreation clearly reflect this hedonistic concept:

> Recreation, in contrast with work, has its own drive and is enjoyable. The chief drive in recreation is the pleasure it affords.[26]

> The chief aim in play is satisfaction or pleasure, but in much the same way it is true of life as well.[27]

> The primary objective of recreation is to give pleasure, enjoyment, and happiness to individuals and groups . . . every other objective is secondary to this one . . . in all matters relating to evaluation, measurements are in terms of the abundance of joy, happiness, and pleasure that accrue to individual and group.[28]

> Play may be defined as activity undertaken for pleasure, or as an expenditure of energy for the pleasure inherent in the process of expending it . . . one cannot imagine or even conceive of play without pleasure, for pleasure is its very root.[29]

The same adherence to hedonism can be found in much of the literature on play and recreation. Many of the writers and theorists

---

[26] Martin H. Neumeyer and Esther S. Neumeyer, *Leisure and Recreation* (New York: A. S. Barnes and Company, Inc., 1936), p. 147. Cf. also, Martin H. Neumeyer and Esther S. Neumeyer, *A Study of Leisure and Recreation in Their Sociological Aspects,* 3d ed. (New York: The Ronald Press Company, 1958), p. 247.

[27] Elmer D. Mitchell and Bernard S. Mason, *The Theory of Play* (New York: A. S. Barnes and Company, 1935), p. 90. Cf. also, A. V. Sapora and E. D. Mitchell, *The Theory of Play and Recreation,* 3d ed. (New York: The Ronald Press Company, 1961), p. 119.

[28] Harold D. Meyer and Charles K. Brightbill, *Community Recreation* (Boston: D. C. Heath and Company, 1948), p. 24.

[29] Austin Fox Riggs, *Play: Recreation in a Balanced Life* (New York: Doubleday, Doran & Company, 1935), pp. 16-17,

have held to surface manifestations of action or behavior rather than seek out the underlying or basic patterns of stimuli influencing behavioral action.

Freud, in his earliest writings, stressed the pleasure principle as motivating individual behavior. However, with the publication of *Beyond the Pleasure Principle,* Freud modified his basic concepts to refute the pleasure principle as the sole force for motivation. The observation that prompted this change was centered around masochism. In his later work he abandoned hedonism as motivational and developed an environmental concept of behavioral stimulation. According to Freud, the situations in which individuals find themselves restrict or prohibit certain actions while requiring others. The individual is compelled to accept reality and face daily living. Under such circumstances no individual could be considered to act merely for pleasure.[30]

Perhaps a more important aspect of Freudian psychology, for an understanding of the meaning of recreation, deals with the psychoanalytic theory of play. Again, catharsis is a part of the phenomenon. The Aristotelian idea of dynamic emotional release in play roles reached its most profound conceptualization in Freud's sublimation theories. In *Beyond the Pleasure Principle,* Freud observed the play of an infant whose activity involved throwing small toy objects away. Seeing this pattern of behavior, Freud investigated and discovered that the child's mother usually left him alone for long periods of time. The child, in an attempt to master this renunciation situation, acted out this frustrating experience by playing a game, i.e., throwing his toys away and out of sight. Psychoanalytic study has shown that the need to master an unpleasant or traumatic experience scores a central part in child's play.[31] As Freud says:

> It is easy to observe how, in every field of psychical experience and not merely in that of sexuality, an impression passively received evokes in children a tendency to an active response. They try to do themselves what has been done to them. This is a part of their task of mastering the outside world, and may even lead to their endeavoring to repeat impressions which they would have good reason to avoid because of their disagreeable content. Children's play, too, is made to

---

[30] Sigmund Freud, *Beyond the Pleasure Principle* (London and Vienna: The International Psycho-Analytic Press, 1922), pp. 15-16.

[31] R. Walder, "The Psychoanalytic Theory of Play," *Psychoanalytic Quarterly,* Vol. II, 1933, 208-224.

serve this purpose of completing and thus, as it were, annulling a passive experience by active behavior.[32]

Although the doctrine of hedonism, as a psychological theory of behavioral motivation, appears to be waning, some important recent developments from experiments by animal psychologists under laboratory conditions have givern rise to some pertinent questions. No explanation of motivation as pleasure seeking would be complete or valid without a reference to the Nebraska Symposium, which involved studies by Harlow, Brown, and Butler on aspects of motivation.[33] Among the experiments reported is the investigation of discrimination learning through visual exploration by rhesus monkeys, by Butler at the University of Wisconsin Laboratories. In light of these experiments it appears that a strong case can be made for the hedonistic or appetitive concept. However, such conclusions as were drawn from these experiments can also be explained in terms of psychological homeostasis.

As explained in Harlow's paper,[34] it is conceivable that a complex organism, when conditioned by certain environmental stimuli, will adjust toward those conditions as either its mental and/or physiological adaptability apparatus undergoes transformation. One of the important factors differentiating higher from lower order of animals is the ability to adjust. Inasmuch as homeostasis is a condition of adjustment and balance in the chemicophysical sense, it is presumably possible to extend such an adjustment mechanism to the mind.

The satisfaction the monkeys received when they were able to look out a window after having solved a particular problem might be explained as an adjustment process to which the animal's mental and physical receptors were conditioned. When deprived of the privilege of looking out the peep-hole, a psychological imbalance may have occurred that resulted in the behavior observed. The deprivation may have produced anxiety factors or tension, or it may have been the animal's attempt to reduce this condition of

---

[32] Sigmund Freud, *Collected Papers*, Vol. V, ed. and trans. James Strachey (London: The Hogarth Press, Sigmund Freud Copyrights, Ltd., and the Institute of Psycho-Analysis, 1950), p. 264.

[33] Harry F. Harlow, "Motivation as a Factor in the Acquisition of New Responses," *Current Theory and Research in Motivation* (Lincoln, Neb.: University of Nebraska Press. 1953), pp. 24-27.

[34] Ibid.

stress to regain balance. Yet this is only conjecture because it is not known whether pleasure seeking as a motive really exists, and if it does, how much or how little a part of the principle may have played in this situation.

Another feature of Harlow's paper is the continual reference to the elimination of homeostatic drives, as opposed to externally aroused drives, which, he states, are of such intensity that they are inimical to learning.[35] However, Brown has challenged this point of view on the ground that the homeostatic drives are rarely of such concentration as to be of importance to human learning.[36] In any case, whether hedonistic drives or biological drives are responsible for behavior manifestations in complex organisms has not yet been clearly indicated. There appears to be fairly good support for the theory that biological drives are the basis for human behavioral acts, whereas, any suggestion that hedonism can safely be validated by experiments already conducted is open to serious question.

Rejection of hedonism as the basis for motivating human behavior and thus play or recreation, is supported on three distinct judgments: First, the theory that the organism is motivated by the prospect of a pleasurable response is, in fact, paradoxical. Seeking behavior has most nearly come to be associated with unpleasant manifestations. What is sought is generally needed or lacking: One seeks rest because of weariness, companionship because of loneliness, food and drink because of hunger and thirst. In these cases the factor that influences action is unpleasant. In many cases the pursuit of pleasure, *per se,* is doomed to failure. Pleasure may be typically generated as a by-product or effect of specific actions.

In questioning Troland's theory of prior hedonism, an example of the act of a parent frantically diving into a body of water to rescue a child could hardly be thought of as the pursuit of pleasure, yet prior experience has modified the neural patterns of the parent and has effectively determined the course of action, which, under the stimulus of the situation, forces the parent into the water regardless of swimming capability. Thoughts concerning pleasant or unpleasant feelings hardly ever arise at the moment of stimulation.

Secondly, a question of semantics becomes a part of any discussion of the hedonistic doctrine. In this instance the difficulty lies

---

[35] Ibid.

[36] J. S. Brown, "Problems Presented by the Concept of Acquired Drives,"*Symposium on Motivation* (Lincoln, Neb.: University of Nebraska Press, 1953), p. 1.

with the terms *seeking* and *avoiding.* Usually, no difficulty is experienced in differentiating seeking from avoiding, but occasionally both terms can be used with identical meaning in a peculiar circumstance: The steelworker seeks safety by avoiding the furnace; the trapped miner seeks air to avoid suffocation. In these cases the individual may not be aware of his objective, but when observed from a disinterested point of view, one is never sure of the goal.

Thirdly, hedonism restricts the behavioral effects of pleasantness and unpleasantness to acts of seeking and avoiding; such a restriction is far too limiting. Pleasantness or unpleasantness is probably encountered as often by passive noncommitment as by active pursuit. Pleasantness or unpleasantness are probably effects rather than causes. These are surface manifestations of many factors that serve as motivational stimuli in human behavior.

HOMEOSTASIS AS MOTIVATION

According to one theory, human behavior is stimulated by a drive to reduce or relieve organic or tissue needs. In the struggle for survival, the organism that does not fulfill the insistent demands of physiological needs soon deteriorates and then ceases to exist. Through conscious desire in some cases, or by general ill-feelings, the body makes known its needs so that the organism can mobilize its functional apparatus for response. The process by which the body continues to produce the chemical balance necessary to maintain life has been called *homeostasis.*[37] This concept holds that the body is an intricate chemical manufacturing plant, limited by organ structure, and dependent on autonomic stimuli for effective maintenance of proper chemical relationships so that organic balance (equilibrium) is preserved. The process by which such equilibrium is maintained is homeostasis, a condition of adjustment designed to satisfy physiological needs.

Rignano has clearly enunciated the principle of homeostasis with this statement:

> Every organism is a physiological system in a stationary condition
> and tends to preserve this condition or to restore it as soon as it is

---

[37] W. B. Cannon, *The Wisdom of the Body* (New York: W. W. Norton & Company, Inc., 1932; rev. ed., 1939), p. 24.

disturbed by any variation occurring within or outside the organism. This property constitutes the foundation and essence of all need, of all desires, of all the most important appetites. All movements of approach or withdrawal, of attack or flight, of seizing or rejecting which animals make are only so many direct or indirect consequences of this very general tendency of every stationary physiological condition to remain constant. . . .[38]

This same principle has been referred to by Raup as *complacency*, an adjustment ratio wherein a consummatory or fulfilling act completes a relationship that has been disturbed. Raup stresses the idea that maintaining homeostasis is the fundamental factor, not only of behavior, but of all life processes. His principle of complacency suggests that behavioral adjustments are related to the organism and its environment. The healthy organism maintains homeostasis through the process of adjustment. Raup further wrote that the condition of equilibrium is continuously interacting, i.e., always dynamic.[39] Thus, this theory considers that human behavior moves away from equilibrium when physicochemical balances are disturbed, toward it when meeting the need, and through it to continue human activity.

In his chapter on complacency and the autonomic nervous system, Raup comes to grips with what might be termed psychological homeostasis. He refers to the psychological state of the organism as the thing that gives rise to behavior. Continuing this line of thought, he introduces the concept of the nervous system as a mechanism that serves the whole organism and eases the condition of stress as the organism seeks to adjust. The whole question of metabolic reaction to environmental stimulation is opened. The nervous system is thought of as the means whereby favorable relationships are maintained.

Relating concepts of equilibria to behavior patterns, Raup asserts that any disturbance of these little known equilibria reveal themselves in the psychological factor of complacency and its imbalances. When equilibrium is fully restored, complacency develops. Maladjustment, therefore, is a disturbance of balance, i.e., lack of equilibrium between the organism and its surroundings. All behavior,

---

[38] E. Rignano, *The Psychology of Reasoning* (New York: Harcourt, Brace and Company, 1923), p. 6.

[39] R. Bruce Raup, *Complacency: The Foundation of Human Behavior* (New York: The Macmillan Company, 1925), p. 42.

then, is the effect of movement toward complacency or restored equilibrium. Because the maintenance of homeostasis affects psychological activities as well as tissue needs, mental adjustments reflected in behavior activities are affected.

Perhaps the most important implication of Raup's view of the dynamism of homeostasis is the progressive nature of this idea. Homeostasis is not stable. As the organism reaches equilibrium, it concurrently creates new tensions, proceeding to throw itself off equilibrium. This would appear to fit present knowledge of both physiological and psychological functions. Thus the physical laws of energetics, principally the second law, would be involved in a system concerning free and bound energy.[40]

> ... whenever there is activity of any kind in the part of the organism considered there is also a using up of energy. The cells are worn down, but there is a corresponding heightened process of building up the cell. This metabolic process goes on just because there is activity in the part, throwing the energy condition off of equilibrium, and thus compelling a drive back toward that state.[41]

Psychological homeostasis is merely the term given to mental complacency or equilibrium and is not separated from physico-chemical effects, because whatever disturbs even the most obscure tissue appears to influence the whole organism. Any type of activity might be an example of psychological homeostasis. The painter may be engrossed for any number of hours in painting and never once be concerned with the function of the brush. The whole self is at ease as far as using the brush is concerned. Yet in the course of the effort, something might occur to the brush relationship, and complacency disappears. The hairs of the brush may become loosened or hold too much paint. Attention is turned toward removing the difficulty to regain the interrupted condition. The brush relationship now enters into those processes that define changes in activity directions; furthermore, it will perpetuate itself until such time as some action so resolves it that the former condition of unconcern is restored. In this example, mental focus was directed toward the disturbing element that served as motivation for behavioral actions. This may be true for all behavior patterns.

---

[40] Ibid., p. 16.

[41] Ibid., p. 65.

If homeostasis is the condition that motivates behavior in human beings, it must also serve as the motivational stimulus for recreation. Just as there are physicochemical needs for equilibrium in the organism, there is also a psychological need for equilibrium, which reveals itself as the environment changes during the daily experience of living. When people consciously or unconsciously realize imbalance in their lives, they tend to move toward a rebalance in which harmony and accord between the self and environment are found. This balance may be restored through recreation.

The distinguishing feature of recreation is the consummatory quality that sets up or regains for the individual the equilibrium lost during impact with environmental forces. The consummatory act is characterized by complete absorption. During such intense concentration consummation displaces any maladjustment so that harmony is restored or re-created in the individual. The whole concept of the consummatory act depends on and helps to explain the principle of homeostasis. In recreation, a need is met and satisfied. The satisfaction continues until some other disturbance enters the psychosomatic field, at which time equilibrium is lost and the process repeats itself. Thus the process is dynamic and perpetual.

The principle of homeostasis has been further refined and classified for inclusion in psychological systems attempting to interpret human behavior. The psychologists Snygg and Combs claim that the preservation of the individual's self, the "I," makes logical and consistent all human behavior.[42] Whether or not action is directed toward life preservation, suicide, or any other activity affecting the physical being, the concept of the phenomenal self can explain human behavior.

> The phenomenal self includes all those parts of the phenomenal field which the individual experiences as part or characteristic of himself.[43]

Thus, all behavior may be explained and even predicted in the light of people's desire to maintain a concept of self, i.e., what they believe to be the actual self. The one basic human need is determined to be predicated on the desire for self-esteem. All other so-called needs or drives are in reality subservient to this one.

----

[42] Donald Snygg and Arthur W. Combs, *Individual Behavior* (New York: Harper and Row, 1949), p. 54.

[43] Ibid., p. 58.

> From birth to death the defense of the phenomenal self is the most pressing, most crucial, if not the only task of existence. Moreover, since human beings are conscious of the future, their needs extend into the future as well, and they strive to preserve not only the self as it exists but to build it up and strengthen it against the future of which they are aware. We might combine these two aspects in a formal definition of the basic human need as: the preservation and enhancement of the phenomenal self.[44]

Seen from the phenomenological view, such seemingly diametrically opposed propensities as a life or death wish can be placed in context and may appear quite logical as a manifestation of the enhancement of the individual's phenomenal self. This means a desire on the part of individuals to gratify some aspect of personal self esteem. They may do this by appearing in one situation with a concern for "What will people think (of me)?" and in another by their reaction to physical privation or to a surfeit of physical goods. The phenomenal point of view is a psychological system based on the impact of culture upon the individual. It is a ready device for the explanation of behavior in terms of environmental pressures on the physical and mental existence of the organism as it attempts to adjust to the culture of which it is a part.

Snygg and Combs also suggest a conceptualization of goals differentiation. As the organism matures and seeks to gain an idea of self in its surroundings, goals arise to which the basic need, preservation and enhancement of the phenomenal self, is directed. Techniques, or the methods by which goal attainments are carried out, develop in the same way and are also differentiated as experience dictates. Three classifications of techniques are suggested.

1. Mastery of people and/or things.
2. Identification with powerful forces, i.e., pressure groups, individuals in control, or dominant ideas.
3. Physical change in the somatic organization.

The first two classes of techniques are self-explanatory, but the third needs some clarification. To regain self-esteem, peer status, or other restoration of the phenomenal self, the individual may seek excitement usually associated with activities ranging from minor sports and games to drug addiction. The inherent stimulus derived from excitement results in an increased feeling of power and effec-

---

[44] Ibid.

tiveness which uplifts the lagging or humiliated self-esteem and gives heightened vigor to the individual.[45] This exhilaration is commonly sought in competitive activities, in exhibition of artistic or creative accomplishment, or in antagonistic and compulsive behaviors that may overstep social taboos in certain circumstances. The explanation offered for human behavior and the motivation stimulating such beahvior is an all-inclusive doctrine of the phenomenal self based on homeostasis. Behavior is produced by the organism's need to maintain a constant.

The great Swiss child psychologist Jean Piaget asserts that two fundamental processes are essential to human development: assimilation and accommodation. Assimilation means the collection or gathering of materials or matter and the rearrangement of them so that they are suitable for use. Thus, physical assimilation is best observed in the digestion process. Food is eaten and processed so that the nutrient content may be chemically broken down for further use by the organism. Psychological assimilation, on the other hand, deals with the information from the world around us and using it so that perceptual meaning is obtained.

Accommodation means the adaptation of the organism to the social or physical milieu that surrounds the individual. Physical accommodation requires bodily adjustment to any changes in the environment. The homeostatic reaction of the body to a drop in temperature might be that of shivering. At a more simple level it could be a postural modification resulting from a parental order to "stand straight." Mental accommodation deals with any intellectual adaptation an organism must perform to assimilate information.

According to Piaget, mental growth develops in consequence of the continuous active interdependence of assimilation and accommodation. The probable danger comes when one or the other type of behavior predominates. Accommodation, which suggests imitation, is the result of passive acceptance. If assimilation tends to dominate, then the child does not adjust to reality situations and engages in fantasy and play. To Piaget, both play and imitation are required if the child is to develop intellectual powers most positively. The fundamental processes should be in balance.

Piaget borrowed some ideas on the stages of human development from Freud. However, Piaget views physical activity or free play as a factor of accommodation in response to the reactions of other

---

[45] Ibid., p. 76.

children and includes imitation as well. Creative play is thought to be chiefly a question of assimilation, i.e., only a "pretend." This aspect of play is very closely associated with Huizinga's concept. In creative play the child sees the world through its imagination. Piaget therefore believes that creative play is the child's way of learning to manipulate symbols rather than objects. The assimilative facet of behavior, with the projection of self into other than real situations, may take the child, figuratively speaking, out of the immediate environment and give it room to roam in a world of its own making. Whatever disassociation that occurs would be effected by the need for complete concentration on the child's part. It is not likely that daydreaming or other fantasizing will take place unless the child is completely absorbed in the intellectual process of creating its own world. Under such circumstances the child reaches a level of harmony between itself and its environment, and a consummatory experience is achieved.

SELECTED REFERENCES

Callois, R. *Man, Play, and Games.* New York: The Free Press, 1961.

Ellis, M. J. *Why People Play.* Englewood Cliffs, N. J.: Prentice-Hall, Inc., 1973.

Freud, Sigmund. *Beyond the Pleasure Principle.* London: The Hogarth Press, 1948.

Huizinga, Johan. *Homo Ludens.* Boston: The Beacon Press, 1955.

Levy, J. *Play Behavior.* New York: John Wiley & Sons, 1978.

Mitchell, Elmer D. and Mason, Bernard S. *The Theory of Play.* New York: A. S. Barnes & Co., 1948.

Piaget, Jean. *Play, Dreams and Imitation in Childhood.* New York: W. W. Norton & Co., 1962.

_____. *Science of Education and the Psychology of the Child.* New York: Orion Press, 1970.

Reilly, Mary. *Play As Exploratory Learning: Studies of Curiosity Behavior.* Beverly Hills, Calif.: Sage Publications, 1974.

Salter, M. *Play: Anthropological Perspectives.* West Point, N. Y.: Leisure Press, 1978.

Chapter 8

Recreation - Definitions and Concepts

Few definitions of recreation or play have been presented in any but stereotyped terms. Most definitions have assumed the innocuous exterior of smoothed-over clay in which any individuality or peculiarity is hidden. Each may be worded differently, but the net effect has been to produce conformity and total identification with what have been considered absolutes.

PROBLEMS OF INADEQUATE CONCEPTUALIZATION

Although a few, indeed too few, recreationists and educational philosophers have hinted at more broadly defined terminology, none has really stated what recreation is. The practice has been to explain recreation in limited terms of function or use; thus, the field has accumulated singularly restrictive definitions. By misapplication or through faulty concept building, common definitions present only the one way, the ultimate way, in which anyone can recreate. It is said that these definitions allow for freedom of choice (if one discounts human conditioning factors as abrogating free choice). Although presumably based on selectivity, they offer only one choice. One can argue that these offer freedom, to act or not to act, but in reality there is no choice.

Traditional definitions of recreation have been founded on five concepts. These include when recreation occurs (in leisure), why recreation occurs (prime motive), how recreation occurs (freedom of choice), what occurs (activity), and in what context it occurs (virtue). On these bases restrictive meanings have been applied to prevent many human activities from being termed recreational in either quality or connotation. The real difficulty in talking about the "where" and the "what" of recreation has been that people have not coined a sharp enough terminology that could be used to guide future thinking and to suggest new possibilities. The problem, then, is not that these questions of when, why, what, and how have been asked, but that they have been answered in such ways that their definitions become useless as a guide to future activities.

In both the past and the present, recreation has been viewed as the antithesis of work or labor. It has been thought of as value derived, contributing to mental health, physical well-being, creativity, personality development, satisfaction, self-assertion, pleasure, and so on. Beyond this, recreation has been subdivided into activity classes that range from antisocial on the lowest level to creativity on the highest. Thus, it has been explained as everything from the universal panacea to mere sports and games or physical exercise and art.

The Leisure Concept. The leisure concept has always had an inordinate following, which, in proportion to its relationship with the recreative experience, is beyond justification. Basing recreation on leisure pursuits, or defining recreation as the use of leisure, distorts the entire picture. Such a narrow view effectively omits the vast possibilities of recreative behavior during time other than leisure.

Recreation has been described as a way for people to supplement and complement their hours of stress and labor with activities that bring relaxation and rejuvenation. It has suffered from being made synonymous with time not required for satisfying the incessant need for food, clothing, or shelter. Historically, therefore, recreation has come to include those activities performed during leisure, i.e., time not spent in vocational pursuits, education, or in attending to natural physiological acts. Thus, even the word *leisure* has been spoiled by being made synonymous with time in which nothing significant occurs. It would appear that what has been described is not recreation but leisure activity. There is a great difference between the two. What has developed is a gross misrepresentation in which a part becomes greater than the whole.

The Neumeyers, in *Leisure and Recreation*, explain recreation in sociological terms as:

> ... including many types of activities which are undertaken for their
> own sake and not for any reward or goal beyond themselves, and
> which are relatively free, spontaneous, and enjoyable. Such activities
> are motivated primarily by interest and give more or less immediate
> satisfaction.[1]

Once again the reader is made aware of an underlying pleasure
principle in the motivation of recreation. However, another significant feature of this definition has meaning for the act itself: No
mention is made of when such activities may be performed. Implied
in this description is the cognition that recreation can be performed
under any circumstances, i.e., at any place in time and not limited
to leisure. Although the definition tends to limit recreative acts to
those pursuits entered into for their own sake, it nevertheless paves
the way for an extremely broad interpretation of recreation as a
manifestation of behavior. According to the Neumeyers' definition,
even vocational, educational, and various physiological activities
could be defined as recreation if, during their performance, they
elicited in the participant pleasure, satisfaction, and enjoyment. One
would have to stretch both the imagination and the precise meaning
of this definition, but such an implication is present.

In the Neumeyers' view, leisure is time free from obligatory
activities; it is not to be confused with idleness or with recreation.
Recreation is recognized as a type of leisure activity. Further than
this, an attempt is made to show the integration possible between
recreation and work:

> Work can be playful and be recreation motivated. All agreeable and
> enjoyable work has a large element of recreation in it. The same can
> be said of education, which may be drudgery or a pleasant experience.[2]

Thus, recreation is conceived as a behavioral act that can be performed at any time the individual wishes. It is not measured or
defined as a specific time, but as an act taking place in time.

Leisure, then, is considered time free from the occupational
hazards of monotony and boredom. It is a time for education, a
time for learning the uses to which leisure may be put. Recreation,
a manifestation of human behavior, can be achieved during leisure.

---

[1] Martin H. Neumeyer and Esther S. Neymeyer, *Leisure and Recreation* (New York: A. S.
Barnes and Company, Inc., 1936), p. 7.

[2] Ibid., pp. 122-123.

It combines the aesthetics and the trades through a spirit of self-expression, thereby uniting two of the more important features of life: the need for activity and the desire for achievement.

In his book *Adventures in Recreation*, W. W. Pangburn states:

> Leisure and recreation are not the same. Leisure is free time after work. It spells opportunity for the activities of life not necessary for making a living.[3]

Pangburn also suggests that recreation is an activity that has its own drive and is carried out without any need of reward. It is its own end and has no ulterior purpose. It means refreshment and, most important, self-expression.

Eugene T. Lies has taken a dictionary definition of leisure as "freedom from necessary occupation or business."[4] He sees a vast amount of free time, produced by the machine age, being used for both creative and recreative ends. His setting is the school where education for the recreational use of time can be taught.

The Prime Motive Concept. Prime motive means the casual factor that determines individual behavior towards a particular activity. Traditionally, recreation has been conceived of as a self-motivating activity, i.e., it differs from all other activities not only in the sense of the values derived when it is performed, but also *why* it is performed. Basic motivation, which includes the individual's attitude toward any given thing, is the criterion that effectively excludes education, various physiological acts, vocation, and religious experience from being recreation. In the view of many, the basic tenet of recreation is that it is primarily engaged in for its own sake and for the fun of it.[5] The activity is executed for the pleasurable feelings aroused. Therefore, primary motive—in this instance, fun—excludes all activities from being considered recreation if they are not engaged in primarily for fun.

There is always the question of the distinction between work and recreation. Both represent activities that may give self-expression,

---

[3] Weaver W. Pangburn, *Adventures in Recreation* (New York: A. S. Barnes and Company, 1936), p. 10.

[4] Eugene T. Lies, *The New Leisure Challenges the Schools* (Washington, D. C.: National Education Association, 1933), p. 18.

[5] James E. Rogers, *The Child and Play* (New York and London: The Century Company, 1932), p. 25.

satisfaction, and fun to the individual; both may contribute to well-being and be totally absorbing. The main difference, as it has been described, is that vocation is motivated by the promise of economic advantage together with certain psychological values, whereas recreation is motivated presumably for its own sake or for the fun of it. The difference between work and recreation is the reason for undertaking the activity.

Recreation supposedly carries with it its own drive, whereas vocation seems to need a reward, prize, or other extrinsic motive to stir the individual to action. If we are to believe this, then many of the activities being carried on by professional leaders under the aegis of recreation are not really recreational. They are vocational because the participant is urged on, not by the inherent interest of the activity, but for the promised reward at the conclusion of the activity. An example would be the common assertion that one ought to exercise or engage in sports for the sake of building a healthy or stronger body. In the sense of this discussion, this is pure vocationalism.

There are two possible reasons for this problem: (1) The activities are presented without any thought of planning that includes potential participants; and (2) activities have been presented in a manner that conflicts with standards of acceptance.

Participation becomes reward-centered; the prize becomes all important. Our leadership has glorified the winner, the hero, the champion to such an extent that anything less than winning is considered failure. Huge bonanzas are paid; the individual is surrounded by commercialized amusements that offer get-rich-quick schemes. Recreational departments that continue to offer league-type tournaments flourishing on the promises of bigger and better trophies, cross-country travel, and audience adulation have helped to create this one-sided value system. As Bucher has written:

> There are other evils which make the practice of stressing the 'winner' educationally unsound. This is true especially in the area of sports. Undue pressure is placed on the participants, parents become over-enthusiastic, immature children become over-stimulated, the health of the individual is overlooked, excessive publicity often times is bad for the 'star' contestant or the 'star' team, unsportsmanlike play is resorted to, and a sound standard of values if disregarded.[6]

---

[6] Charles A. Bucher, "Must There Always Be a Winner," *Recreation Magazine*, Vol. XLIX, October, 1956, p. 364.

Few will quarrel with competitive activities or even recognition for being best in a class, game, event, or other participatory act; the quarrel is rather with the amount of emphasis placed on the incentive so that a completely biased view is brought about. In another aspect of this reasoning, too much stress has been placed on the mass or crowd activities and not enough time or importance has been placed on individual encouragement and stimulation. The thinking behind this emphasis of mass versus the individual has been centered in the public recreational agencies and schools. All too often budget-minded boards or other authorizing agencies have to be "sold" by the number of participants engaged in the activities of the department or system. This has led to thinking in terms of numbers. If a department can receive so much money for x number of participants, then it follows that more participants mean greater budgets.

The result of this all too common situation is that spectator sports and other mass activity enterprises are programmed while individual opportunities and services, or even small groups of people and their needs, are generally overlooked in the rush for the large crowd. Thus, the differentiation between extrinsic and intrinsic values is somewhat overlooked, probably unintentionally, by "promoters" or "businessmen" operating in the guise of recreationists. This unintentional identification of work and recreation is of considerable significance in the dogma of the field.

There are several volumes concerning play and recreation that do not differentiate between work and recreation, i.e., that assume that work and recreation have overlapping content. This bone of contention between the traditionalists and the more progressive writers takes the form of defining both work and recreation in terms of time performed, motivation of the individual, and the opportunity for choice.

The traditionalist defines work in terms of its being performed in nonleisure, being of an obligatory or compulsory nature, and having an economic motive. The progressive may be aware of relative distinctions between work and recreation, but minimizes that distinction; in general, the progressive focuses attention on the fact that any work requires periods of rest even though such work allows the individual to maintain a high level of intellectual activity. Although creative work is not something to be avoided, there should be periods that may be termed relaxation. Even though creative work may produce complete satisfaction and pleasure in the participant and thus be similar to play, time must be taken to refresh and restimulate the individual.

In analyzing this concept of the relationship between work and recreation, one must recognize that the majority of practitioners in the field of recreational service regard their organized, or even privately conducted, activities performed in leisure as recreational. It is only on the theoretical or educational level, and then in too few instances, that thought is given to the shading between these two types of behavior. A typical pronouncement that shows the position of those who view work and recreation as overlapping is taken from *Principles of Education* by Chapman and Counts.

> The line between recreational and other activities, however, cannot be rigidly drawn, because by imperceptible gradations the one type of activity shades off into the other. . . . Even in the field of vocations there are many cases where, because the individual expresses himself fully in his calling, work becomes identified with play.[7]

A typical statement showing the position of those who view recreation and work as completely distinct is taken from Riggs:

> Work might be defined as the purposive expenditure of energy toward objectives to which the worker holds himself responsible, whereas play is the expenditure of energy just for the joy of expending it in that particular way. . . . In short, play must not only give pleasure in itself, but must also be utterly carefree. . . . To complete the definition by contrast, work is activity bound by purpose and responsibility and may or may not be pleasurable.[8]

Regardless of how the work-recreation concept is viewed, both schools of thought agree that recreation must produce satisfaction for the participant, whereas such is not necessary for work, however desirable it might be. Both are convinced that work demands conscious effort over a sustained period of time, whereas recreation is an immediate experience demanding only the moment.

This same thinking is also met in another important area of human activity, religion. Generally religion is not considered a form

---

[7] J. Crosby Chapman and George S. Counts, *Principles of Education* (New York: Houghton Mifflin Company, 1924), p. 296. Reprinted by permission.

[8] Austin Fox Riggs, *Play: Recreation in a Balanced Life* (New York: Doubleday, Doran & Company, Inc., 1935), p. 18.

of recreation even though there are many similar aspects between
the two. Again primary motive or individual attitude is taken as the
criterion for stating whether or not this activity is recreational. There
can be no question that early human experience in religion with its
rites and ceremonies had significant recreational overtones, just as
there are ceremonies in various religions of today that contain
predominantly recreational themes. However, for all intents and
purposes, all of the recognized religious sects, groups, or denomina-
tions have as their primary purpose the glorification and adoration
of their god-symbol, whatever it might be. Under these conditions
and with primary motive explained in this way, religion could not
be conceived of as recreation.

Problematically, the question of recreational value must arise
when prime motive is concerned. This question is: What value is
derived from recreation if it is entered into only for fun? Is not fun
to be construed as value? If fun is the value, then doesn't it rule
out the aspect of prime motive?

A thing has value for us, as individuals, because we know from
experience its worth. We evaluate both material objects and intangi-
bles—i.e., feelings, attitudes, pleasure, or pain—on the basis of prior
experience, seldom if ever at the moment of experience. We are
prone to say that a thing is good or bad depending on our previous
experience or learning and relative to the particular situation in
which we are placed. We appear to seek activities that afford us
pleasure and satisfaction rather than the opposite. This is also true
of the values derived from recreation. However, the value received
from a recreational activity as opposed to a nonleisure activity, it
is said, is that in the former the activity is engaged in for its own
sake, it is valuable for itself for what it does to or for the individual.
Nonleisure activities, on the other hand, are engaged in primarily
for the latent value to be received, be it economic reward or some
other asset. Notwithstanding the fact that nonleisure activity may
be just as enjoyable, satisfying, or self-expressive to the individual
concerned, it is not recreation.[9]

By its very tone, the common usage of recreation would have
the world believe that the elemental reason and main purpose for
its being is fun regardless of the seriousness involved in the activity.
It is unequivocally stated that recreation is desired for the pleasura-

---

[9] George D. Butler, *Introduction to Community Recreation* (New York and London:
McGraw-Hill Book Company, Inc., 1948), p. 3.

ble feeling created in the individual. Happiness is its characteristic.[10] Thus, when all the derived values are removed, when the camouflage and pseudopurposes are stripped away, then, we are told, only fun remains, there being no other urge to act.[11]

Other problems arise with the concept of primary motive, for some antisocial acts as well as low order escapist activities then come under the heading of recreation. This enigma is neatly sidestepped by some writers who include such activities in a scale, stating that they are recreational if they carry within them their own drives to action, i.e., if they are ends in themselves regardless of how vulgar such acts are and how low on the scale they are placed.[12] However, only the most broad-minded professionals would dare thus to classify as recreation acts that are antisocial in nature. In the majority of cases the entire area of immorality is disposed of by placing the word *wholesome* or *worthy* before the rest of the definition. In this way the profession maintains an aura of ethics and moral pride.

Yet a true definition of the word *recreation* must spell out explicitly what recreation is. It must include negative aspects, if such there are, as well as the positive. If the prime motive concept is valid, then education, work, physiological acts, and other activities not performed in leisure must be excluded. Most of the above-mentioned activities are performed either to keep the individual alive, to propagate the species, or to gain profits other than fun. Even though these acts may have pleasure or satisfaction as a secondary aim, perhaps even as a primary aim, they are not to be considered recreation. Eating and sleeping, which under certain circumstances are extremely pleasurable, or the eliminatory process, which under varying psychological conditions becomes pleasurable, are considered only in terms of their supposed primary purpose, whether consciously desired or not, and are therefore nonrecreational.[13]

One considers physiological activities to be those that are necessary to keep the individual alive. In this way the implication of

---

[10] Harold D. Meyer and Charles K. Brightbill, *Community Recreation* (Boston: D. C. Heath and Company, 1948), p. 24.

[11] Riggs, *Play*, p. 25.

[12] J. B. Nash, *Philosophy of Recreation and Leisure* (St. Louis: C. V. Mosby Company, 1953), pp. 93-95.

[13] J. F. Brown, *The Psychodynamics of Abnormal Behavior* (New York: McGraw-Hill Book Company, 1940), p. 190.

societal taboo is averted by classifying the procreative act with physiological functions. Nevertheless, there still remains the stumbling block of explaining sexual relations when social taboos are not present. In this instance the sex act presents every indication of being a recreational activity inasmuch as it meets all the requisites of definitions now in current use.

The Virtue Concept. The virtue concept of recreation draws upon the heritage of the early Greek society where leisure was used so that a man could perform worthy acts, enhance his culture, and live an ethical life. From that period and having that concept to live up to, all professional definitions have adhered to the virtue concept by insisting that its activities be worthy or wholesome. This is most clearly seen in the numerous volumes and pamphlets written on character building through recreational experience and in the adoption by a National Education Association committee of the wording "worthy use of leisure." This standard has been so ingrained that its inclusion as part of the *Recreation Platform* issued by the combined committees of the American Recreation Society, American Association for Health, Physical Education and Recreation, and the American Association of Group Workers, was almost mandatory.[14]

The virtue concept inevitably grows out of the prime motive concept. It has been stated that most crime is eliminated from the recreation definition even though many antisocial acts have fun or pleasure as their basic motivation. Various acts of juvenile delinquency, such as vandalism or fighting, may have fun as their primary motive, at least outwardly. The inner psychological problems manifested in these acts may be quite different, but individuals who engage in immoral or criminal acts may actually believe that such activity is fun or that it evokes pleasurable sensations for them. By the clever insertion of "worthy" or the phrase "not antisocial in nature," the whole issue of unethical practices, immorality, and crime is completely disposed of; as if the field could, by definition, eliminate the fact that many antisocial acts may be recreation for the individual pursuing that line of conduct.

Among the values that have been ascribed to recreation has been the bolstering of ego and self-esteem in individuals, especially children who have experienced failure in school or in other social

---

[14] Office of Education, *Cardinal Principles of Secondary Education* (1918, Bulletin No. 35).

contexts.[15] Recreation is valued because it develops character in the individual, strengthens personality, and helps the person achieve satisfaction in making a social adjustment to the environment. Although this may be true, it is not recreation itself that deserves such tribute, but activities performed by individuals in the hope of attaining recreation.

This may appear a radical thought, but on closer inspection it may prove quite logical. It would be inconsistent with current recreation definitions to explain recreation in any way other than activity performed during leisure, along with other qualifications. If, however, recreation is defined in terms of human behavior, i.e., as a nondebilitating consummatory experience, motivated by equilibrium-seeking within the organism, then the entire picture changes. Asserted in this manner, all human activities become potentially recreational, and the activities engaged in, regardless of their moral qualities, become steps in attaining recreation. They have inherent values in themselves, whatever they might be, but these values are incidental to achieving recreation. Hence a criminal bent on lawbreaking would be attempting to find his phenomenological self in criminal pursuit in order to regain his organismic balance. If while committing a criminal act, he did achieve recreation, that act would have value for him in relation to his need, provided there is no following sense of guilt. If, on the other hand, a police officer played at collecting stamps in order to assert his phenomenological self and did not achieve recreation, the act would have no value for him in relation to his need. Thus, human actions, whether socially acceptable or not, may have recreational value depending upon the individual's psychological need and in relation to one's personal ethics in satisfying that need. In other words the virtue concept is null and void when speaking of recreation as a product of human behavior.[16]

This does not mean that recreationists advocate unethical conduct, nor does it mean that immoral, criminal, selfish, or other negative behavior is necessary in order to achieve recreation. It implies that recreation as behavior may include all human activities and must be so considered in order that a true definition be given.

---

[15] S. R. Slavson, *Recreation and the Total Personality* (New York: Association Press, 1946), p. 23.

[16] Clarence E. Rainwater, *The Play Movement in the United States* (Chicago: The University of Chicago Press, 1922), p. 8.

The Freedom Concept. The typical axiom recited by professionals and laypersons alike is that recreation is indulged in on a purely voluntary basis. It is free, not in the economic sense, but on the foundation of independence of thought, movement, and action. It carries with it the idea of liberty, personal and social. Within acceptable bounds individuals do what they want to do when they want to do it. Various members of the recreational service field have stated that recreation cannot be prescribed, ordered, or forced, for to do so would prejudice its meaning and deny its attractiveness.

> Although there are countless activities that may be considered recreation, it is generally agreed that all recreation activity has certain basic characteristics. One is that the person engages in it because he desires and chooses to do so, without compulsion of any type other than an urge from within.[17]

In this way, recreation is strictly defined and limited to those acts that are elected. If recreation, however, is defined in terms of consummatory experience, it does not matter whether the individual is forced into an activity or enters into it for any other reason. Any activity has potential recreational value if it demands some clear-cut action as well as thought.

One of the more difficult problem areas concerning recreation and the freedom concept has been in the field of therapeutic recreational service, i.e., recreational activities conducted in mental, general medical and surgical, long-term custodial, chronic, rehabilitation, and penal institutions. There has generally been a lack of acceptance of recreational service on the part of other professions in the institutional field. Only in recent years have there been any breakthrough and the granting of peer status to recreationists. The problem can be stated in terms of effects. Has recreational activity been used as simple diversion, or is it therapeutic?

Another question in this area involves the use of prescription. Those who feel that recreational activity can be prescribed see no conflict between prescription and voluntary participation because of the way in which prescription is defined. Others oppose prescription on the basis that prescribed recreational activity immediately ruins any value that voluntary participation has on the participant. If therapy is defined as anything that helps or aids recovery, then

---

[17] Butler, *Community Recreation*, p. 4. Used with permission of McGraw-Hill Book Company.

assuredly recreational activity is therapy. If, on the other hand, therapy is defined as the scientific treatment of the application of specific remedies for diseases, then it is unlikely that recreational activity as presently practiced is therapy.

In any case, with recreation defined as behavior, in contradistinc tion to particular activities, it no longer matters whether recreational activity is prescribed. It may very well be taken as therapeutic, and the obtaining of individual prescriptions for patients will not destroy the value that it has for them. Prescribed recreational activity, provided it is recreational, may prove just as effective and thera-peutic as activities voluntarily entered into. In many observable cases, recreational experiences that have been prescribed for various patients have proven very stimulating and absorptive for them, although at first there was resistance. When this occurs, it is gener-ally due more to unfamiliarity with the activity or subject than to any inherent dislike because of prior experience. Strangeness or unfamiliarity breeds fear of failure or anxiety; thus, the unwilling-ness and apparent hostility toward new outlets. Any human activity may potentially be recreation or have recreational value whether an individual consciously seeks it or not.

Objections to this concept might well take form as farfetched questions to test the validity of this statement. Samples of these tests could consist of questions concerning war, crime, forced labor, or other occupations that usually carry distasteful connotations. Does war have potential recreational value? Yes! But the conse-quences of combat or the strain undergone in the manifold emer-gencies one finds in a battle atmosphere would appeal only to a certain type of individual. Yet, because recreation is so highly personalized, some people could conceivably find in a war activity a consummatory experience (not death) and achieve recreation. Huizinga realized that there was play in war:

> Ever since words existed for fighting and playing, men have been wont to call war a game. . . . The two ideas often seem to blend absolutely in the archaic mind. Indeed, all fighting that is bound by rules bears the formal characteristics of play by that very limitation.[18]

Huizinga always refers to war as a cultural function that pre-supposes certain rules recognized by all. Once war becomes total

---

[18] Johan Huizinga, *Homo Ludens* (Boston: The Beacon Press, 1950), p. 89. Copyright © 1950 by Roy Publishers. Reprinted by permission of Beacon Press.

war, as we know it today, it loses its limiting rules and becomes simply criminal violence. Notwithstanding the fact that war today is total war, some individuals still regard it as a game. One is reminded of that unnamed British officer who, during the Suez Canal dispute in 1956, stated that the fight was "jolly good sport," taking the view that war is a sport with rules to observe. This might lead to a consummatory experience, but only where the activity involves complete absorption.

This possibility can also hold true for other activities that are in the main distasteful. The very fact that a human being is engaged in the action clears the way for recreation to take place. The dullest, most repetitious job imaginable might require an automatic control for hand manipulation but still leave the mind free to wander. In such circumstances the dull mechanical job performance can pave the way for free flights of the imagination, which at later times may be transformed into action. Thus, thought leading to action or action leading to thought may characterize the consummatory experience.

The criminal act may also be recreation under certain qualifying circumstances. If a burglar is intent upon looting a safe, the opening of that safe may be completely absorbing. Concentrating on the clicking tumblers might require such intense effort that the burglar could be completely absorbed in this pursuit. The thought of financial gain may enhance the act, but it is the act itself that provides the thought access to recreation.

It does not matter in which activity individuals are engaged as long as they attain a state beyond tension or stress. Although it may be possible to reach consummation through total absorption in any activity, external stress or internal body chemistry reactions can cause dissolution within the individual and prevent total absorption. The unity and harmony achieved during moments of consummation may be withheld because of tension factors.

Whether or not individuals feel guilty because of participation in activities of dubious ethical value depends on their own value systems and the type of conduct acceptable in their communities. Thus, an habitual thief, liar, cheat, prostitute, or other immoral individual can feel perfectly free of tension or other stresses while engaging in antisocial activities as long as their culture accepts such conduct. Even if the culture does not accept immoral behavior, such individuals may still regard their behavior as normal and acceptable because of a complete absence of moral standards or pathological factors. If such is the case, immoral action might well lead to recreation. On the other hand, where actions, regardless of social acceptability, cause feelings of guilt or tension, unity or harmony is not possible and complacency will not be attained.

When an individual steals time from one activity to participate in another, there may be guilt feelings. When this happens the unity derived from recreation and the value that this has for the individual cannot be attained, regardless of surface feelings of pleasure. People may fool themselves into thinking they are having fun or even that they have received something of value for their misbegotten efforts, but in reality they have only succeeded in repressing their true feelings of guilt or other tension-producing factors. They may, therefore, feel they are attaining recreation, but they do not emerge from the activity with a reborn feeling, which one receives from recreation, because the unity feature is lacking.

This reborn sensation is better described as the "ahhh" feeling experienced by countless millions engaged in various and sundry activities since time immemorial. It is the feeling that the dedicated golfing "duffer" receives when, for the first or hundredth time, he or she hears the sweet click of club head meeting golf ball and watches as the sphere rises straight and true to hum down the fairway and alight some two hundred plus yards away. It is the feeling doctors, lawyers, teachers, researchers, businesspeople, and all other professionals and laypeople have achieved in their respective callings. It is "the job well done." Yet this feeling is produced only when complete absorption occurs. Stated more simply, it means that the degree of concentration leading to total absorption is not as great when some guilt thought or other tension-producing strain is present. More often than not recreation will not be obtained by individuals engaged in activities in which they have no right or should not be. Any part of the mental process that prohibits complete unity of mind and body also prohibits recreation. Only when there is a consummatory activity leading to unity does recreation exist.

This concept does not eliminate the fact that many antisocial acts have recreational value for the individual who pursues them. Antisocial acts seldom contribute to the unity of human nature. Unethical practices and degrading activities seldom produce a sound mind in a sound body, nor are they conducive to peace of mind for the individual concerned. Criminal and immoral practices probably cause more worry and tension than acts that are in line with moral behavior and conduct, but such feelings of guilt or lack of guilt depend on the value system of the individual and the social environment. To a lesser extent other delinquent acts or minor breaches of a given society's code are also included in this class.

A unique characteristic of the re-created feeling is that it can be repeated. This duplication or reproducing quality can elicit the same satisfying response or feeling of well-being regardless of the number of times the action is performed. The same responses to certain acts may be eternally evoked in the same person, and more wonderful still, the act is never dulled or boring, nor is the consequence tarnished or jaded in any way. Once the recreational act has been discovered, it never loses its ability to consume fully or absorb the participant, especially, although not necessarily, if it is highly competitive.

This does not say that interests never change. One is aware that the changes in an individual's interests are somewhat determined by emotional, environmental, and physiological growth factors. These factors push forward several interests or bring about an interest in a different set of objects, as illustrated very clearly at the onset of puberty or menopause. Nevertheless, it can be indicated just as clearly that adults, whatever the changing interest pattern is, at times revert to activities and interests that once held their attention as children. Witness some of the social gatherings that adults attend or the convention tactics and antics that some adult males go through. The solemn rites in various orders and organizations are throwbacks to the love of secrecy that children have.

Having defined recreation in terms of values that are derived, time of performance (leisure), and free choice, the term is carried to extreme proportions. It is described as basic to the democratic process of individualism, as a cure-all for the ills of mankind, as the sociological answer to mental illness, juvenile delinquency, high blood pressure, and personality difficulties.[19] No one has spelled out this type of thinking more clearly than G. Ott Romney in *Off The Job Living.* He states:

Release from strain, translation from self-concern to absorbing interests and the concurrent discovery of the friend you can be to

---

19 John E. Davis, *Play and Mental Health* (New York: Barnes and Company, 1938), pp. 60-61, 64, 135, 139.

yourself, by *rest, play* or *doing* something you really want to do—
such is the insurance recreation writes against the mill-run miseries
and ills of too much self.[20]

The definition most used in this context, or the one that typified
the current trend of thinking in the recreational service field is:

> . . . a voluntary participation in any wholesome activity for the per-
> sonal enjoyment and satisfaction derived from the doing, producing
> a refreshment of strength and spirit in the individual.[21]

This definition is a composite of all those that have been described
in the preceding pages and that are in use up to this time. It neatly
side-steps all activities having any moral taint, delimits the scope
of activity to include only leisure activities, and states that the
democratic ideal of free choice or electivity must be present.

The Activity Concept of Recreation. One of the least innocuous
concepts of recreation in current use is that which sets up the criterion of action as the measuring rod by which experience will be
known as recreation. In this instance recreation is set up as a going,
doing, active type of behavior. Preeminent in this outcry against
passivity has been Jay B. Nash, an outstanding educator in the
fields of recreational service and physical education. In his book
Spectatoritis, published in 1932, he laid down several explicit
points concerning the recreative act as an active process.

> Recuperation may be defined as the rejuvenation of the body after
> work. It is, however, not wholly relegated to inertia—doing nothing.
> Recuperation is obtained in action—action with a 'glide-stroke rela-
> tionship.' The body recuperates, regains its equilibrium, much more
> quickly in an atmosphere of happiness, joy—the play attitude.[22]

He further stated that "the thesis of this discussion is that the
central motive of our behavior is struggle—doing."[23]

---

[20] Romney, *Off the Job Living*, p. 16.

[21] American Recreation Society, Hospital Recreation Section, *Basic Concepts of Hospital Recreation* (Washington, D. C.: The Society, September 1953), p. 4.

[22] Jay B. Nash, *Spectatoritis* (New York: Dodd, Mead and Company, Inc., 1932), p. 65.

[23] Ibid., p. 195.

Nash's concept rests upon the Greek formula inscribed on the façade of the Olympic stadium—"strip or retire." This meant either prepare for active participation or withdraw from the arena, as there was no place for spectators. He questions the majority who sit in the stands, admire skills they do not possess, and secure whatever exaltation lies in the vicarious thrill of escape and in shouting:

> The looker-on, the victim of spectatoritis, brings neither joy to himself nor heritage to his people. Living is struggle, competition—a hope-fear relationship. Remove that and you remove satisfaction. Competition exists not only in sport, but in every zestful act.[24]

In another book, Nash depicted leisure activities in terms of level or status drawn in a pyramid or triangular form. This drawing represents not only levels of behavior, but also the amount of activity or passivity that the individual exhibits in participating. Thus, at the base are antisocial acts and inertia, whereas at the apex are socially acceptable acts, creative acts, and participating acts.[25]

Although it seems logical to assume that active participation would bring about a deeper absorption and lead to a consummatory experience, such is not always the case. Passive appreciation, intellectual browsing, so to speak, may be as deeply absorbing and recreational as any active participation can be. It might be stated that contemplation is really active because it requires some effort and may be equally exhausting as hard labor or other strenuous activity. However, in the way that Nash used the term, it appears that what he means by active is actual physical participation. This concept also restricts the definition of recreation but not so completely as other concepts mentioned in preceding pages. Although it is true that Nash conceived of recreation as activity performed in leisure, he nevertheless is willing to include activities that would ordinarily be classified as non-recreation. His thesis is mainly concerned with leisure activities, and although he attempts to solve the problem of deciding which activities are better suited for individual choice, he recognizes the semantic problem of delineating work from play and recreation from education.

---

[24] Ibid., p. 190.

[25] Nash, *Philosophy of Recreation and Leisure*, pp. 93-96.

The activity concept is not a negative restriction. It has been formulated to associate participation with the recreative act in opposition to activities that promote loafing or other completely passive amusements.

Harold Rugg and William Withers have this to say about the action concept as it relates to recreational activity:

> We are an active and creative people, yet we have increasingly tended toward conformity and group behavior in recreation. . . . Perhaps Americans find the trend toward passivity and 'spectatoritis' wholly satisfying. But recreation has a greater social significance than mere escapism and relaxation. Recreation is one of the realms in which creative powers are developed and broader perspectives discovered.[26]

Rugg and Withers and Nash have hit upon one of the more complicated features of recreational life, which in the action concept becomes more and more assertive. The problem of the spectator is one that needs a fully detailed explanation. Out of the action concept grows the problem of the spectator: empathy or escape. At certain times and in specific places the problem of empathy asserts itself. Does the spectator escape his surroundings or empathize with them? Is it catharsis through participation or vicarious pleasure through escape?

The difference between these two terms is characterized by the psychological implications for the individual. Escape is a behavior pattern that acts as a mechanism for adjustment. Like other forms of behavior, it is part of the homeostatic process. The individual initiates this type of behavior to ease the tension of inner stresses or environmental pressures. In this attempt at adjustment the individual may call upon the mechanism of escape. Escapism may be the method by which a desired end can be attained, and it is usually carried on outside the world of reality. It is sealed off, as it were, from the hectic struggle for existence in that it is compensatory, through the imagination, for physical or mental inability.

For some people escape may be a way of "getting out of themselves." They drop the cares and burdens of daily living and either play at or become somebody else. This type of activity is generally pleasurable. It may be observed in many of the spectator-type events in which skilled individuals are in competition, although it

---

[26] Harold Rugg and William Withers, *Social Foundations of Education* (Englewood Cliffs, N. J.: Prentice-Hall, Inc., 1955), pp. 600-601.

may occur whenever or wherever admired qualities are found. The spectator may have had the skill at one time and no longer possesses it or never had it and would have liked it.

Such behavior reflects satisfaction through imagery representations that are not attained in true experience. Thus, the imagination compensates for certain personal lacks and achieves success quite easily. The spectator may slip from the confines of strain and frustration to the fancy and make-believe of leisure activities. Regardless of the activity, whether it is highly developed sports and games or daydreaming, individuals tend to forget themselves and identify with being someone or something else. In this way they satisfy their longings or desires to be what they are not and thus achieve vicarious pleasure.

Empathy, in opposition to this, is an identification from actual experience. It is a process by which the individual completely identifies with the object of immediate experience because a past experience under similar or identical circumstances has occurred. Thus, a person can say to another who is undergoing some trial or tribulation or an extremely happy event, "I know exactly how you feel." This should not be confused with sympathy, which is a feeling for, i.e., a sympathizer wishes that the misfortune never occurred; an empathizer feels with the individual because of having actually experienced the sensation, which may be pleasurable or unpleasurable. In the present context the spectator may empathize with the performer, competitor, or artist and gain a certain freedom of expression through cathartic reaction.[27] This can be illustrated by college football. Graduates or former players may receive immense satisfaction by shouting and armwaving as they cheer their team on. In some instances such individuals may empathize with an on-field player, feeling the tension, reliving the force and drive of straining bodies and pounding pulses. They may re-create in their mind's eye the movements and pace that they once knew. Outwardly this pent-up emotion may give way to shouts and hysterical body contortions to release the tensions that have been built up during the identification process. Empathetic catharsis, in the spectator sporting events, is most usually pleasurable. It consists of physical effort and exertion as an outcome of psychophysical stress. The physical reaction of outburst stimulates the entire organism and results in a feeling of well-being.

---

[27] Wilhelm Worringer, *Abstraction and Empathy* (New York: International Universities Press, Inc., 1953), p. 6.

The empathic reaction may also occur during exhibitions of an aesthetic nature. Thus, the same physical reactions may occur from stimulating effects of an opera, art exhibit, dramatic production, or other spectator performances. Whereas the cathartic expulsion may be of a more quiet nature, i.e., no shouting or violent body contortions, there may still be the physiological expression of quickened breathing, perspiration, faster pulse rate, and other physical manifestations of some physical exertion taking place. This reaction may occur during the performance or make its appearance immediately upon its conclusion. Thus, the wild out-burst of applause and hysterical acclaim that accompany a spectacu-lar performance by some artist may be not only an appreciation of the artistic accomplishment, but a cathartic release of pent-up emotion.

The concept of action poses the problem of empathy or escape in citing what would appear on the surface as a manifestation of passivity or at best active appreciation. No definite conclusion can be drawn concerning this phase of leisure activities, because only the participating individuals can make known the type of response or behavior mechanism they use at a particular point in time. The action concept is then incomplete because it considers only physical activity as a criterion for making a judgment. Action may be of the intellectual variety as well as the physical. True recreation, however, combines both of these elements. Clear-cut action developed out of purposive thought as a consequence of past action allows individuals to re-create themselves.

This is the consequence meted out to all the activities that confront human beings in their efforts to adjust to the constantly changing scene of daily living. The professional definition is strict in its interpretation because it cannot afford to be associated with any other meaning. Although a few professionals on the fringe of the practicing field discern conflicts or gray areas between what is called recreation and other activities, the great majority see only black and white. Yet this black and white pattern reflects a distorted image of what recreation really is.

PLAY AND RECREATION

Recreation is so highly personalized that any effort to assign its usage and limit its area to a small segment of human action is fruit-less. Yet this restraint continues to be applied. When the term *recreation* is mentioned, the word immediately suggests pictures of relaxation, entertainment, spectator sports, and any nonserious activity. Used in this way it connotes a strictly nonutilitarian type of activity.

Play and recreation express the same idea. Much confusion has resulted from differentiating these words, which are in fact interchangeable. Play has been used by many to show contempt for an individual's action, i.e., one disparages another by saying,"All he does is play." One speaks of acts that do not seem appropriate by saying, "Don't play around! Be serious!" People continually place the words *play* and *seriousness* in opposite categories. One generally speaks of play as something a child does. One says to a child, "Stop playing like a baby and act like a grown-up." What one really meant is: "Your actions are bothering me, and I have no time to understand them." To children, their actions may be perfectly intelligible; they are playing. They play in all seriousness, i.e., with fixed attention. The rude voice of the adult shatters this play-existence because, not understanding the profoundness of what is occurring, the adult assumes it is meaningless.

Children play with all the devotion and energy of which they are capable. Whether the play is concerned with listening to a story, chasing another, manipulating objects, or just dreaming, children are intently and completely absorbed in what they consider real and therefore serious. Children are probably aware that they are only playing at being something or somebody, that such play is not real life; but nevertheless, during the course of the play they may empathize with whatever they imagine and, for that short instant, may be what they play at being. Children exalt their play in the same manner as the adult who pays homage to the tee and golf ball. Such play is deadly serious to the player. The same feelings are evoked in child play as in what adults call their play, the only difference being that adults have dignified their play by calling it recreation. There is no difference between the two symbols. Whatever results from this intense preoccupation, the feelings, sensations, or effects are the same. This is not to say that play is nonserious. Many times child and adult play are light and frivolous, but behind the façade of the tensionless and comic is the probability of serious purpose.

Another confusing aspect concerns attitudes toward work and play as each infringes on the other. Some people putter or work around the garden, tool shed, or kitchen at the end of a working day. Some people work at perfecting their skill at any number of sports, games, or musical pursuit. Others work at play. These people try hard to have fun, to divert themselves, to find relief from boredom. They invest their leisure, money, and effort to achieve a modicum of satisfaction, and they work hard to attain that feeling. Is this work or play? Conversely, there are those who do all of these things and consider that they are merely playing around, i.e., getting their recreation. What is the standard by which one can say that one thing is work and another is play?

According to Ellis, "Play is that behavior that is motivated by the need to elevate the level of arousal towards the optimal."[28] He then explains that both work and play are on the same continuum. This complicates the matter of definition because what the observer calls work or play may be identical behavior. The idea of arousal to explain play motivation may be valid, but the view of work as stimulus reduction does not follow. There is no reason to believe that work cannot stimulate arousal, particularly if it is of a type that entertains new experiences, elicits anticipatory behaviors from the worker, produces an environment that is constantly changing, or continually challenges the curiosity of the worker. All of these characteristics may be part of one's work and be intensely arousing despite another's observation. As Ellis indicates, under these circumstances it would be difficult to differentiate between work and play, if play were defined in terms of arousal.

There is no reason to believe that work and play are indistinguishable at any time, for the individual so involved. The outside observer may only guess at the behavior of the individual, although obvious clues, insofar as setting is concerned, may be of some assistance. Only the individual undergoing the experience is in a position to indicate whether or not the behavior is work or play. There is an excellent likelihood of distinguishing between any behavior and play by the expedient of classifying play as a consummatory activity that is beneficial to the player. Thus, any activity may provide the basis for play/recreation to occur. Of course, this can only be evaluated after the fact, but it is certainly possible for play to grow out of any activity that can totally concentrate the individual's attention for a period of time. It is not that play and work occur simultaneously, but rather, that work or any other experience, under specific

---

[28] M. J. Ellis, *Why People Play* (Englewood Cliffs, N. J.: Prentice-Hall, Inc., 1973), p. 110.

conditions, may become the vehicle for the achievement of complete absorption and therefore play.

Brian Sutton-Smith has accentuated absorption as the essence of play. He feels that play may be characterized by its ability to capture the attention of the player to such extent that the experience is capable of lifting the person out of his or her tasks. This lifting out may be elaborated as the process of consummation within an activity. The individual is so thoroughly involved with the task, game, or subject under consideration that the world slips away and for that magical moment is suspended while the person is enmeshed in the intellectual processes of play. The fundamental or essential feature that distinguishes play from all other forms of behavior is total immersion to the point where everything else in the environmental milieu disengages.[29]

The same attitude prevails with regard to work and recreation. Many people express the view that recreation is the antithesis of work, that its main function is to divert, relax, and rebuild the individual's strength for another round at the strenuous task of living and working. Statements have been made to the effect that recreation is the wholesome use of leisure, time free from work. Some definitions concerning play, recreation, and work show how ambiguously they are used.

> But the word 'recreation' is broad enough to include play in its every expression and also many activities not thought of as play—music, the drama, the crafts, every free activity and especially creative activity for the enrichment of life.[30]

> Summing up the formal characteristics of play we might call it a free activity standing quite consciously outside 'ordinary' life as being 'not serious' but at the same time absorbing the player intensely and utterly.[31]

> There is a very common misunderstanding of the play of children among adults which arises from their confusing it with recreation. Recreation is relief from toil. It is intended for the rest and rebuilding of wearied muscles and nerves and spirit. It may take any form,

---

[29] B. Sutton-Smith, "Child's Play—Very Serious Business," *Psychology Today*, (December 1971), pp. 67-69.

[30] John H. Finley, "What Will We Do With Our Time?" *Recreation*, November 1933, p. 367.

[31] Huizinga, *Homo Ludens*, p. 13.

but it is always lacking in seriousness and usually has value only in re-creating the mind and the body for the more serious work of life. The play of the child does not correspond to the recreation of the adult, but to the work of the adult. Play is the most serious activity in which the child engages.[32]

As one reads over the preceding statements from authorities in the field, a certain confusion must result from there being no clear distinction between play and recreation. The experts do not agree. They tend rather to disagree on what constitutes the proper definition for the terms involved. Witness the following: attitude, time, activity, or value difficulties that accrue when discussing the separate structure of play and recreation. Each is supposed to take place during leisure. Each is composed of a peculiar attitude that expresses itself in pleasure. Each is set in a free-choice atmosphere. Each is self-activated, i.e., motivated or carried along by its own drive. Each completely absorbs the individual. Each takes many forms. Each has been interpreted as being broader or larger in scope than the other and therefore includes the other. Each is serious. Each is not serious. Each is different but the same. In other words, no one knows precisely where the difference lies, or for that matter what makes the difference; yet a few claim that there is a decided difference. That difference would appear to be artificial. Every characteristic that has been listed in the name of play has also been attributed to recreation.

Not only has there been a great confusion in the semantics of play and recreation, but much of the literature of the field has intensified the confusion rather than alleviated it. Prior to the early 1930s, there was a preponderance of literature on the meaning, nature, psychology, and value of play; today the literature of the field has come to focus on recreation and its exploration. Before 1900 few writers even mentioned the term *recreation* as a subject for discussion; after that time the two terms were treated with recreation in the subordinate position. Today in many of the books on education and recreation, major import is given recreation, its structure, meaning, and value; whereas play is included only as a secondary consideration.

Probably the most valuable suggestion would be to accept or to assume that recreation and play are synonymous. For all practical

---

[32] Henry Curtis, *Education Through Play* (New York: The Macmillan Company, 1916), p. 12.

purposes, when individuals speak of their play, they refer to recreation, and when they recreate, they do so in the spirit of play. They do not give any thought about whether they play or recreate; they just exhibit a pattern of behavior. The main consideration is that these symbols are interchangeable and have the same meaning, structure, and value.

The Unity Concept of Recreation. It is not surprising that the professional definition and interpretation of recreation, as an act, should be what it is, inasmuch as the entire field has been conditioned by and is a logical outgrowth of Aristotelian precepts and philosophy. Any definition or philosophy based on the teachings of the absolute, unchanging, immutable truth placed within human reach, such as the Aristotelian world view, can under no circumstances be anything but biased toward what it considers to be that truth or absolute good. In the contemporary views of many, the truth regarding recreation is that it consists of voluntary participation performed in leisure for pleasure or satisfaction as a means of gaining recreation or refreshment. Everything else is ignored regardless of the values derived from participation or lack of participation by the individual.

In defining recreation, it must be realized that there are no absolutes! Secondly, one must remember that any definition is a concept of the subject concerned, initiated in the mind, and projected or developed as a consequence of acts, or ideas of acts, that may prove fruitful if adapted to human experience. Finally, it must be remembered that any concept of recreation is developmental in content; factors involved in its substance are subject to change and are continually changing. Recreation, then, may be said to be dynamic.

In most subject matter whatever is depicted as its essence is the thing that gives is meaning. If the essence of a subject or substance is meant to be its primordial element which, if removed, so changes the structure or form of the subject that its original character becomes so completely altered as to defy description, then essence is a final end. In terms of this explanation and under these circumstances, recreation could have no essence. It must be defined in terms of a *concept of essence.* Concept, by its inclusion, changes the interpretation from finality to an on-going or changing product. The obvious intent for explaining the essence of recreation in terms of conceptualization is to show it as evolutionary rather than as an absolute. Recreation is any consummatory experience, nondebilitating in character.

The conceptual essence of recreation is theorized as being oneness or unity. This unity or physical and mental harmony that one captures by a consummatory experience appears to be a constant or finality because it does not seem to change within the life span of any human being. Nevertheless, it is always changing. It is continually translated in people's minds from an idea to a reality, but it is still different in each individual's view. Such an idea may be likened to a flowing stream. The water maintains a basic appearance; the channel, except for deepening, holds true; but the stream continues to flow. It never is the same at any two times. Its chemical properties vary by the second; yet for all practical intents and purposes, the stream looks and is the same.

In analyzing what recreation is, it is found that only one condition is necessary to bring about unity or harmony. An intense absorption must seize individuals' attention so that everything outside of whatever they are participating in loses its significance for the period of time in which their whole attention is engaged. This can never be a piecemeal affair; it is either all or nothing. In losing themselves, individuals find themselves.

The anthropologist Leo Frobenius knew well the intense absorption that play had for the individual. In his book *The Cultural History of Africa,* he devoted a section to the subject, calling it "To Be and To Play." He stated that human beings behave according to the dictates of their own nature, that they attain complacency, which is a product of an absorbing interest, and that their complacency gives way to disharmony under the influence of internal and external interferences. The characteristic feature of human animals is their ability for absorption and dissolution, which influence the development of ethos. In relating the completeness of absorption to children at play, Frobenius says:

> I have shown . . . what devilish power lies in the game that children play. Whoever has naturally active children knows what it means to tear the child away from the game and tell him he has to go home. In fact, when we are dealing with the intensive play of children we work with the basic source out of the holiest ground waters of all culture and with one of its greatest powers for creation.[33]

---

[33] Leo Frobenius, *Kulturgeschichte Afrikas, Prolegomena zu einer historischen Gestaltlehre: Schicksalkunde im Sinne des Kulturwerdens* (Zurich: Phaidon Verlag, Inc., 1954), p. 24.

In this manner Frobenius explains his concept of the consummatory act. For him consummation is the grace of play, where people are engrossed by the nature of things, and where the highest grace is the capacity for devotion. Thus, the consummatory act is intimately connected with aesthetic creation, and it is through this medium that culture develops. He conceived of the development of culture as a process of living experience in which the individual was completely absorbed in the natural ebb and flow of creativity and extinction. The consciousness was enmeshed in this rhythmic pattern, compressed through reflex action to an outward expression of emotion in aesthetic form. In this way play served to bring about the consummatory act. This consummatory process is possible because the mind is free to concentrate on the pursuit at hand without mental reservation that time taken up in the immediate act should be spent on or devoted to other more useful, necessary, or mandatory activities.

Finally, recreation is absorption leading to unity, balance, or harmony. One follows the other as surely as day follows night. Without absorption or consummation there can be no unity or equilibrium; if unity is not the outcome of the consummatory experience, it is not recreation. In this respect, total absorption may be brought about by almost any activity or pursuit engaged in by human beings, and when achieved, will result in varying degrees of complete and intense concentration. In any case, unity or equilibrium, i.e., the uniting of the physical with the spiritual or mental processes, is complete at the time of consummation. It is from this vital sensation or dynamism of feeling that the receiver truly becomes reborn, reawakened, or re-created. However, it must be remembered that equilibrium is not nirvana, quiescence, or lack of action, but a dynamic balance between the individual and all stimuli. It is an adjustment that is satisfying to the organism.

Thus, the only truly recreative value is that of absorption or consummation. In other words, recreational value arises from the consummatory experience the individual may undergo in any activity. Recreation, however, is the unification of mind and body brought about by consummation. Such a distinction is not only logical but necessary. If consummation was the end product, this concept would be just as biased as the leisure-time proposition. With unity as the base and post behavior as an outcome, this is a dynamic concept.

The basic difference between recreational value and recreation is one of time rather than degree. Recreational value will be noted after the consummatory experience has occurred, whereas recreation occurs at the time of the consummatory experience. With this type of definition to go by, primary motive is no longer a consideration or criterion by which an act may be classified as recreation. As has been implied, antisocial acts as well as socially acceptable activities including religion, education (schooling), vocations, various physiological acts—in fact, most human activities that have long been classified as non-recreational—have potential recreation value and are indeed potentially recreation.

In defining recreation as a progression or pragmatic concept, the logical consequences that such a definition has for human activities and conduct must be explained. The unity of mind and body (psyche and soma) brought about at the time of consummation is recreation. This unity or wholeness is predicated upon the organism's continual attempts to attain equilibrium. Because all behavior is a product of the organism maintaining organization and manifesting itself in acts seen by the individual as phases of phenomenological self, then any act may become recreation. Recreation as a product of behavior is also a part of behavior. This is explained by understanding recreation as the aim of organismic action, i.e., as equilibrium and as a functional process of thought and action.

SUMMARY

Theorists who have favored instinct as motivation for human behavior do not include play as one of the human instincts. However, several psychologists have felt that if instinct is thought of in terms of responses to stimuli and environmental conditions that have not been learned through past experiences, then recreation or play might well be instinctive. Suggestions have been made that people instinctively turn to play to satisfy racial habits, to practice for later life skills, to fulfill the need for relaxation, or to expend surplus energy.

That human beings possess certain prenatal characteristics that influence the kinds of traits that each will display during life is almost universally accepted. Much of the controversy over instinct boils down to the question of whether that concept really explains anything and whether so-called instincts are, in fact, instincts at all. A human being, being a complex product of psychosomatic energy in dynamic form, cannot be anything but active. It would be an unwarranted assumption that innate human nature should be one of inactivity.

Psychologists' views on the problem of instincts differ. Freud's theory of the death instinct seems to have been influenced by the biological theories current at that time. These theories were largely based on the second law of thermodynamics, which applies only to closed systems. Because the phenomenon of life can only occur in open systems, the principle of entropy is not applicable in these circumstances.

There is to be found in the various psychiatric views the unitary theory of instinct. According to this theory, there is a single primary instinct, the life instinct, the aim of which is to keep the life processes of living systems in continuous operation. This is accomplished by driving negative entropy from the environment. Death results from environmental interferences with the life instinct. The same idea was expressed by Ferenczi as early as 1913, and Freud's earlier writings were dominated by similar views. Following *Beyond the Pleasure Principle*, Freud's observation of a behavioral manifestation, which he called *masochism*, caused him to modify his basic concepts.

Instead of using the term *instinct* to explain behavior activity, other psychologists refer to stimuli, the structure of the nervous system, the internal chemistry of the body, past behavior, and similar determinants. This occurs because instinct has accumulated such a wide variety of meanings that no scientific exactness can be applied to it. Historically, the concept of instinct has become so encrusted with customary meaning and ambiguity that its utility as a scientific term has been lost. Consequently, many behavioral scientists have dismissed explanations of behavior as instinctive and have substituted other terms with more explicit and descriptive meanings.

The whole question of the hedonistic doctrine as the motivational stimulant appears to have been proved either obsolescent or not quite valid. The paradox contained within the doctrine prevents its continued acceptance. Because seeking activities are generally conceded to accompany unpleasant conditions or situations, the basis for the doctrine of pleasure-seeking presents difficulties of logical explanation. It has been found that conscious and active pleasure-seeking usually makes realization of such a goal impossible to

achieve. Pleasure more often accompanies an activity as an affect
or a by-product and is not considered causal.

The principle of homeostasis has come to receive wide acceptance, especially among scientists who deal with biochemical, physico-
chemical, or electrochemical phenomena. It has been accorded wide
popularity among psychologists, who see in homeostasis the fundamental basis for human behavior. It has been noted that body
chemistry continually seeks to maintain equilibrium among its
products, and therefore within the organism as a whole. Directly
related to this aspect is the metabolic condition of the organism
upon which behavioral activities are built. Just as the physicochemical balance is concerned with equilibrium in the somatic field,
psychological homeostasis is concerned with maintaining equilibrium
in the psyche or mental field. Psychological homeostasis, also called
complacency, attempts to direct the mental state into a condition
in which there is unawareness of tension or stress. In an individual
this is achieved during moments of complete concentration or absorption in any activity that does not subject the organism to mental
or physical debilitation, guilt, or degradation. During this period
of consummation individuals are restored to a state of harmony
within themselves as well as toward their environment, a mind-body-
situation relationship.

Recreation is characterized by its consummatory nature. It has
the power to seize and hold the individual's attention to such an
extent that the very meaning of subjective time and environment
disappears from view. In this respect it fulfills the need for psychological homeostasis. Recreation receives its motivation from the
organismic movement toward equilibrium, based on metabolic and
environmental conditions. As such it is part of human behavior.

There are many aspects of psychology that can be explained in
terms of biology and physiology. It is also true that in the more
complex organisms there are blank spaces or unsupported assertions
and analogies in the relationship between psychology and physiology.
There is, however, an increasing acceptance of homeostasis and the
implications that this concept has for behavioral motivation. If
psychological homeostasis is an acceptable explanation for recreational motivation, then it abrogates the pleasure principle as its
main aim and instinct as the drive that causes spontaneous action.
Under these circumstances a new definition must be offered for
recreation to be meaningful.

The concept of essence provides the basis for a definition of recreation. It is the realization of totality, i.e., complete integration of the individual with the self. This is the recreational focus. Unity is its conceptual essence—the re-creation of human sensitivities, sensibilities, and rationale. What individuals lose during moments of frustrating experience, their equilibrium, and sense of proportion may be regained through the unifying power of recreation. By broad identification, the consummatory concept defines recreation as the product and process of equilibrium-seeking within the human organism. It provides the basis for a theory of recreation and a concommitant philosophy using the social psychology of pragmatism. A complete and radically new idea of the meaning, value, and process of recreation has been postulated: It is any nondebilitating, consummatory experience.

SELECTED REFERENCES

Csikzentmihalyi, Mihaly. *Beyond Boredom and Anxiety: The Experience of Play in Work and Games.* San Francisco: Jossey-Bass, Inc., 1975.

Forbenius, Leo. *Kulturgeschichte Afrikas.* Zurich: Phaidon Verlag, 1954.

Garvey, Catherine. *Play.* Cambridge, Mass.: Harvard University Press, 1977.

Huizinga, Johan. *Homo Ludens.* Boston: The Beacon Press, 1955.

Norbeck, Edward, et al. *The Anthropological Study of Human Play.* Houston, Tex.: Rice University Press, 1974.

Raup, R. B. *Complacency: The Foundation of Human Behavior.* New York: The Macmillan Company, 1925.

Rignano, E. *The Psychology of Reasoning.* New York: Harcourt Brace and Company, 1923.

Salter, M. *Play: Anthropological Perspectives.* West Point, N. Y.: Leisure Press, 1978.

Index

Accommodation, 177
Aelfric, 52
Agriculture, 14-15, 17
Akkad, 23, 26-27
Alaska, 12
American Revolution, 85
American Association for Health, Physical Education and Recreation, 188
American Association of Group Workers, 188
American Recreation Society, 188
Archery, 16
Ârété, 39, 42
Aristippus, 107
Aristocracy, 45, 46, *et passim*
Aristotle, 103, 106, 107, 108, 109, 111, 112, 166, 169
Aristotelianism, 143
Aristotelian precepts, 204
Art, 9-11
Art as play, 148
Artists, 8
Asia, 12
Assimilation, 177
Assyria, 34-35
Augustus, 46, 47

Babylon, 32-34
Bacon, Roger, 67
Bagley, William C., 151-152
Barnard, Henry, 131, 132, 137, 138
Bentham, Jeremy, 88
Bernard, L. L., 165
Biological clock, 5, 6
Blue laws, 49
Brameld, Theodore, 157
Brown, J. S., 170-171
Brueghel, Pieter, 80-81
Bubonic plague, 69
Bucher, Charles A., 183
Burg, 56
Butts, R. Freeman, 141

Caesar, G. Julius, 46
Campfire Girls, 131
Calvin, John, 77-80, 109
    on leisure, 79
Calvinism, 98, 104
Calvinists, 82, 83, 84, 85
Canaan, 35
Carthage, 44
Castiglione, Baldasare, 72
Catharsis, 142, 197, 198

Chaldea, 34, 35
Chapman, J. Crosby, 185
Charlemagne, 55, 56
Chattle art, 11
Chaucer, Geoffrey, 74
Cicero, Marcus Tullus, 69
Cicadien time, 6
Civilization, 21-23
Color, 8
Combs, Arthur W., 175, 176
Communication, 5, 15
Complacency, 173
Consummatory concept, 143-150
Consummatory effect, 136, 173
Consummatory experience, 136, 137,
    149-150, 201, 202, 205, 206, 209
Consummatory quality, 164
Constantinople, 60, 67
Contemplation, 109, 112, 113
Cooking, 5
Counts, George S., 185
Creativity, 93-95, 121
Cremin, Lawrence A., 141
Crete, 37-38
Cro-Magnon man, 7-9
Crusaders, 65
Cutten, George B., 109, 110
Cyclical history, 15
Cyrus, the Persian, 34, 36

Dance, 25
Dark Ages, 51
David, 36
da Vinci, Leonardo, 70, 72, 75
Darwin, Charles, 91, 92
de Grazia, Sebastian, 111
Delinquency, 104
Dewey, John, 14, 131, 142, 144, 145,
    146, 147, 148, 149, 150, 153, 155
    on play, 144-150
Diocletian, 47
Dordogne, France, 7
Domestic animals, 13, 17

Drums, 16
Dumazadier, Joffre, 115, 116, 117, 118,
    119
Dürer, Albrecht, 74

Economics, 95-96
Egypt, 26, 27-32
Ellis, M. J., 201
Empathy, 197, 198, 199, 200
Energetics, 174
Enlightenment, 87
Entropy, 208
Erasmus, 74
Eridu, 23
Escape, 197-198, 199
Etruscans, 43
Eudaemonism, 166-167
Euphrates River, 23
Europe, 51 et passim
Experimentalism, 131, 141, 143, 144
Faculty psychology, 140, 163
Feudalism, 54
Fire, 5, 6, 7
Fishing, 12
Flood, 35
Florence, 71, 74
Folk Dance movement, 131
France, 7, 8
Freedom, 59, 61, 111, 114, 132, 137, 190
Free time, 116, 117, 118
Freud, Sigmund, 108, 167, 169, 177, 208
Frobenius, Leo, 166, 205, 206
Frobel, Friedrich August, 137, 155

Genesis, 35
Gilgamesh Epic, 33
God, 141
Goethe, Johann Wolfgang von, 155
Greece, 103
Greeks, 39-42
Groos, Karl, 108, 134, 136, 154, 161,
    162, 163
Grushin, B. A., 122

Guilds, 62
Gulick, Luther Halsey, 113, 133, 134,
   135, 136, 137, 138, 139, 147, 163
Gutsmuths, Johann, 160, 161

Hall, G. Stanley, 134, 147, 165
Hamilton, Edith, 41
Hammurabi, 32, 33
Handaxe, 16
Happiness, 107
Harlow, Harry F., 170, 171
Hebrews, 35-37
Hedonism, 107, 108, 135, 164, 166-172,
   208
Hegel, Georg Wilhelm Friedrich, 140
Hellenic, people, 39
Hittites, 34, 35
Holidays, 57, 58, 59
Holy Roman Empire, 55
Homeostatis, 139, 149, 156, 170-177, 209
   as motivation, 172-178
   complacency as, 173, 174
   defined, 172-173
Homo Erectus, 4, 5, 6, 7
Homo Habilis, 4
Homo Sapiens, 6, 7, 8, 9
Horace, 45
Huizinga, Johan, 48, 73, 111, 153, 178,
   191
Human sacrifice, 24
Humanism, 69, 74, 88-89, 131
Hunting, 13

Idealism, 131, 160-141, 152
Industrialization, 91-93
Instinct, 139, 142, 154, 158-166, 207-
   208
   definition of, 159
   play theories of, 161-162, 164, 165
   recreation theories of, 160
Islam, 55
Israel, 36

Jacks, L. P., 113

Jacob, 35, 37
James, William, 131, 140, 141, 142, 143
Jamestown, 83
Jericho, 14, 16
Johnson, George E., 147, 165
Joshua, 35
Judah, 36
Judea, 35

Kames, Lord, 160
Kant, Emanuel, 140
King-priest, 23
Kings, 24
Kish, 23
Kitto, H. D. F., 40
Knossos, 37
Knox, John, 80

Labor, 132
Labor specialization, 21
Lagash, 23, 34
Larsa, 23, 34
Lascaux, France, 10
Law of effect, 167
Law of frequency, 167
Law of recency, 167
Lazarus, Moritz, 142
Leakey, Richard, 4
Lee, Joseph E., 163, 164
Leipzig Trade Fair, 63
Leisure, 3 *et passim*
   acceptance of, 98-100
   aristocratic, 64-68, 81-82
   as function, 115-119
   as pleasure, 106-109
   as rejuvenation, 109-110
   as recreation, 103-106
   as social stratification, 119-123
   as state of being, 111-115
   as time, 105, 113, 118, 123-127
   burger's, 62-64
   human development and, 3-20
   in Colonial America, 83-85

Leisure — *Continued*
  in Medieval Europe, 51-67
  peasant's, 80-81
  Reformation influence on, 75-80
  Renaissance influence on, 68-75
Leisure time, 118
Liberalism, 88
Lies, Eugene T., 182
Livy, 45
Locke, John, 155
Luther, Martin, 76-77, 78, 80

Magdalenian, 9
Magic, 9
Magna Carta, 66
Manorialism, 54
Martel, Charles, 55
Marxism, 122
Masochism, 169, 208
Medievalism, 51-67
Mesolithic era, 12
Mesopotamia, 22, 23
Metal, 17
Michelangelo, 70
Mill, John Stewart, 107
Moscow, 122
Moses, 35
Motivation, 157-178
Mycenae, 38

Nash, Jay B., 195, 196, 197
National Education Association, 188
Neanderthal, 8
Nebraska Symposium, 170
Nebuchadnezzar II, 36
Neolithic, 14, 15
Neulinger, John, 114, 115
Neumeyer, Esther S., 180, 181
Neumeyer, Martin H., 180, 181
Nineveh, 34
Nippur, 23
Nomadism, 6
Nomads, 7

Overstreet, H. Allen, 113

Pack, Arthur N., 114
Paideia, 112
Paidia, 112
Paleolithic period, 7 and ff.
Palio, 71
Pangburn, Weaver W., 182
Parker, Stanley, 127
Patrick, G. T. W., 161
Pentateuch, 35
Pfeiffer, John, 14
Phenomenal self concept, 175, 189, 207
Philistines, 35
Philosophy, 131-156
Piaget, Jean, 177, 178
Pierce, Charles S., 140
Pisa, 71
Plato, 39, 103, 108
Play, 112, 114, 131, *et passim*
  as catharsis, 162, 169
  as instinct, 159, 160
  consummatory quality of, 164, 166
  practice theory of, 162, 164
  recapitulation theory of, 165
  recreation and, 133, 138, 139, 140
  relaxation theory of, 160, 161, 162
  sublimation theory of, 169
  surplus energy theory of, 161, 162, 164
  synonymous with recreation, 157
  work and, 200-201
Pleasure, 106-109, 139
Pleasure principle, 167
Pleistocene, 4, 7
Plymouth Bay, 83
Poitiers, 55
Pragmatism, 131, 141, 143, 144
Prescription, 190-191
Priests, 24
Puritans, 82, 83, 84

Quintilian, 69

Raup, R. Bruce, 173, 174
Realism, 131, 150, 152
Recapitulation, 133, 135
Recreation, 105, 114, 157 and ff.

activity concept of, 195-199
consummatory quality of, 175
definition of, 157, 205, 209
freedom concept of, 190
hedonistic motivation for, 171
homeostatic motivation of, 175
leisure as, 180-182
play and, 200-202, 203
prime motive for, 182-183
synonymous with play, 157
unity concept of, 193, 204-207, 207
virtue concept of, 188-189
work element and, 181, 182-183, 184, 185, 202
Recreational activity, 118
Recreational service, 91, 92-93
Recreational service movement, 153, 163
Recreationist, 165
Recuperation, 134
Reformation, 75-80
Rejuvenation, 109-110
Renaissance, 51, 68-75
Riggs, Austin Fox, 185
Rignano, E., 172
Rome, 42-48, 51, 103
Romney, G. Ott, 105, 194
Rousseau, Jean Jacques, 88, 155
Rugg, Harold, 197
Russell, Bertrand, 153, 154, 155

Sabbath, 37
Saint Augustine, 49
Sargon, 26, 27
Saul, 36
Savonarola, 72
Schiller, J. C. F. von, 161, 162
Schola, 41, 107, 112
Sectarianism, 98
Serfdom, 52, *et passim*
Settlement, 14-15
Shalmaneser, 36
Siena, 71
Slaves, 40, 44, 45, 46
Syngg, Donald, 175, 176
Social stratification, 119-123

Socrates, 39
Solomon, 36
Song, 16
Spain, 8
Spencer, Herbert, 107, 161, 162
State of being, 111-115
Sumer, 23, 26-27
Surplus energy theory, 161, 162
Survival, 15
Susa, 23
Sutton-Smith, B., 202

Terramara people, 42
Therapeutic recreational service, 191
Thermodynamics, 208
Thorndike, E. L., 108, 167, 168
Tiglath Pileser I, 34
Tiglath Pileser III, 34
Tigris River, 23
Time, 123-127
Toil, 57-59
Tool making, 8-9
Tools, 13
Town growth, 59-61
Troland, L. T., 167, 171
Truth, 141, 144, 151
Twain, Mark, 136

Ucello, Paola, 72
Ur, 23, 27, 34, 35
Urbanization, 96-98
Uruk, 23, 34
Universality, 70
Utilitarianism, 87, 89-90

Van Sickle, C. E., 45, 47
Veblen, Thorstein, 119, 120, 121
Venus of Willendorf, 10
Villon, Francois, 74
Virgil, 45
Viricenzo, Rustice, 71

Withers, William, 197
Work, 109, 113, 115, 132, 145, 148, 151

Work — *Continued*
    leisure dichotomy and, 126
    play and, 200-201

Worship, 9

Yugoslavia, 8